THE BIBLE NOW

THE
BIBLE
NOW

RICHARD ELLIOTT FRIEDMAN
& SHAWNA DOLANSKY

OXFORD
UNIVERSITY PRESS

OXFORD
UNIVERSITY PRESS

12/14

Oxford University Press, Inc., publishes works that further
Oxford University's objective of excellence
in research, scholarship, and education.

Oxford   New York

Auckland   Cape Town   Dar es Salaam   Hong Kong   Karachi
Kuala Lumpur   Madrid   Melbourne   Mexico City   Nairobi
New Delhi   Shanghai   Taipei   Toronto

With offices in

Argentina   Austria   Brazil   Chile   Czech Republic   France   Greece
Guatemala   Hungary   Italy   Japan   Poland   Portugal   Singapore
South Korea   Switzerland   Thailand   Turkey   Ukraine   Vietnam

Published by Oxford University Press, Inc.
198 Madison Avenue, New York, New York 10016

www.oup.com

Oxford is a registered trademark of Oxford University Press

Library of Congress Cataloging-in-Publication Data
Friedman, Richard Elliott.
The Bible now / Richard Elliott Friedman and Shawna Dolansky.
p. cm.
Includes bibliographical references and index.
ISBN 978-0-19-531163-1
1. Ethics in the Bible. 2. Bible. O.T.—Criticism, interpretation,
etc. 3. Ethical problems. I. Dolansky, Shawna. II. Title.
BS1199.E8F75 2011
241—dc22   2010035681

DEDICATION

DAVID NOEL FREEDMAN 1922–2008

We dedicate this book to David Noel Freedman, our senior colleague, friend, and teacher.

Noel had the second-largest entry in *Who's Who in the World*.

Noel was the greatest biblical editor since Ezra. As everyone whom he edited knows, for every page of manuscript you sent him, he sent back one double-spaced page of comments, typed on an IBM Selectric typewriter. He once said, "Give me any book, and in five minutes I'll find a typo." In one of our books, it took him less than one minute.

Noel was the greatest conscious sleeper since Jacob at Beth El. He was famous for falling asleep at every lecture he ever attended, but he could still make an incisive comment. He once complained to us at a conference that all he was doing was attending meetings. He had attended no papers, and he had gotten no sleep. We said, "Forget the papers. Get some sleep." He said, "No, the papers are where I sleep."

Noel said we saved his life when we brought him from the cold of the University of Michigan to warm San Diego, California. That's funny; we thought we were doing it out of self-interest. At the University of California, San Diego, Noel was the highest-ranking member of the faculty of arts and humanities and social sciences, and his nephew Michael Freedman was the highest-ranking member of the faculty of mathematics and natural sciences, having won the Fields Medal and MacArthur awards. Noel came from a good family. His father was known on Broadway as the king of the gag writers, writing for Fanny Brice and Smith and Dale and Eddie Cantor. The family lived in Manhattan in the Beresford, a building where now reside the likes of Jerry Seinfeld and John McEnroe, who got Noel's family's old apartment. Where the likes of Ira Gershwin came to play poker with his father. Where

Herman Wouk was his father's apprentice—and later wrote a novel in which Noel and his father are characters. With his father's untimely death, Noel's older brother, Benedict, put his career in mathematics on hold and wrote for Al Jolson and Red Skelton. So the family moved to California, and Noel went to the University of California, Los Angeles—at the age of sixteen by the way. And Noel's younger brother, Toby, became the team doctor of the Los Angeles Rams.

With much of his father's skill at humor, Noel could keep an audience in stitches while making a significant scholarly presentation.

With much of his brother's skill at mathematics, he raised the level of calculation in our field. He used to say, "If you count anything, you'll find something interesting." When he and Frank Moore Cross did a retrospective session together at a national conference, Cross said about their work in syllable counting in Hebrew poetry, "We both do it, and we both think it doesn't mean anything." That received an appreciative laugh, but the truth is that Noel actually *did* think that it means something. And if you read him, you'll see that he showed it.

With a real scholar's ability to transcend simple answers, he noted in textual criticism that haplography (dropping words out by accident) is the most common scribal error, yet insensitive scholars still apply the principle of *lectio brevior praeferenda est* (the shorter reading is preferable) as if it were a law from Sinai. Noel said, "We don't get the truth of a biblical text from a Latin proverb."

For his eightieth birthday, Noel asked us to have all of his books in the room. It was done. And there were over three hundred books—the ones he edited and the ones he wrote.

Some need to derive their status from being at a particular institution, but not Noel. If there were two epicenters to our field in North America during the lives of Freedman and Cross, those centers were wherever those two men happened to be. Where Noel was, that was the center of the Anchor Bible, his baby, the most successful commentary series in the history of the Bible, with over three million copies bought. Where Noel was, that was where well-trained students came out. Where Noel was, that was where scholars from all over the world came to meet, consult, and talk and learn. Where Noel was, that was where colleagues were inspired and improved. Where Noel was, one was reminded of the pure joy of the life of scholars. And, above all, where Noel was, that was where the most learned man on the Bible in this world was. He simply knew more about the Bible than anyone else on earth. Name a verse, and he rattled off the range of views on it, and then he showed you why they were all wrong and why a view that only he had thought of was right. Often his idea sounded far-fetched at first hearing, but if you had the courtesy and the sense to listen or read on, you might well be persuaded that it was the most likely answer.

And knowing the most about the Bible did not make him a one-trick pony. He could analyze the intricacies of current economics and politics, and he could discuss with insight the history of the British monarchy. And in our case, he could advise us about life, human relationships, and keeping fixed on what is important in a life.

In the end, we could describe Noel like Bogart's description of Captain Renault in *Casablanca*: "He was a man like any other man, only more so."

CONTENTS

PREFACE

This book is about what the Bible has to say about major issues of our time. We shall address five current controversial matters: homosexuality, abortion, women's status, capital punishment, and the earth.

There have been many books in recent years about the literary qualities of the Bible, about who wrote the Bible, and about the Bible in light of history and archaeology. Literary study of the Bible is a focus on what was written *then*. History and archaeology are the study of what happened *then*. But this book is about what the Bible means now. The Bible's value, above all, is as a guide to lives. And we mean to all of our lives, whether one is religious or not, whether one is Christian, Jewish, or from another religion or no religion. Some people think of fundamentalist Christians and Orthodox Jews as the ones who connect their decisions to the words of the Bible. But that is not correct. One finds scholars, clergy, and just folks, from all across the religious spectrum, who read, study, and care about what the Bible says on things that matter to them. And one finds many who have never read or studied the Bible, who still share a cultural sense of its importance as a foundation for morality and virtue. The Bible is a source of human experience and of wisdom, and wisdom is something we need. We can argue about which biblical passages are historically accurate, but, still, it is the first history writing on earth. The Bible's oldest prose was written when Herodotus's great-grandmother was not yet in preschool. We can question the morality of any given story or law, but still the Bible is an extraordinary repository of remarkable stories, exquisite writing, and revolutionary laws. Indeed, when we argue about these things, we are participating in a two thousand-year-old process that the Bible itself started us doing.

You don't have to be Christian. You don't have to be Jewish. You don't have to be religious. You just have to be aware that this ancient text—the Bible—makes a difference. It makes a difference partly because of its qualities, partly because of the status it has come to have in Judaism and Christianity, partly because of the status it has come to have in world literature. You can feel any one of a thousand feelings about it, but one thing you should not do is ignore it.

One may say, "But there have been times in history (and the present) when people used the Bible for harm: burning 'witches,' attacking 'infidels,' defending slavery." True, but that, precisely, proves that we cannot ignore it. The fact that it has both inspired people to do great good and been used by people to do great harm means that it is really important for us to pay attention to it—and to get it right. The Bible is electricity, and it should be handled with care. The stakes are high enough that we cannot afford to be ignorant or sloppy about it. The topics in this book are not theoretical. They are "hot" at the present time because they affect so many of us.

What we are doing here: It is not our job as scholars to take a side and then look for evidence to back it up. Our job is not to persuade you to be for or against abortion, for example. But whatever position you take on abortion, you should be better informed of the evidence from this book. And you should be able to explain your position to yourself and others. And you should be able to defend your position in arguments better. You may change your mind. You may not. But our goal is to give you as much good information as possible. You can do with it what you will. We may have personal opinions, but our job as scholars is not to sell our own opinions. Our job is to seek knowledge, which is to say to seek the truth, through evidence and logic, and to make this knowledge known. This is not what a number of people want in a book on these subjects. They want to read books by people on their side of an issue, who will give them arguments to back up their side. That is their right, and that is their business. But this book is not for them. For all they know, this book might contain some evidence that would support their view. Or it might not.

We shall treat many of the common, popular arguments on these subjects. We shall look at verses that people often cite. We can tell you in advance that a good many of these are misunderstood, misquoted, misinterpreted, misread, mistranslated, and misused. If we show that some classic argument against capital punishment is wrong, you should not assume that therefore we are for capital punishment. And if we show that some classic argument *for* capital punishment is wrong, you should not assume that therefore we are against capital punishment. We are scholars, not politicians. We may have positions, but they have no business in our scholarship. A scholar's job is to tell the truth. Everybody should tell the truth, but a scholar's *profession* is to tell the truth. Nobody should lie, but when a scholar lies it is particularly awful.

Yes, the Bible has often been misused. People have used its authority for harm, for justification of political and social agendas. But that does not mean that we cannot use it. It means that we must use it with integrity—and humility. It means we have to recognize what it teaches even when that teaching goes against what we want. Better to reject the Bible's teaching than to twist it to make it say what we prefer. *The Bible Now* must therefore be judged by how much readers will feel that we have been skillful and honest in our readings.

There have been two tremendous developments in recent generations: the archaeological revolution and the arrival at a new stage in biblical scholarship. We shall bring in very recent developments and conclusions in biblical scholarship, which sometimes make a great deal of difference. People speak about these things—and even write about them—without knowledge of the languages of the Bible or of the world of the Bible or even being aware of how very complex biblical studies are. One would not go to amateurs for drug prescriptions (we hope) or many other things, but folks still listen to people who have not been trained for these fairly important decisions.

We shall apply historical-critical methods, philological and literary analyses, text criticism, source criticism, redaction criticism, anthropological perspectives, archaeology, and ancient languages: Hebrew, Greek, Akkadian, Ugaritic, Aramaic—the variety of tools of our trade—to address these questions. We are not doing this out of some antiquarian curiosity with ancient things. As much as the Bible is an ancient artifact, it is also a present one. The Bible matters to people. More than twenty centuries after its production, the Bible is still brought to bear on practically every important social and political issue in the Western world (and much of the Eastern world). In the eighteenth and nineteenth centuries, both proponents and opponents of African slavery quoted chapters and verses to support their positions. In the twentieth and twenty-first centuries, all sides of every hot issue—from stem cell research to homosexual marriage—regularly include biblical interpretation to support the truth of their stance. How is it possible that those who are pro-choice and those who are anti-abortion can both point to the same text to support their arguments? How can some Jews and Christians use the Bible to justify the subordination of women and other Jews and Christians base feminist reforms and the emancipation—and even ordination—of women on the very same Scripture? Biblical scholars are thus in the position of treating a classical text with tools and skills like those of a scholar of Homer or Aristotle but at the same time dealing with immediate, relevant issues like those in each morning's news.

We were both trained in critical biblical scholarship, but that does not mean that we cannot write for orthodox and fundamentalist readers with courtesy and respect. And as long as we keep to the facts and to honest method, what we have to share from our research should be useful to both traditional and critical, religious and not-religious, readers.

We are dealing only with the Hebrew Bible (also known as the Old Testament, Holy Scriptures, or Tanak) because that is the area of our expertise. We have had the experience of people asking us all sorts of questions about matters that lie outside of our area of expertise: about the New Testament, about rabbinic Jewish texts, and much more. Don't go to a gynecologist for a broken leg. And don't turn to a scholar for answers outside of his or her area of knowledge. Our hope is that this book will prompt scholars who are specialists in the New Testament (and perhaps the Qur'an and other sacred books) to write about these things as well. That was what happened with *Who Wrote the Bible?* It dealt only with the Hebrew Bible, but then other scholars wrote books titled *Who Wrote the New Testament?*, *Who Wrote the Gospels?*, and *Who Wrote the Dead Sea Scrolls?* We also look forward to other books, by ourselves or others, that will treat additional important matters besides the five that we chose here: war, race, evolution, teaching the Bible in schools, posting the Ten Commandments in public spaces. We chose five that have come up a great deal in our recent experience: in mail we have received, in lectures, and in discussions with clergy and colleagues.

There are so many books and articles discussing these subjects and their biblical connection. We have no interest in only citing the same texts or repeating the same points. In every chapter we expect to bring something that you have not already heard a hundred times: either new texts or new perspectives or new evidence.

In approaching these topics, are we afraid? Absolutely. It is impossible to address these things without offending *someone*. But they really need to be addressed. What we can promise is to try to do so with humility and with sensitivity to people's feelings.

A few technical points:

1. Translation. All English translations of the Bible are our own.

2. The chapters are of unequal length. We gave each chapter whatever length it needed to say what we had to say. The chapter on women's status is the longest, but that makes sense. Women, after all, are half of the people on earth.

3. Why we use YHWH for the name of God in the Bible. We do it this way in English because this is how it is done in the original Hebrew. These are the equivalents in our alphabet for the four Hebrew letters that spell the divine name in the text (the Tetragrammaton). When reading aloud, those whose tradition is not to pronounce the divine name usually read "the LORD" when they see this name.

4. Verse numbers. The verse numbers in various English Bible translations may differ by a verse or two from each other or from the original. We follow the verse numbers of the Hebrew (the Masoretic Text). If you look up a verse that we cite and it does not seem to match what we have quoted, take this factor of numbering into account.

THE BIBLE NOW

ONE

Homosexuality

There is more than one reason for turning to the Bible in controversial matters, and there is more than one kind of person who will do so. One might do it because, in one's religious view, the Bible is the final authority and one must do what it says. But also people who do not see the Bible as having this authority, and people who do not believe that the Bible is divinely revealed, may turn to the Bible because they believe it contains wisdom—wisdom that might help anyone, whatever his or her beliefs, make wise decisions about difficult matters.

The first question is: which biblical texts are relevant and potentially helpful to people when forming their views? There are three kinds of texts in the Hebrew Bible: prose, poetry, and laws. In the matter of homosexuality, *and in all matters*, we must distinguish among these. It is one thing to tell a story about something. It is another to write a poem about it. And it is a very different thing to write a law that says, "Thou shalt not do it!" When you tell a story, the story may have a lesson that you want your readers to learn from it. Or it may not. When you write a poem, it is more subtle. A great teacher of ours once said that the difference between prose and poetry is that prose calls our attention to the thing that it is *about*—to its referent—while poetry calls our attention to *itself.* That is, even more than prose, poetry does not need to teach us anything. It needs us to see itself, to see its particular way of expressing something. This matters. In the present generation there has been a surge of literary studies of the Bible. The phrase "The Bible as Literature"—what in the world does that mean? Often it has just meant that professors of literature wanted to get to write and dare to teach about the Bible even though they had no training as biblical scholars. They often could not even read the Bible in its original

1

languages unless someone else translated it for them. After all, is there ever a course called "*Hamlet* as Literature" or "*The Brothers Karamazov* as Literature"? The very title "The Bible as Literature" reflects the fact that the Bible is in fact something else. Still, at its best, literary study of the Bible can bring out some really important things. The significance of different genres of literature is one of them. In other fields of literature this is so obvious that it hardly needs mentioning. But in the Bible it needs saying: a story about homosexuality, a poem about homosexuality, and a law about homosexuality are three different things.

If that is clear, then we are ready to look at the first text that people often mention in connection with homosexuality. It is a story. It is the story of Sodom.

Prose

The story comes in Genesis 19, but it is already introduced six chapters earlier. There it says:

> And the people of Sodom were very bad and sinful to YHWH.
> (Gen 13:12)

Very bad? Sinful? It does not say what sort of things they do. This very general picture of their wrongdoing comes again a few chapters later, where God says,

> The cry of Sodom and Gomorrah: how great it is. And their sin: how very heavy it is. Let me go down, and I'll see if they've done, all told, like the cry that has come to me. And if not, let me know.
> (Gen 18:20–21)

The picture is still unspecific. Its concern is whether the people of these towns are virtuous or wicked, without naming any single act of which they are guilty. Thus far no one would connect this story with any particular act, be it homosexual or anything else.

And this continues during the famous dialogue that follows, in which Abraham questions his God about who is good and who is bad in Sodom:

And Abraham came over and said, "Will you also annihilate the virtuous with the wicked? Maybe there are fifty virtuous people within the city. Will you also annihilate and not sustain the place for the fifty virtuous who are in it? Far be it from you to do a thing like this, to kill virtuous with wicked—and it will be the same for the virtuous and the wicked—far be it from you. Will the judge of all the earth not do justice?"

And YHWH said, "If I find in Sodom fifty virtuous people within the city, then I'll sustain the whole place for their sake."

And Abraham answered, and he said, "Here I've undertaken to speak to my Lord, and I'm dust and ashes. Maybe the fifty virtuous people will be short by five. Will you destroy the whole city for the five?"

And He said, "I won't destroy if I find forty-five there."

And he went on again to speak to Him and said, "Maybe forty will be found there."

And He said, "I won't do it for the sake of the forty."

And he said, "May my Lord not be angry, and let me speak. Maybe thirty will be found there."

And He said, "I won't do it if I find thirty there."

And he said, "Here I've undertaken to speak to my Lord. Maybe twenty will be found there."

And He said, "I won't destroy for the sake of the twenty."

And he said, "May my Lord not be angry, and let me speak just this one time. Maybe ten will be found there."

And He said there, "I won't destroy for the sake of the ten."
(Gen 18:23–32)

There is still no hint of any single offense here. The idea that homosexuality has something to do with this story comes in the next part, where two angels arrive in Sodom and are taken in by Abraham's nephew, Lot. Here is the first part of the story:

And the two angels came to Sodom in the evening, and Lot was sitting at Sodom's gate, and Lot saw and got up toward them, and he bowed, nose to the ground. And he said, "Here, my lords, turn to your servant's house and spend the night and wash your feet, and you'll get up early and go your way."

And they said, "No, we'll spend the night in the square." And he pressed them very much, and they turned to him and came to his house, and he made a feast and baked unleavened bread for them, and they ate.

They had not yet lain down, and the people of the city, the people of Sodom, surrounded the house, from youth to old man, all the people, from the farthest reaches. And they called to Lot and said to him, "Where are the people who came to you tonight? Bring them out to us, and let's know them!"

And Lot went out to them at the entrance and closed the door behind him, and he said, "Don't do bad, my brothers. Here I have two daughters who haven't known a man. Let me bring them out to you, and do to them as is good in your eyes. Only don't do anything to these people, because that is why they came under the shadow of my roof."

And they said, "Come over here," and they said, "This one comes to live, and then he *judges*! Now we'll be worse to you than to them." And they pressed the man, Lot, very much and came over to break down the door. And the people reached their hand out and brought Lot in to them in the house, and they closed the door. And they struck the people who were at the house's entrance with blindness, from smallest to biggest, and they wearied themselves with finding the entrance.

And the people said to Lot, "Who else do you have here—son-in-law and your sons and your daughters and all that you have in the city—take them out from the place, because we're destroying this place, because its cry has grown big before YHWH's face, and YHWH has sent us to destroy it."

(Gen 19:1–13)

Now, on first reading, one would not necessarily think that this story has anything to do with sex of any kind, either heterosexual or homosexual. Interpreters have understood it to be about sex because the people of Sodom call for the two guests in Lot's home to be sent out "so we may know them." The word *know* in biblical Hebrew can indeed mean to know someone with sexual intimacy. (Joke: An ancient Greek says to an ancient Jew: "Know thyself." The ancient Jew punches the ancient Greek.) For example, an earlier text says, "Cain knew his wife, and she became pregnant and gave birth" (Gen 4:17). It can also mean any other kind of knowledge, but sexual knowledge is likely here in the Sodom story because Lot responds by offering them his virgin daughters, and he says, "do to them as is good in your eyes"—which means "do whatever you want to them."

Another reason for thinking that the story is about sex is that there is a parallel story later in the Bible. In Judges 19 is a story with many obvious similarities. In this story, a Levite man is provided hospitality by a fellow Israelite in the town of Gibeah. The other people of Gibeah, although Israelite as well, do not take kindly to strangers, and they surround the house where the Levite and his concubine and his servant have been welcomed for the night. As the unwelcoming crowd gathers around the host's house demanding that the stranger be sent out so that they might "know" him, the owner of the house pleads, "Don't, my brothers. Don't do bad. Since this man came to my house, don't do this foolhardy thing. Here are my virgin daughter and his concubine. Let me bring them out. And degrade them and do to them what's good in your eyes, and don't do this foolhardy thing to this man." Like Lot in Genesis, the host offers his virgin daughter and the traveler's concubine in place of his guest. But in this story the concubine is actually handed over to the crowd by her man. The crowd "knew her and abused her all night until morning and let her go at sunrise. And the woman came toward morning and fell at the entrance of the house where her man was, until it was light." And there she dies.

In this horrifying story the "knowing" that the crowd wants is manifestly sex, and the parallels of story line and specific wording are so close to those of the Sodom story that they certainly indicate that the Sodom story is about sex as well.[1] But, granting that the story is about sex, one still would not read it and automatically think that it is about anything homosexual. Interpreters have taken it to be about homosexual sex because they understand the text to say that the *men* of Sodom call for the two *men* in Lot's home to be sent out so that the crowd may know them. But the Hebrew text in this chapter speaks of two "people" (not necessarily both male) in the house, and it speaks of all the "people" (not necessarily just the males) of Sodom wanting to know them. It does not necessarily have anything to do with homosexuality. The misunderstanding arose because Hebrew, like many other languages, uses the masculine when referring to mixed groups. That is, in Hebrew the word for "men" and the word for "people" are the same. (The word in Hebrew is *ănāšîm*.) Likewise, when Lot says, "Don't do bad, my brothers," the word *brothers* need not refer to just males. Like the word *brotherhood* in English, it has the meaning of fellow humans, not just fellow males. Outside of this story, the word *ănāšîm* occurs in twenty-one places in Genesis with this indefinite meaning, in which it could mean either people in general or just males.[2] In two places it must mean both males and females.[3] And in fifteen places it means just males.[4] English translators quite commonly translate almost all of these as "men." But that is not correct. In most Bible stories, this does not make a big difference. But here in the case of the story of Sodom, it makes all the difference in the world. It is only because the interpreters and translators understood the word to be *men* that people thought that the story was about something homosexual. The most cautious statement would be: it might mean just men, and it might mean people. We do not know.

Those who are aware of this problem but still think that it means men, not people, here say that the issue is homosexual because the crowd rejects Lot's offer of females—his daughters. But the offer and rejection of his daughters are more probably about ancient Near Eastern bargaining than ancient Near Eastern sex. When Lot offers his daughters and says, "Here, do whatever you want to them," we cannot assume that he means it. As in many other cases in Genesis, this story is consistent with the going conventions of bargaining.[5] When buying the cave of Machpelah as a tomb for his wife, Abraham says, "I'll pay full price." The owner responds, "Pay nothing. I've *given* it to you!" Abraham insists, "I've *given* the money." The man says, "Well, what's four hundred shekels between you and me!" Abraham understands the man's point and pays the four hundred shekels. Likewise in the story of Jacob: when Jacob is about to face his brother Esau, whose blessing he appropriated twenty years earlier, Jacob sends a tremendous gift in advance. Esau declines the gift. He says, "I have a great deal, my brother. Let what's yours be yours." But Jacob insists, and the text concludes: "And he pressed him, and he took it." Likewise in the story of Esther: at Esther's soiree, King Ahasuerus says, "What do you ask, Queen Esther, and it will be given to you! What is your request, up to half my kingdom, and it will be done!" (Esth 7:2). But he is not offering her one half of the Persian Empire, and she does not accept it. And so on: Abraham's servant bargains over the acquisition of a wife for Isaac (Genesis 24). Jacob bargains with his future father-in-law, Laban, over the bride-price for Laban's daughters, and later they bargain again over the compensation for Jacob's work (Gen 29:15–19; 30:28–34). Jacob and the king of Shechem bargain over the fate of Jacob's daughter Dinah and the relationship between their two communities (Genesis 34). Judah bargains with Tamar for sex with her (Genesis 38). When a king says, "I'll give you half my kingdom," he does not mean it, and you are not supposed to take him up on it. That has been the way of the Near East for thousands of years. Anyone who has been there knows this. Some find it fun; some find it annoying; some find it challenging. But if one does not understand it, one is at a disadvantage there today, and one can misinterpret several stories of that world in Bible times.

Some think that Lot's offer of his daughters reflects Near Eastern traditions of hospitality. But offering your daughters for rape is far beyond what almost anyone in any culture would consider to be an obligation of hospitality. Neither Lot's offer of the young women nor the crowd's rejection of it proves anything about what the crowd is after. It is not good evidence on which to conclude that the rest of the story is about homosexuality.

Likewise in the Gibeah story, the host offers his virgin daughter, but the crowd does not take him up on his offer. The guest gives his concubine, conceivably to protect the host (and his virgin daughter?) from suffering on the guest's account. This story, too, has been thought to be about homosexuality because again the "people/men" (*'ănāšîm*) want to "know" the guest. But they in fact accept and rape the concubine. Moreover, they do not ask for the guest's male servant, and neither the host nor the guest is pictured as ever considering or mentioning the male servant rather than the female concubine. The Gibeah story shockingly establishes the sexuality of both stories, but it does not establish homosexuality.

Another thing that may possibly shed light on this is the fact that all the people of Sodom are destroyed—male and female, young and old. This fits with the emphatic statement in the text that

> all the people of the city, the people of Sodom, surrounded the house, from youth to old man, all the people, from the farthest reaches

as well as the statement that the angels

> struck the people who were at the house's entrance with blindness, from smallest to biggest.

The text is taking pains to emphasize that everyone is involved. That is what justifies what happens, namely, that God destroys "all of the residents."[6] This point favors the reading that Hebrew *'ănāšîm* here more probably means the people, and not just the men, of the city.

Indeed, if we were to read the story as meaning "men" rather than people, then this would mean that Sodom is pictured as a place where the entire male population is homosexual (or bisexual). And if homosexuality is the great sin for which God seeks to destroy Sodom, the same would presumably apply to the other "cities of the plain" that are destroyed along with Sodom (Gomorrah, Admah, and Zeboim). Why would the biblical author picture such a thing, where every single man is gay (or bisexual), which is contrary to all human experience? And what in the world is Lot doing there with his family? Why would he go there? Why would they accept him? Is he their token heterosexual?

Moreover, the Sodom episode is not found only here in Genesis. Many other biblical books speak of the destruction of Sodom and the other cities.[7] Not one of them connects it to homosexuality. They do not mention this at all.

Ironically, the very word for anal sexual intercourse in English, "*sodomy*," derives from this unsubstantiated understanding of the story of Sodom.

And in any case, the story is about rape—whether homosexual or heterosexual—not just about having sex. The ongoing criminality of the people of Sodom and its neighbor cities is never identified, and this story that conveys the degree of their corruption is about abuse and violence. It does not mean that the whole town was gay.

However one feels about homosexuality, one should not base his or her view of it on this story.[8]

Poetry

The other text that is commonly mentioned on the subject of homosexuality among biblical persons is in poetry. It is about David and Jonathan. This poem is taken to support the opposite view, that is, that homosexuality is acceptable. Some understand it to imply a homosexual relationship between these two friends: Jonathan the crown prince of Israel and David the future king. Why? Because, when Jonathan dies, David's lament includes the words "Your love was more wondrous to me than love of women."[9]

Are there grounds for taking this expression of David's love for his friend in a song to mean a physical sexual relationship? Actually, there are none.

One of the authors of this book (Friedman) notes: I myself have a great male friend whom I have known since childhood. He is like my brother. I could say that I love him, and I could say that this kind of love between men who are friends is "more wondrous to me than love of women." But I have no sexual interest in him. Those words in themselves do not prove anything about the sexual views of the man who says them. On matters as significant as this, one should be circumspect about reaching a conclusion about an entire relationship between two famous biblical persons because of a line in a song.[10] Not to mention that David is married to Jonathan's sister. He lives a lusty life in which he twice takes married women, one before her husband's death and one immediately after. And he has other wives and at least ten concubines.[11] Now one might suggest that he may be a homosexual man who has all of these women as a way of covering or denying his homosexuality. Or one could suggest that he is bisexual. But these are big conclusions to draw out of the poetic line in the song. Moreover the final story of David's life, which involves sex, further argues against these suggestions. At the end of that account, the text pictures David, now very old, as sexually impotent. (The old King James English translation says, "He was old and stricken in years and he gat no heat.") Several biblical texts besides this one indicate that a king's ability to continue to rule was tied to his sexual potency.[12] So they bring the beautiful woman Abishag for sex with the king, but "he knew her not," and, sure enough, his kingdom falls to his son (possibly that very day). The story is interesting in a hundred ways, but the main point for now is: they bring him a beautiful woman, not a man, when his sexual potency urgently needs to be established.

The David-and-Jonathan poem should not be used in an argument for male homosexuality, and the Sodom story should not be used in an argument against it. Our conclusion is: the prose and poetry texts that people most often mention with regard to homosexuality do not shed any light at all on this subject.

Law

Now the law, on the other hand, is explicit: male homosexual acts are prohibited. There are two legal texts, both in Leviticus. A literal translation of them comes out as somewhat crude in English, but we shall use it here because the precise wording is extremely important, and scholars have argued about them in great detail. The texts say:

> You shall not lay a male the layings of a woman; it is an offensive thing.
> (Lev 18:22)

> And a man who will lay a male the layings of a woman: the two of them have done an offensive thing. They shall be *put to death*. Their blood is on them.
> (Lev 20:13)

Some have tried to interpret these words to mean something other than prohibiting homosexual intercourse. Some have suggested that these words may prohibit only some, but not all, homosexual acts. The lines in Hebrew certainly appear to be a straightforward prohibition of male homosexuality. This brings several questions to mind. First, why does the law prohibit male homosexuality but not female? Second, what is the reason for prohibiting it? And, third, can this law change, or is it an eternal prohibition that can never be different?

Why prohibit male homosexuality but not female? People have proposed various answers:

1. Some think that it has to do with a biblical concern for wasting a man's seed. That is, in homosexual sex the man's semen does not produce children.[13] These scholars conclude that the reason why female homosexual sex is not forbidden is that it does not have this "nonproductive spilling of seed."

This concern is hard to establish, though, here in these texts in Leviticus. After all, there is no reference to seed in these verses. They do not use the phrase "an intercourse of seed," which is the phrase that is used elsewhere for sex that could produce children.[14] In fact, the phrase "your intercourse of seed" is used just two verses before this one, where the law says, "And you shall not give your intercourse of seed to your fellow's wife."[15] So its absence here stands out. Also, there is no prohibition of many other things that waste semen too, for examples: sex with a pregnant woman, sex after menopause,[16] masturbation, sexual acts between a man and a woman that do not involve vaginal intercourse, and birth control of various sorts.

Some might consider masturbation to be an exception to this list of things that waste semen but are not prohibited. This is based on the biblical story of Onan in Genesis 38. It is a strange story of a levirate marriage, which is when a man dies childless and so his brother marries the widow, and their first son is regarded as the son of the dead brother, not the son of the actual biological father. Here is the text:

> And Er, Judah's firstborn, was bad in YHWH's eyes, and YHWH killed him. And Judah said to Onan, "Come to your brother's wife and couple as a brother-in-law with her and raise seed for your brother." And Onan knew that the seed would not be his. And it was when he came to his brother's wife: and he spent on the ground so as not to give seed for his brother. And what he did was bad in YHWH's eyes, and He killed him, too.
> (Gen 38:7–10)

The very term *onanism* for masturbation in English comes from this story. But, in the first place, this story does not involve masturbation. It is a case of withdrawal in the act of sex with a woman. Second, the nature of Onan's offense is not clear. It may possibly be the withdrawal itself, but it is just as likely to be his refusal to provide seed for his brother. And, third, the offense is strictly Onan's and nobody else's. One cannot conclude from this episode that, biblically, it is wrong for any man to spill seed in any situation. It is a very specific story about a singular case in a family's history. It has no broader application, and there is in fact no law against masturbation or withdrawal during sex anywhere in the Bible's law codes. Masturbation is not forbidden according to the Bible.[17]

Also, one can argue that in homosexual sex the female egg is no more or less "wasted" than the male semen. The ancients may have known less than we do about anatomy, but they were able to know that there was something going on inside a woman that interacted with a man's semen to produce pregnancy. One might respond that the ancients may have thought that the woman's body was just built to receive the man's seed, to provide the environment in which it could develop into a human being. In that case they would not have imagined that the woman's body contained anything that could be wasted in the way that male seed could. But, after all, they could observe that children were born with just as many traits in common with their mothers as with their fathers. With centuries of experience of children who looked like Mommy, they did not have to be the first-millennium BCE equivalent of a rocket scientist to figure out that mothers somehow contribute something to the children who come out of them.

Also, the text twice calls male homosexuality "an offensive thing" (in Hebrew: a *tōʿēbāh*). Older translations use the harsher word *abomination* to translate *tōʿēbāh*. But from the softest possible understanding of this word to the strongest, it suggests that there is something about a homosexual act itself—about two men being together sexually the way a man and a woman would be—that bothers the author of this law, not just the waste of seed. (More on the meaning of *tōʿēbāh* below.)

Finally, we can know that spilling seed is not what bothered the author(s) of the laws in Leviticus because there is a specific law about this:

> And when a man's intercourse seed will come out from him: he shall wash all of his flesh in water and will be impure until evening. And any clothing and any leather on which there will be intercourse seed: it shall be washed with water and will be impure until evening. And a woman with whom a man will lie—an intercourse of seed—they shall wash with water and will be impure until evening.
> (Lev 15:16–18)

The seed that comes out of a man is not treated here as something bad or forbidden. It is treated exactly the same as seed in intercourse with a woman. Namely, it is a matter of purity. In both cases, the people involved are just required to wash.

2. Some think that women may have been sufficiently controlled in that culture that there was no need to prohibit females from having homosexual sex. But, in the first place, there is no reason to think that women were that thoroughly controlled in ancient Israel. There are, after all, many other commandments that apply to women in the Hebrew Bible. Women were not so controlled as to make all of those unnecessary. Indeed, the very next verse after this one in Leviticus prohibits sex with an animal, and it prohibits this for both men and women. There is no biblical idea that any laws need to be stated only for men while women are so controlled that the law need not even be stated. And, second, the fact is that even in extremely restrictive societies homosexuality takes place. The sex drive is very

powerful, and people will do this even in communities that are much stricter than ancient Israel was. One cannot assume that male control in ancient Israel was so overwhelming that women would never have an opportunity to do this.

3. Some might say that the law includes female homosexuality implicitly: even though it is formulated in terms of man-and-man, one should understand it to mean woman-and-woman as well. Even if we were to grant that such an understanding is possible, though, it is a big leap to make without definite proof. This is not a small matter. This is a question of what kind of sex women might have for their entire lives. As a basic principle of Bible understanding, we should not draw a conclusion on an important life issue based on a possible secondary implication of a verse. Moreover, as we saw above, the next verse after this one (a law prohibiting sex with animals) is careful to include women—not by implication but explicitly. So, if the law tells us when women are included and when they are not, we are on dangerous ground if we conclude that they are suddenly implicitly included in this one case.

4. The biblical scholar Jacob Milgrom rightly rejects a view that this law comes from male authors who simply had no knowledge of or interest in female sex. Milgrom calls this view a "stab in the dark," not based on any evidence.[18]

All of these proposals are interesting, but they do not seem adequate to explain this distinction that forbids male homosexual acts but not female. We do not think that these things derive from a failure of men even to have it occur to them or from the Israelite men thinking that they could be the only ones in human history to regulate it. Mores and laws about sex are more likely to derive from actual conditions and actual feelings. We think that the probable reason for the distinction has to do with *the most prominent difference between sexual relations in the biblical world and in our world*, namely: polygamy.

In Israel (and among many other peoples) in biblical times, men could have many wives. They could also have other women—concubines—in their homes along with their wives. Men with two wives, or even harems, had opportunities for group sex and for voyeurism of female homosexuality. This is a common male fantasy. One especially sees it in our generation, in which barriers to seeing this have, to a large extent, melted away. Scenes of women being with other women are common in films with sexual content. One sees it not only in pornographic films. It is in mainstream movies, in popular television programs, and in advertisements in magazines. Sometimes it is subtle. Sometimes it is outright. It is a regular feature of popular magazines for the entertainment of men. It is on Internet sites that reveal various degrees of sexual content. It may be hard for us to grasp how very different it was to live in a world of polygamy. Today it is a fantasy for men, which they can view in these venues, but for men in the ancient world it was an option, at least for the men of wealth who could afford it. They could arrange it, see it, even participate along with it on any given night. For those who believe that the biblical law codes were written by men, men were not about to forbid female-to-female contact. It was a part of their world. For those who believe that the biblical law codes were revealed to humans by God, the case is more complex, but the laws favor men's role in marriage in many places—most notably allowing polygamy in the first place—so the point may possibly be similar.

Thus just a few verses before the law about male homosexuality there is a law that says:

> You shall not take a woman to her sister to rival, to expose her nudity along with her in her lifetime.
> (Lev 18:18)

The law here forbids a man only from having sexual relations with two sisters at the same time. There is no prohibition against having sexual relations with two unrelated women at the same time. We are therefore persuaded that this fact of sexual life in the ancient Near East is a far more probable explanation for why the Bible does not prohibit female homosexuality than any of the more theoretical reasons given above. But even for those who disagree as to whether this is the prime reason, the fact remains: whatever the reason, female homosexuality is not forbidden in the Bible.

Now, the fact that biblical law prohibits male but not female homosexual acts tells us something important: it was not something about homosexuality itself—about relations with a person of the same sex—that was the issue. It was rather something specifically about *male-to-male sexual contact*. It is not that acts of sex between like and like were offensive to them. It is that acts of sex between male and male were offensive to them. Now who is bothered by the idea of male–male sex but not female–female sex? Who? Many men. What is this something that bothered them?

1. Waste of seed. We have already indicated above that we do not see evidence that this is what is at stake behind this commandment. One might respond: what about "Be fruitful and multiply and fill the earth"? It is, after all, considered to be the first commandment in the Bible. God says it to the first humans and then again to Noah after the flood. Does it not show a concern for increasing the human population? It certainly does. We should be cautious, though, of deriving too much from it. In the first place, in both the creation and the flood contexts it is presented as a blessing from God, not a requirement of each and every human being:

> And God blessed them, and God said to them, "Be fruitful and multiply
> and fill the earth. . . ."
> (Gen 1:28)

> And God blessed Noah and his sons and said to them, "Be fruitful and
> multiply and fill the earth."
> (Gen 9:1)

Filling the earth does not require that every couple have as many babies as possible. And in fact that is what has happened: humans have filled the earth, and they did it despite the fact that not all of them had children. One cannot take the words of this blessing at the beginning of the Bible and understand it to show something about the motive for a law about homosexuality in Leviticus. (We will have much more to say about this famous passage in our chapter on the Earth.)

2. Distinction. Recognizing distinctions among things is tremendously important to the priestly authors of the Torah. In the creation account in Genesis 1, God starts out with all matter being the same, undifferentiated. This primal matter is called in Hebrew *tōhû wābōhû*, traditionally translated as "unformed" in English. Creation takes place when God makes distinctions between one thing and another: between light and darkness, between water and dry land. This principle of the significance of distinctions returns in Leviticus, where the task of priests is:

> to *distinguish* between the holy and the secular, and between the impure
> and the pure.
> (Lev 10:10)

Several mixtures are forbidden in this text. These mixtures would bring together things that are otherwise distinguished. One cannot mix animal species: for example, mating a horse and donkey to make a mule. One cannot mix various seeds to make a new plant. One cannot wear clothing that is *shaatnez*—a mixture of fabric from a plant (flax) and an animal (wool) in the same garment. Now one might make the argument that we can understand the ban on homosexual intercourse as deriving from this priestly interest in keeping the categories of male and female distinct. This is an interesting argument, but one must be cautious about it. In the first place, it is rather in heterosexual sex that the mixing of the sexes takes place! Now one can argue that it is still in homosexual sex that the concern for the *distinction* between the sexes becomes an issue. However, if this matter of distinction were the reason for the law, then female homosexuality should have been prohibited as well. The biblical law's limitation to male–male sex but not female–female sex makes it hard to argue that the concern for distinguishing the sexes is the motive for the law. In fact this is demonstrated by a biblical law against cross-dressing. Men in drag and women dressed like men are more clearly a mixing of categories. And precisely here the law mentions both men and women:

> There shall not be a man's item on a woman, and a man shall not wear a woman's garment, because everyone who does these is an offensive thing of YHWH, your God.
> (Deut 22:5)

A second reason for caution is that sometimes a good argument can be overdone. People have spoken of "Israel's proclivity for keeping categories separate." As we have seen, there are passages and laws that involve distinction. The passages are the creation story in Genesis 1 and the line about the task of priests in Leviticus 10. But these are the only two occurrences of the phrase "to distinguish" (Hebrew *lĕhabdîl*) in the Torah. And the individual laws that we mentioned about *shaatnez* and crossbreeding animals are the most obvious examples. One should not derive from these things a basis for explaining all kinds of laws in the Bible, including the law about male homosexual acts. The case that people often bring up as showing distinction as a concept pervading an entire set of laws is the forbidden animals (in Leviticus 11 and again in Deuteronomy 14). They cite the work *Purity and*

Danger by the anthropologist Mary Douglas. They frequently cite Douglas uncritically.[19] She argues that the reason certain animals are forbidden as food (including pigs, camels, horses, rabbits, rodents, eagles, owls, and fish that do not have scales) is that they do not fit distinct categories of what the Jews considered to be appropriate to eat. As we have explained elsewhere, however, our friend Professor Douglas's model of such distinctions and categories was based on incorrect information that she received from her informants. Dependent on others for the meaning of Hebrew words, she misunderstood a description of many of the forbidden animals. Incorrectly informed about the character of life in biblical Israel and especially about the author(s) of these laws, she was led to logical but erroneous conclusions. The reason why Jews in biblical times did not eat ham or rabbit or crow or lobster was not that they had a "proclivity for keeping categories separate." The reasons lie elsewhere. And one should certainly not use this matter to shed light on a law about homosexual sex.[20]

Moreover, something feels wrong about this argument: it is purely theoretical. Does anyone who opposes or forbids homosexual sex take this view because he or she is concerned for *keeping categories distinct*? People do not hold a meeting to discuss distinctions and then conclude that homosexuality should be banned because it fails to keep things distinct enough. People rather oppose it for cultural and personal reasons, for gut-level psychological reasons, for reasons of power, fear, control, acceptance in a group, having someone on whom to look down, instinctive abhorrence that they themselves cannot necessarily explain—reasons of which we may approve or disapprove. We are not psychologists, and we do not propose to analyze here all the reasons why individuals feel negatively about others having homosexual sex. We are simply accepting the fact that such feelings of antipathy are in the first place visceral (and culturally conditioned), not intellectual.

Further on this matter of distinction: Some say that the ultimate purpose of that entire code of laws in Leviticus is to distinguish Israel from others.[21] This is simply wrong. In the first place, this law code says ten times that the law is to be the same for Israelites and for aliens:

And if an alien will reside with you in your land, you shall not persecute him. The alien who resides with you shall be to you like a citizen of yours, and you shall love him as yourself.
(Lev 19:33–34)

> You shall have one judgment: it will be the same for the alien and the
> citizen.
> (Lev 24:22)

The law code does include a statement that Israelites are not supposed to engage in a number of practices of the Egyptians and the Canaanites. But the goal in that statement is specifically that following their God's laws instead of those other two cultures' laws will be a path to a better life:

> You shall not go by their laws. You shall do *my* judgments, and you shall observe *my* laws, to go by them. I am YHWH, your God. And you shall observe my laws and my judgments which, when a human will do them, he'll live through them!
> (Lev 18:3–5)

So distinction may be a *result* of Israel's keeping the biblical commandments, but that does not mean that distinction is itself the whole purpose of the thing.

Some have even taken this matter of distinction to the extreme, thinking that Israel was thus setting itself apart from other people. We should take care to note that there is a difference between distinction (*mabdîl*) and "setting apart." There is no reference to "setting apart" anywhere in this body of laws in Leviticus—or, for that matter, in the entire Torah. The assertion that the Jews set themselves apart is one of the most persistent anti-Semitic claims, and one should be careful not to suggest that such a thing has a historical basis in the Torah. The Israelites are forbidden to practice certain acts that are attributed (not always correctly) to the Canaanites. That is different from separation or setting apart—which was never required by the Torah and never practiced by Israel in biblical times. One might cite the passage in which the Moabite prophet Balaam calls Israel "a people dwelling separate and not reckoned among the nations" (Num 23:9). But that is presented as a poem by a foreign prophet, not a goal of the Israelites themselves. And it applies only to the Israelites in the wilderness on the road back from slavery in Egypt. In that situation they really are literally separate and not yet thought of as a nation by anyone. That line of poetry should not be used to prove anything about biblical ideas of distinction or separateness.

3. Morality. In connection with the discussion in our age, some people say that homosexuality is immoral. This especially comes up when people on the other side of the issue say to these people that discrimination against homosexuals is the same as discrimination against people of other races or religions. They respond that the difference is that homosexuality is immoral. So the question is: what is immoral about it? In the case of murder or theft or false witness, we can see pretty readily what is wrong with these things. Likewise in some sexual matters, we can see, with very few of us disagreeing, what is wrong with incestuous abuse of children. The harm that occurs in all of these is visible. But homosexuality is different. The harm is not obvious in the first place, and, on the other side, there are questions of harm that is done to homosexual persons when they are ill-treated by the heterosexual majority. When we have heard people assert that homosexuality is immoral, the most common thing we have heard them say to back that view up is precisely to cite the fact that the Bible forbids it (at least for men). That, however, is not the answer. It is the question! Our original question about the biblical law was: what is immoral about it? The law does not say. It just says that homosexual acts are a *tōʿēbāh*. But, as we shall discuss below, the word *tōʿēbāh* does not mean that something is immoral. It means that it offends some group. In the absence of the obvious harm that other laws involve, we cannot conclude that this law regards homosexuality as immoral. It regards it as offending. We shall discuss morality further in connection with culture below.

This is not to say that the general population in biblical society was homophobic. There is absolutely no evidence to suggest that. In fact, what is striking about this particular law against male homosexuality is that we find it only in the law code of one biblical author. There are at least four separate authors of biblical law, writing over a period of centuries in ancient Israel. The stratum of legal texts in which we find prohibitions of male homosexual acts is the latest. The other three are the Covenant Code (Exodus 21–23), the J Decalogue (Exod 34:14–26), and the Deuteronomic law code (Deuteronomy 12–26). None of these contains any law at all about homosexuality. The law prohibiting it is part of the Priestly laws and in particular the section of these laws known as the Holiness Code (Leviticus 17–25). Some scholars trace this code to a different author or even a different group from the rest of the Priestly laws.[22] There is a considerable variety of views of when these laws were written. This would require at least a chapter for us to treat here.[23] For our present purpose, though, we can say that (1) these laws come from an Aaronid priest in ancient Judah and (2) it is the latest of the major law codes. We cannot say why the other law codes do not mention homosexuality. All we can say is that it does not appear to be a concern in biblical law until a fairly late stage, and therefore we cannot know how people in biblical society overall regarded homosexuality. We know only that this one author in this one community stated that it was an offensive thing.

4. Purity. Now why does only this author of the Holiness Code raise the matter of homosexuality? How does it differ from those other law codes?

1. They were written earlier.
2. They do not deal with sex very much in general.
3. The Holiness Code comes from the Jerusalem priesthood.
4. The Jerusalem priesthood was closer to the monarchy: favorable to it, intermarried with it.
5. The Priestly laws in general and this section called the Holiness Code in particular are concerned with purity, and this law about male homosexual acts is a matter of purity to these priests. As we quoted above, in Leviticus purity is placed alongside holiness in importance to priests ("to *distinguish* between the holy and the secular, and between the impure and the pure").

So what is the significance of purity to a Jerusalem Temple priest, backed up by the monarchy, centuries after the founding of the country? This section of his law code forbids male homosexual acts, other sexual acts, and sacrificing one's children. It says:

> You shall not become impure by all of these, because the nations that
> I am putting out from in front of you became impure by all of these.
> (Lev 18:24)

Now, this does not appear to be historically correct. The archaeological evidence is that the nations did *not* do these things. For example, there is no archaeological evidence at all of human sacrifice among any of the peoples of the ancient Near East except the Phoenicians at their colony in Carthage.[24] The priest who gave us these laws was concerned with purity, so he framed the laws in terms of it: these acts will make the land impure;

the people who lived here before us did these things and made the land impure; we must not do that. But he did not base this on actual historical memory of such things. So the motive for forbidding homosexuality cannot just be derived from the biblical claim that it makes one impure or is contrary to Israel's holiness or will result in polluting the land and getting the Israelites thrown out. The law was formulated by the author of Leviticus 18, like the human sacrifice (Molech) prohibition, as a reason to give to the people. But the specific reasons for each law lie elsewhere.

The biblical scholar Saul Olyan proposes a more specific reason for the prohibition of male homosexual acts with regard to purity. He has combined the matter of improper mixtures, discussed above, with the matter of the pure and impure. He argues that the laws in Leviticus applied only to one act—anal sexual intercourse, and he suggests that the concern was with mixing two separate "defiling substances," namely, semen and excrement. To discuss Olyan's arguments requires that we speak openly of bodily matters. Some find such discussions unpleasant, but we really have no choice if we are to give due treatment to a serious subject.

Olyan's case, then, comes in two steps. In the first step, he argues that the laws in Leviticus refer only to anal sex and to no other acts. In the second, he argues that the issue is a matter of purity and of unacceptable mixing of the two impure substances: semen and excrement. We disagree with Olyan, so we want to say first that his is probably the most thorough, carefully researched treatment on this subject, with a rich bibliography in the notes citing conservative and critical works from medieval times to the present. There is a lot of irresponsible—which is to say, bad—work on various sides of this matter. We take the trouble to challenge and refine Olyan's work precisely because his work is exceptional. He is a serious, important scholar; but we believe that his conclusions are not correct.

Regarding his first step, Olyan bases his case on a very refined analysis of the Hebrew phrase that appears in both of the verses quoted above that prohibit male–male sex. The phrase is "a woman's layings," which in Hebrew is *miškĕbê 'iššāh*. Olyan notes that in another verse we get the parallel phrase for sex between a man and a woman: *miškab zākār*, which means literally "a male's laying."[25] So Olyan sees the two phrases as parallel:

miškab zākār   a male's laying
miškĕbê 'iššāh   a woman's layings

Now in that parallel verse, Olyan says, the phrase *miškab zākār* means specifically only a man's reproductive intercourse with a woman—meaning through vaginal penetration. So he sees the phrase in our verses, which uses the same word, *laying*, to mean likewise only vaginal penetration. He concludes therefore that the law that says not to lay a man like a woman's layings must mean not to penetrate the man—meaning, namely, anal sex. He therefore claims to be the first to show this meaning of the phrase on philological (i.e., linguistic) grounds. An honest scholar, he acknowledges that "several readers of prepublication versions of this manuscript raised the possibility that *miškĕbê 'iššāh* could refer to acts other than vaginal receptivity." But, he says, "I think it unlikely." Why? Because, he writes, "to assume this, one would have to assume that *miškab zākār* also refers to a range of sexual acts."[26]

This is where we disagree, and our point is also philological. Precisely the most blatant difference between the phrase that means "a male's laying" and the phrase that means "a woman's layings" is that the woman's layings are plural. The phrase "a male's laying" is a singular because it occurs in biblical passages about ending a woman's virginity—so it means specifically vaginal sex and nothing else in those places. The phrase "a woman's layings," on the other hand, as a plural, means the opposite of the male phrase. That is, it means all kinds of sexual acts, not just basic penetration of another person. Singular means one act; plural means many. So we believe that Olyan drew the exact reverse, wrong conclusion. He focused on what the two phrases have in common, and he is right about that. But he did not give enough weight to what is an essential difference between the two phrases: a singular act versus a number of acts.

We should acknowledge that nearly all translators have translated this Hebrew plural as a singular in English. And in a moment of honesty, this includes one of the authors of this book, Richard Elliott Friedman: I, too, made it a singular in my translation of the Torah, probably for the same reason as all the other translators. Namely, it makes a less awkward English.[27] But I admit that what I gained in felicity I lost in accuracy. That may be all right for a translation in general, but for our present purpose of relating the Bible to important issues we need to put accuracy first.

Next we turn to Olyan's second step, that the reason for forbidding male–male sex is that it mixes two impure substances, semen and excrement. (Olyan suggests that this is why female–female sex is not prohibited: because it does not involve a mixing of defiling substances.) Now if his first step is not correct (that it is only about anal sex), then this second step does not work. The homosexual sex could mean acts that have nothing to do with excrement. But, in any case, Olyan was mistaken in thinking that human excrement is like the other things that are called "impure" (in some translations "unclean"; Hebrew ṭāmē') in the Bible. These things include semen and menstrual blood. When a woman has a menstrual period she is in a ṭāmē' condition for seven days. When a man has a flow of semen, he too is ṭāmē' and must wait a day and then bathe. Excrement (solid and liquid), however, is not ṭāmē'. It cannot be ṭāmē'. If it were, then humans would all be ṭāmē' almost every day of their lives! Olyan blurs the distinction between excrement and the ṭāmē' fluids by using the phrase "defiling liquids" to describe all of these. But excrement absolutely cannot be "defiling" in the way that the others are. It is never grouped with them in the law. And it is never referred to as ṭāmē' in the Torah. Olyan bases his claim that it is connectable to the impure fluids on a passage in Ezekiel. There God tells Ezekiel to eat a disgusting concoction of cake made with human excrement. God explains the meaning of this symbolic act: "So the children of Israel will eat their bread impure (ṭāmē')." Ezekiel, who has done a lot of things for God, finally balks. He pleads with God on the grounds that he has never eaten anything ṭāmē' or any animal that is found torn or dead. God meets him halfway. God lets him use animal excrement instead of human (Ezek 4:9–15)! What does this have to do with the laws about homosexual sex in Leviticus? Olyan attributes these laws to the "Holiness School" (called H for short), and he says that the prophet Ezekiel "is widely viewed as sharing H's purity system (in other words, Ezekiel belonged to the Holiness School)." He therefore concludes: "I will assume from Ezek 4:9–15 that excrement defiles in H circles, even though this is not evidenced in the Holiness Source itself."[28]

With due respect, this set of connections has too many weak points for such a big conclusion. A story of an extreme symbolic act by a prophet cannot be used to establish a point of law. Ezekiel's act is a metaphor. We cannot conclude that it meant that the Jews were really supposed to end up eating bread baked with anything impure in Babylonian exile. We cannot know that it meant that the specific cake that Ezekiel himself was supposed to eat was actually in the category of ṭāmē', just as it did not in fact fit the other two categories that Ezekiel mentions (torn or found dead). Olyan also cites Zech 3:1–5, Deuteronomy 13–15, and 2 Kgs 10:27. These verses all have to do with excrement, but none of them connects it with impurity. They do not support Olyan's case. They rather underscore the point that, in all the Bible, excrement is never connected with impurity in any way except in the single case of the metaphor in a unique vision of the prophet Ezekiel.

Also, as a more general point of method in biblical scholarship, we have said elsewhere that we must all be careful about imagining "Schools" in ancient Israel.[29] Various scholars speak of the Wisdom School, the Priestly School, and the Deuteronomistic School. These are very speculative constructs. We do not know if a Holiness School existed, let alone if Ezekiel was a member of it.[30] What we do know for sure is that human excrement is not and cannot be in the Bible's category of impurity.

We therefore have good reason to doubt the explanations that have been proposed for why sex between a man and another man is prohibited in the Bible. We may never know for sure what the reasons were. The text does not say, and so much time has passed since these laws were given. As we indicated above, we think that the reasons are more probably visceral and cultural, not theoretical or intellectual.

Proposals for permitting homosexuality biblically

What reasons have scholars given for still finding male homosexual acts to be acceptable, even by those who recognize the force of the biblical commandment against them? Some have tried to interpret the words of these laws to mean something other than prohibiting homosexual intercourse. Some have suggested that these words may prohibit only some, but not all, homosexual acts. For example:

1. The biblical scholar who is widely thought of as the most learned on the book of Leviticus is Jacob Milgrom. His three volumes of commentary on that book are indeed impressive. Milgrom also concentrates on the phrase "like a woman's layings" (*miškĕbê ʾiššāh*), but he sees it differently from Olyan and from us. Milgrom argues that this plural term, *miškĕbê*, is a technical term and that it never means just sexual relations in the Bible. It means illicit sexual relations. That is, in every place where it occurs it refers to something that is illegal. It never means just ordinary sex. It means forbidden sexual relations. He therefore concludes that the law forbids for homosexual men only those sexual relations that are also illegal for a man

with a woman. In practice, this would mean that a man is forbidden to have sex with males who are close relatives, just as he is forbidden to have sex with females who are close relatives, but a man is not forbidden to have sex with any other male.[31]

That is a clever argument, but it does not really have a sufficient basis. When Milgrom says that in every single occurrence of the phrase *miškĕbê 'iššāh* it means something illicit, he is right. But the fact is that the number of occurrences of the phrase is only three. And two of the three are the very two passages about homosexual sex in Leviticus that we are studying here. So he is basing his understanding of these two verses on just the one other time the phrase occurs in the Bible. Such an argument simply will not hold up.

2. Milgrom also makes the point that this law applies only in the land of Israel.[32] As a matter of fact, that is true. Both chapters in which these laws appear make the point that these are laws that the Israelites are supposed to obey when they arrive in the promised land. Both chapters conclude with a warning that if the people do not follow the laws, they will be thrown out of the land.[33] However, even though Milgrom's point is well taken, this is a reading of the letter of the law that almost no one will accept. Jews who live by the laws of the Torah have always understood the laws in these chapters to apply both in the land of Israel and everywhere else on earth. These laws include prohibitions of incest and human sacrifice, and no one would say that these things are forbidden in Israel but permissible everywhere else. Conservative readers of the laws about male homosexual acts would almost unanimously say that these laws express principles that would apply everywhere. Liberal readers, also almost unanimously, would not be satisfied with the idea that men can perform homosexual acts outside of Israel but not inside it.

3. One of our students once pointed out that it is, after all, impossible to lie with a man in the way one does with a woman—namely, vaginal sex—so no one can violate this commandment.[34] That is a clever, even fascinating idea, but why then would the commandment exist if it prohibits something that is impossible anyway? And besides, as we said above, the plural phrase "a woman's layings" (*miškĕbê 'iššāh*) implies that many acts, not just vaginal sex, are included here.

4. Similarly, a daughter of one of the authors of this book (Friedman) pointed out that a homosexual man may not mind a commandment that

tells him that he cannot lie with men the way he lies with women because he does not lie with women! This, too, is not a compelling argument, but it is clever.

We do not think that we can define our way out of the problem or get around it by looking for such loopholes in the law. The law really means what pretty much everyone has taken it to mean for centuries. Whatever view one takes, one must address the law fairly in terms of what it says.

Law and prose

There is a related matter that involves both laws and narrative passages in the Bible's history of the kingdom of Judah. This is the case of homosexual prostitution. The legal passage says:

> There shall not be a sacred prostitute from the daughters of Israel, and there shall not be a sacred prostitute from the sons of Israel. You shall not bring the price of a prostitute or the cost of a dog to the house of YHWH, your God, for any vow, because the two of them are both an offensive thing [tō'ēbāh] of YHWH.
> (Deut 23:18–19)

The understanding of the Hebrew term qādēš in the first sentence is uncertain. It may mean a sacred prostitute, as translated here, but it may not.[35] It has been claimed that the prohibition of homosexual sex was about cult prostitution, that it was part of the worship of pagan gods. However, we do not have sufficient evidence to think that there ever was cult prostitution in that region. This claim comes from a time when scholars believed that ancient Canaanite pagan religion included such things, that people would go to a place of worship and perform sex there. This idea was spread popularly in a best-selling novel, James Michener's *The Source*. Scholars today are more skeptical about the existence of such a thing. The ancient texts and archaeological record do not support it.[36]

The narrative passages that refer to this come later, in the history of the kings of Judah. During the reign of King Solomon's son Rehoboam, it is said that there was qādēš in the land and that the people were doing the offensive things (tô'ăbōt) that the Canaanites had done.[37] The historian credits Kings Asa, Jehoshaphat, and Josiah with ridding the country of the *qĕdēšîm*.[38] We simply cannot be certain if this means sacred male prostitutes or not.

To complicate things further, even if they are male prostitutes, we cannot be certain whether their clients were understood to be male or female. So we are not even sure that this has to do with homosexual matters at all. And to complicate things even more, even if they are male prostitutes, and even if their clients are men, these passages would only be expressing opposition to male cultic prostitution, not to homosexuality in general.

The second sentence forbids anyone from bringing "the price of a (female) prostitute or the cost of a dog" to the Temple. That is, if the going price for sex with a prostitute is fifty dollars, it would be crude to come to the Temple and say, "I pledge fifty dollars." Those present might snicker, or they might get angry. No matter what their reaction, though, the whole thing would be unseemly. As for the price of a dog, the term *dog* is usually understood to be a pejorative term for a male homosexual prostitute, placed in parallel here with the female prostitute. As with the first sentence, we can learn very little about male sexuality from this. Assuming that we are right that the term means a male homosexual prostitute, it is still not the homosexuality but, rather, the prostitution that is denigrated here. It is the same for both the female and the male prostitute. The issue is that one should not use their price for a vowed donation to the Temple. This law does not even forbid one to be a prostitute, male or female. The issue is respect for God and the Temple. Once again, therefore, we advise caution in making any conclusions about homosexuality in the Bible on the basis of these texts.

Culture

For one thing, one must address the law in its context. There has been an archaeology revolution in the past century and a half, which has enabled us to know more than any generation before us what the biblical world was like. There have also been significant developments in anthropology, which have enabled us to appreciate more the impact that cultures have on the individuals within each society. How do these new bodies of knowledge affect this particular question?

The word *homosexuality* is commonly understood today to be a category separate from, and in opposition to, *heterosexuality*. We tend to take these categories for granted, as though there are two kinds of people, those who prefer sexual relationships with people of the same sex and those who do not; or at most we add a third category, "bisexual," to refer to people who are sexually attracted to members of both sexes. Although history shows us that same-sex relations have always been a part of human culture and society around the world, the idea of categorizing people according to sexual preference is actually a modern invention. In most ancient societies—and also among many non-Western cultures at the present time—homosexuality is not a distinct and separate category of identity or existence. Sexual preferences were certainly acknowledged, but they did not serve as a means by which to classify people. In fact, historical texts from Europe and the Mediterranean show that identity was not defined in terms of sexual preference before the seventeenth century CE, and homosexual activities were simply viewed as temptations of the flesh to which certain people may have been more prone than others.[39]

In ancient cultures of the biblical region we find a particularly different way of seeing homosexuality than the way in which we tend to understand the category today in the West. Historical texts from the ancient Hittites, Babylonians, Assyrians, Egyptians, and Greeks describe legal and cultural boundaries pertaining to male homosexuality, and male homosexual intercourse is actually depicted in art from Uruk, Assur, Babylon, and Susa from as early as the third millennium BCE. But none of these ancient cultures of the biblical region understood homosexuality as a lifestyle choice or as a marker of identity. None of them referred to people as "homosexual" in opposition to "heterosexual," and none of them condemned homosexual behavior categorically.

So while historical texts attest to the experience of homosexual desire throughout human existence, the interpretation of this desire and of same-sex activities varies considerably from culture to culture. What this means is that when we think about homosexuality, and when we read about homosexuality in an ancient text like the Bible, we need to understand what connotations and interpretations that concept might have brought out in people in ancient Israel before we can think about how to apply the biblical perspective on homosexuality to current issues.

We know from combining biblical references with archaeological discoveries and ethnographic data that ancient Israelite society was structured around extended family units, household compounds consisting of a patriarch, his wives, his concubines, his sons and their wives and families, and often his brothers and nephews and their families.[40] Although children were considered a gift from God and a blessing, the reality was that infant and child mortality rates were high.[41] Since most homesteads were self-sustaining units, many hands were needed, and the production of many children was encouraged.[42] Passing on one's patrimony to male children was extremely important.[43] Many women died in childbirth.[44] Having more than one wife, in addition to concubines by which one could sire more children, simply made sense in this world. On the other hand, a way of life that did not encourage the production of many offspring, such as gay marriage, would not. Now this may not explain the Holiness Code's firm prohibition on male homosexual acts, but it does provide some insight into the societal emphasis on heterosexual marriage found throughout the Bible and elsewhere in the ancient world.

If the opposition between "homosexual" and "heterosexual" as categories of people's identity is a recent construct, then when we look at these biblical texts that people perceive as relating to our current category of homosexuality, we need to try to understand how the ancients talked about same-sex acts. In other words, if homosexuality was not a separate category of existence—and, in fact, living an exclusively homosexual lifestyle was not really an economic option for many in the ancient world—then how did people of the ancient Near East perceive same-sex desire? What was their construction of homosexuality?

Now this is not to say that the Bible's authors thought about homosexuality in the same ways that those other ancient cultures did. In some cases, more than a thousand years separate those other ancient literatures from the Bible's writings; and the Greek literature, though separated from some of the biblical literature in question by only a century or two, was still produced a thousand miles away. But an overview of ancient Near Eastern and Greek attitudes toward homosexuality from times both before and shortly after the biblical texts were written offers us an alternative way of understanding homosexuality in the Bible from the way in which we might be inclined to see it from a twenty-first-century Western perspective. Although separated in time and space from biblical Israel, stories, laws, and other ancient Near Eastern texts still provide a nearer context in which to understand the biblical injunction against homosexuality than our modern world does.

As in the Bible, there are actually very few laws from the rest of the ancient Near East regulating homosexuality. Extant legal collections from Babylon and Egypt are silent on the matter. A Hittite Law from the mid-seventeenth century BCE prohibits sexual relations with mother, daughter, or son, but the context indicates that kinship, rather than gender, is the basis for this prohibition.[45] But the existence of this law suggests that male homosexuality was known, and the lack of other laws prohibiting such activity may indicate that same-sex relations were simply not subject to legal regulation.

Male homosexual intercourse is discussed as either auspicious or inauspicious (but not moral or immoral) in a Middle Babylonian divination text, *Šumma Ālu*:[46]

> If a man copulates (*iṭeḫḫe*) with his equal (*meḫrīšu*) from the rear, he becomes the leader among his peers and brothers.
> If a man copulates with an *assinnu*, a hard destiny will leave him (?).
> If a man copulates with a *gersequ* (courtier, possibly a eunuch), terrors will possess him for a whole year but then they will leave him.
> If a man copulates with a home-born slave (*dušmu*), a hard destiny will befall him.[47]

There is no moral condemnation of homosexuality here. There is only a concern with the roles and statuses of the men involved. It seems that, for the Babylonian author in this period, being the active partner in homosexual intercourse with someone of high social status (an equal, a cult prostitute, a courtier) brought good luck, while being homosexually involved with one's slave, or being the receptive partner in a noncultic context, was considered bad luck.

Two Middle Assyrian Laws (mid-second millennium BCE) also discuss male homosexuality. The first reads:

> If a man started a rumor against his neighbor in private, saying "People have lain repeatedly with him," or he said to him in a brawl in the presence of (other) people, "People have lain repeatedly with you; I will

prosecute you," since he is not able to prosecute (him) (and) did not prosecute (him), they shall flog that seignior fifty (times) with staves (and) he shall do the work of the king for one full month; they shall castrate him and he shall also pay one talent of lead.[48]

The law that precedes it provides a similar penalty (forty floggings) for a man who makes unsubstantiated accusations against a neighbor's wife, saying, "People have lain repeatedly with your wife." In both cases, sexual libel is a punishable offense; and in fact, accusing a "neighbor" (meaning a fellow seignior or aristocrat) of being repeatedly receptive to homosexual intercourse earned one ten more stripes than accusing a neighbor's wife of promiscuity.[49]

The law that follows reads:

If a man lay [by force?] with his neighbor [*tappā'u*—a man of equal status], when they have prosecuted him (and) convicted him, they shall lie with him (and) turn him into a eunuch.[50]

The crime here seems to be not the homosexual behavior but, rather, the subjugation (or possibly forcible rape) of a man of equal status to the passive/receptive role in intercourse. The punishment for this is to be homosexually raped oneself—and then castrated.

It is possible to read these laws as looking down on male homosexuality in general, of defining homosexual behavior categorically in the terms of our day. However, these laws occur in the context of a series of laws concerning crimes committed against married women, and so Assyriologists have concluded that this context suggests that the passive/receptive partner in male–male intercourse was perceived in Middle Assyrian culture as the equivalent of a woman. This culture is making a major distinction between the two men: the one who penetrates and the one who is entered by him. The laws and cultural norms do not seem concerned with homosexual behavior itself. They are concerned rather with the issue of social status and the shame of being feminized when a freeborn male citizen assumes the passive/receiving role in a homosexual partnership.

Literary evidence from ancient Egypt demonstrates the same set of associations. In *The Contendings of Horus and Seth* is an extraordinary sexual account: Horus, the son of Osiris and Isis, vies with his uncle Seth for the throne of Egypt. As the older male, Seth repeatedly tries various tactics designed to demonstrate his dominance and superiority over Horus to the other gods. At one point he attempts to dominate Horus sexually. Horus, tricking Seth into thinking that he has succeeded, manages to catch Seth's semen in his hand. Horus then brings the semen to his mother, Isis, who cuts off Horus's hand in outrage and throws it into the marshes. By use of magic, Isis then makes Horus's phallus rise and catches the semen in a jar, spreading it on lettuces that Seth later eats. Seth informs the gods that he has humiliated Horus by having homosexually dominated him, but Horus asks the gods to call forth Horus's and Seth's semen from where each is located. The god Thoth does this, and Seth's semen emerges not from Horus but from the marshes where Horus's hand had been thrown by Isis. Horus's semen appears as a gold disc on the head of Seth, who is now the one who has been humiliated.[51]

Similarly in other Middle Kingdom and New Kingdom literature, an Egyptian man who assumed a passive role in a homosexual encounter was culturally perceived to be weak, feminine, and cowardly.[52] Those who took this role were categorized as "back-turners" (ḥmjw).[53] But the sexual element of being a back-turner was a symptom of being a coward, not a cause: sexual acts between men were expressed only when they concerned the acceptable defilement of enemies and the enforcement of power hierarchy. On the other hand, homoerotic relationships between men of equal rank were considered scandalous.

In contrast with the ancient Near East, a wealth of material relating attitudes toward homosexuality survives from ancient Greece and Rome, including literature, philosophy, art, and legal texts. From this evidence, it seems that erotic love between males was socially sanctioned, if not expected, among the Athenian aristocracy, from at least the sixth century BCE through the fourth. Commoners, on the other hand, may have been more ambivalent on the subject. Many of Aristophanes's comedies demonstrate popular prejudice against homosexuality as an elite practice, but most of the barbs are aimed at adult men who assume the passive role, especially to younger partners.[54]

With all of this, however, Greek society also did not label homosexuals as a distinct category of people, set apart from a cultural norm by their sexual preferences. All aristocratic men were expected to marry and raise families; so their relations with other men did not constitute a "deviant" choice of lifestyle. The great gods Zeus, Apollo, and Poseidon were themselves known to fall in love with and/or rape human men as well as women. In Sparta, homosexuality seems to have been universal among male citizens. Rather than distinguish sexual desire or behavior by the gender of the participants, the Greeks were concerned with the extent to which such desire or behavior conformed to social norms. These norms were based on gender, age, and social status. An adult male citizen could choose to have sex with a male youth, slave, or foreigner—all categories of socially inferior men—as long as the citizen was the active, penetrating partner and not the passive recipient of another man's penetration. In Greece as in the Near East, to be on the receiving end of sex with a male was considered shameful, reserved only for those of lower status (including all women). It was not the homosexuality. It was being the man who was penetrated by another man.[55]

The most common and idealized form of homosexual relationships between aristocratic males in Greece was known as *paederastia*: "boy-love." An older male citizen, known in Athens as an *erastes*, would court a young adolescent youth of a good family much in the way a man might court a future wife. If his courtship was successful, the youth would become the *eromenos* to the *erastes*, and the *erastes* would educate, protect, and offer love to the *eromenos*. Social conventions dictated that when the youth became a man, the sexual nature of the relationship must end in order to avoid the shame associated with a full-grown male citizen being penetrated by a social equal. One could be an *eromenos* only in one's youth, before becoming a citizen. In fact, while the *eromenos* must honor and respect his *erastes*, even as a youth he was never to reciprocate the sexual desire of the *erastes*, for this would bring shame on himself and his family. In Plato's *Symposium*, Xenophon states that "the boy does not share in the man's pleasure in intercourse, as a woman does; cold sober, he looks upon the other drunk with desire."[56]

Thus the ancient Greeks did not conceive of sexual orientation as a marker of social identity. They rather subsumed sexuality under the more important social categories of gender, age, and status. It was considered shameful for a man of status to be penetrated by another man, but among the aristocratic elite there was no shame in being the active partner in a same-sex relationship. Aristophanes's complaint about adult men who engage in passive homosexuality is that they act like women, something real men should not do. Plato asks, "Will not all men censure as womanly him who imitates the woman?"[57] This attitude remained long into the Roman era as well: Plutarch writes, "We class those who enjoy the passive part as belonging to the lowest depth of vice and allow them not the least degree of confidence or respect or friendship."[58] But there were certainly no laws against homosexual behavior or any condemnation of homosexuality as immoral. Plato thought highly of those who "love boys only when they begin to acquire some mind—a growth associated with that of down on their chins. For . . . those who begin to love them at this age are prepared to be always with them and share all with them as long as life shall last."[59] Male prostitutes were actually taxed, as they would be in later Rome under Augustus (who also granted them a legal holiday).

Thus it would seem that in the ancient world there was no category of people classified as "homosexual." There were only homosexual behaviors that were either socially condoned or condemned depending on the status of the men involved in them. Acting as the aggressor/penetrator in a male homosexual encounter was a sign of manhood, dominance, and superiority and was often socially acceptable *if* the aggressor acted upon a man of lower rank. When we read the Bible for clues as to the ancient Israelites' understanding of homosexuality, we should do so with this larger context in mind, as they may well have thought about homosexuality in terms more similar to their neighbors' than to ours.

The law in Leviticus against "laying a male the layings of a woman," if understood as prohibiting any homosexual intercourse between men regardless of rank, is unique in the ancient world. However, we need to understand it within the wider cultural context in which the denigrating nature of male homosexuality is not tied to homoerotic desire but, rather, is regarded as a violation of a penetrated man's dignity and thereby a socially degrading act. In other words, what the authors of Leviticus 18 and 20 may be prohibiting is not homosexuality as we would construe the category today but, rather, an act that they understood to rob another man of his social status by feminizing him. This particularly makes sense in the context of the greater legislative text in which Leviticus 18 and 20 are embedded, the Holiness Code. Underlying these texts' general theology, that all who settle on God's land are entitled to His protection, is an insistence that both ritual and moral laws are binding not only on the Israelites but on all who dwell in the promised land, citizen and alien alike.[60] The existence of one law for all men is a unique phenomenon in the ancient world. The law codes of Babylon, Assyria, Egypt, Greece, and the Hittites all assume that laws apply differently to men of different social classes. Israelite society did something revolutionary in the degree to which it treated all residents as equal. So homosexual domination of a social inferior by a social superior, as a socially acceptable institution, had to be modified in Israelite society. In the Holiness Code, therefore, there can be no homosexual acts at all in Israel, since by cross-cultural perception such intercourse would necessarily denigrate the passive partner and violate his equal status under God's law. The laws in Leviticus thus make no distinction between the penetrating male and the passive male the way the other ancient law codes do. The entire range of homosexual acts is forbidden, and both males are equally instructed not to do them.[61] In biblical terms, this would bring pollution to the land, causing it to "vomit" out the Israelites as it had the previous inhabitants.[62] Olyan makes this point effectively: that other ancient cultures make distinctions—between classes, between penetrator versus recipient—while the law in Leviticus makes no distinctions; the law is the same for any two males. He suggests that the reason may be that the entire law code in Leviticus emphasizes the equality of all. It does not have the class distinctions that are in the other cultures' laws. One Torah for the citizen and the alien. There is even equal treatment for slaves in some matters. So the law on homosexuality likewise does not make the distinctions that we find just about everywhere else. Cultural comparison, then, suggests that any immorality attached to male homosexuality in the Hebrew Bible has to do with the violation of a fellow social equal and not with the nature of homosexual desire itself.

Our contribution to the subject

Now, we want to contribute another perspective that we believe can be helpful on this subject. Let us return to the point that the text identifies male homosexuality by the technical term tōʿēbāh, translated in English as "an offensive thing" or "an abomination." This is important because most things that are forbidden in biblical law are not identified with this word. In both of our contexts in Leviticus (chapters 18 and 20), male homosexuality is the only act to be called this. (Other acts are included broadly in a line at the end of chapter 18.[63]) So this term, which is an important one in the Bible in general, is particularly important with regard to the law about male homosexual acts. The question is: is the term *tōʿēbāh* an absolute—meaning that an act that is a *tōʿēbāh* is wrong in itself and can never be otherwise? Or is the term relative, meaning that something that is a *tōʿēbāh* to one person may not be offensive to another, or something that is a *tōʿēbāh* in one culture may not be offensive in another, or something that is a *tōʿēbāh* in one generation or time period may not be offensive in another—in which case the law may change as people's perceptions change?

Elsewhere in the Bible the term is in fact relative. For example, in the story of Joseph and his brothers in Genesis, Joseph tells his brothers that if the Pharaoh asks them what their occupation is, they should say that they are cowherds. They must not say that they are shepherds. Why? Because, Joseph explains, all shepherds are an offensive thing (*tōʿēbāh*) to the Egyptians.[64] But shepherds are not an offensive thing to the Israelites or Moabites or many other cultures. In another passage in that story, we read that Egyptians do not eat with Israelites because that would be an offensive thing (*tōʿēbāh*) to them.[65] But Arameans and Canaanites eat with Israelites and do not find it offensive.[66] See also the story of the exodus from Egypt, where Moses tells Pharaoh that the things that Israelites sacrifice would be an offensive thing (*tōʿēbāh*) to the Egyptians.[67] But these things are certainly not an offensive thing to the Israelites.[68]

A former student of ours pointed out that right here in the list of laws that we are considering in Leviticus 18, naming acts that are *tōʿēbāh*, are some that prohibit actions that the great patriarchs of the Bible had done.[69] For example, Abraham marries his half sister Sarah. He says:

> She is, in fact, my sister, my father's daughter but not my mother's daughter, and she became a wife to me.
> (Gen 20:12)

But the law in Leviticus explicitly forbids such relations with a half sister:

> Your sister's nudity—your father's daughter or your mother's daughter, born home or born outside—you shall not expose their nudity.
> (Lev 18:9)

So what is not a *tōʿēbāh* in the generation of the patriarchs has changed and become one in the generation of Moses. In a somewhat different way, the land itself can change from not being a *tōʿēbāh* and can become a *tōʿēbāh* as a result of the behavior of its residents on it. The prophet Jeremiah says:

> You defiled my land, and made my possession into an offensive thing (*tōʿēbāh*).
> (Jer 2:7)

An act or an object that is not a *tōʿēbāh* can become one, depending on time and circumstances.

Now one might respond that the law here is different because it concerns an offensive thing to God—and therefore not subject to the relativity of human values. But that is not the case here. The Bible specifically identifies such laws about things that are divine offenses with the phrase "an offensive thing to the LORD" (*tōʿēbāt yhwh*).[70] That phrase is not used here in the law about male homosexual acts. It is not one of the laws against things that are identified as a *tōʿēbāh* to God![71]

From another perspective, it may even be that a *tōʿēbāh* against God is still relative, not absolute. Pagan worship by an Israelite is a *tōʿēbāh* according to Deuteronomy—and it is identified as a breach of God's covenant with Israel.[72] But it cannot be a *tōʿēbāh* for a pagan, who is not a party to that covenant. On the contrary, there are texts that say that God apportioned the nations to the gods.[73] This means that worship of other gods is a *tōʿēbāh* only for the Israelites, not for the pagans who worship those gods in their own religions.

And to take this one theological step further: Why do people assume that things relating to God must be absolute and unchanging? Even for a person who believes in God wholeheartedly, why should that person imagine that God is never free to change? That is certainly not the biblical view of God. God regrets. God changes divine decisions. God listens to humans and reconsiders.[74] The idea that God must be absolute and unchanging seems to be more an application of Greek logic to religion. That is pretty ironic, since the Greeks classically pictured many gods, and the gods were changeable.

If this is right, then it is an amazing irony. Calling male homosexual acts a *tōʿēbāh* was precisely what made the biblical text seem so absolutely anti-homosexual and without the possibility of change. But it is precisely the fact of *tōʿēbāh* that opens the possibility of the law's change. So, whatever position one takes on this matter, Left or Right, conservative or liberal, one should acknowledge that the law really does forbid homosexual sex—between males but not between females. And one should recognize that the biblical prohibition is not one that is eternal and unchanging. The prohibition in the Bible applies only so long as male homosexual acts are perceived to be offensive. This will depend on further presentation of evidence and arguments about whether it is inborn or not, whether it is properly regarded as psychologically healthy or unhealthy, and whether most people in a community are or are not in fact offended by it. Those arguments are for specialists in biology, psychology, and culture. They are beyond our range of expertise as Bible scholars. Our task here has been to make the biblical evidence known.

People are free to deal with this evidence in a variety of ways. One response to the Bible's view on this or anything can be that even one who respects the greatness of the Bible does not necessarily follow its view on everything. We have treated this subject thus far in terms of those who turn to the Bible as the authority in their lives. Most people on earth, though, including most Christians and Jews, do not accept the Bible as an absolute authority in their lives. For those persons within this majority population who accept or even practice homosexuality, they may say, "I can learn from the Bible. I admire its literary qualities. I recognize its profound place in human history for millennia. I shall not steal or murder or commit adultery. I shall honor my parents. But I reject the Bible's prohibition of male homosexuality." In their position, the Bible can still be the Bible without our having to insist that it is right 100 percent of the time. This position requires a good deal of human responsibility and wisdom. That, after all, is one of the main lessons of the first story in the Bible, the story of the Tree of Knowledge of Good and Bad in the Garden of Eden. In that story, at a huge cost, humans acquire the ability to make judgments of what is good and what is bad—which until that point only God could do. (God says, "Here, the human has become like one of us, to know good and bad."[75]) But with great power comes great responsibility.[76] It means that humans must be wise enough to make their own judgments about what is right and wrong. In this, the Bible can still be a guide, a significant guide, but human beings must accept the benefits and the burdens of becoming their own authorities in the end.

Other responses can come from those who believe in the Bible as a literal and infallible teaching. These communities and individuals will decide for themselves what the textual evidence means for them.

Other responses may come from those who do not respect the Bible. There are those who say that the Bible should not be a moral authority. They are critical of its standing as a great work. In our view, these people are simply wrong, especially when they pick out the passages that they find objectionable and use them to disprove the worth of the whole. Given what we have learned in the last two hundred years about who wrote the Bible, such an approach is uninformed and unjustifiable. It was composed by 100–150 persons, spread over a thousand years for the Hebrew Bible alone and centuries more for the New Testament. (In the matter of homosexuality, one of those authors of the Hebrew Bible—and only one—wrote an objection to male homosexuality, and none objected to female homosexuality.) One can argue about any given passage in the Bible and claim that it is good or bad, but one cannot denigrate the whole book—especially when one lacks expertise in the book and the world that produced it—as being unworthy as a social and moral source.

Above all, from this discussion we learn, at minimum, that understanding these passages is difficult. It is complicated. It is more difficult and more complicated than one might think when one first reads the verses. Our purpose is not to talk you into one side or the other in these matters. Our purpose is to reveal that this is not a matter for amateurs, and it is not easy. You cannot just open a Bible—especially in translation—and find an obvious answer.

This applies whether you believe the Bible is a revealed text from God or you believe that it is a human composition. Either way, the reader should recognize how careful and thoughtful one must be in learning the text. We hope that people who hold any of these positions—or many other possible positions—will all benefit and clarify their thinking in response to the discussion here.

Postscript: A related issue, homosexual marriage

Homosexual marriage is a current issue, and it is a step further than the question of attitudes toward homosexuality itself. It also brings female homosexuality back into the discussion because, even though the biblical law does not prohibit female–female sex, the matter of two women marrying one another introduces an additional question about the nature of marriage. The most direct answer to questions about homosexual marriage in terms of the Bible would be to say that the Hebrew Bible does not address the matter. The laws in the Torah in fact hardly address any matters of getting married at all. There is not even anything about the wedding ceremony. Some who oppose gay marriage would say that the Bible's conception of the way marriage is supposed to be is a union of a man and a woman. Genesis 2:24 is cited in this regard. There it recounts how the first woman is brought to the first man, who finds her to be a mate, and the text concludes:

> On account of this, a man leaves his father and mother and cleaves to
> his woman, and they become one flesh.

This text is not a commandment or a definition. It is a part of a two-chapter section of the Bible that contains stories of the origins of things. These are called etiologies. It contains the etiology of why people wear clothes, why snakes do not have legs, why women have pain in labor, why roses have thorns, and why men work. This verse, too, is an etiology, telling a story of why men and women mate. It has no bearing on whether humans might have homosexual mates as well. It also does not prevent a man from having multiple wives. This was permissible in the biblical world, but this verse in Genesis does not address that matter one way or the other. Indeed, since most Jews and Christians have given up polygamy, this suggests that they do not feel bound by the Hebrew Bible's conception of marriage.

Since the Bible does not address homosexual marriage in its laws, its stories, or its poetry, we advise much caution in basing one's views on either side of this question on the Bible. Other kinds of arguments are likely to be more productive.

TWO

Abortion

The egg: is that a human being? No. But it has the possibility of becoming a human being if it is joined by a sperm cell and nurtured in a particular way.

The sperm cell: is that a human being? Roughly the same answer.

What about an egg and sperm in the second after they have joined: same question. Roughly the same answer.

Is it a human being when it gets a heartbeat? Or when it starts to have the *shape* of a human being? Or at *any* moment before it comes out? Or at the first instant after it comes out? Or at the first breath? Or at the moment of consciousness? Or of first self-awareness? (But when is that?) (There is an old Jewish joke: when does it first become a human being? When it graduates from medical school.) The movement from egg to human being is a *continuum*, a process. No one single point is the *turning*-point, the moment of definition.

But we humans are symmetrical. (Some are a little more or less symmetrical than others.) We think in twos. We want definitions: something is X, or it is Not-X. And we construct our laws on the basis of these twos, these definitions. And then, since so much of life is continua, processes, and not "twos" (either-ors), we refine these laws as we go—as this refining becomes necessary.

So with abortion, we are trying to draw a line—to *find* the line—where there is in fact no line. So the battle "line" is drawn, and it is a trap.

Some of us do not want to hurt an innocent little thing that has not tasted life yet, a little thing that each of us once was. Others of us do not want to impose pregnancy, labor, and a complete change of a life on a woman (and sometimes on a man and sometimes on their other children as well),

41

and we are willing to stop a life that never was conscious—or to prevent a conscious life from coming into being—rather than impose that huge change of a life where it is not desired.

What wisdom does the Bible offer on this?

A discussion of abortion in the Bible is disadvantaged at the outset. In the case of homosexuality the Bible has a stated law that we can examine in cultural and cross-cultural contexts. In gender issues we can invoke many biblical stories, poems, laws, and prophetic works. In capital punishment we can look at an array of laws and stories. But on the subject of abortion the Bible is practically silent. Is this because it was unknown in ancient Israel? Is it because it was known but not regulated or discussed?

The Bible plays different roles in the ways that people formulate their views on different current issues. In the matter of homosexuality or of capital punishment there are those passages of law that rule on aspects of it, and there are those stories that may involve it. So, even though we still suspect that most people's views of these things are more visceral and cultural, it is possible that the Bible genuinely influences some persons' decisions about the positions they take on these matters.

On abortion, however, the biblical passages are few, and they are questionable. Abortions were always performed in human history, but, after all, it was a revolution in technology that made the procedure safe enough and common enough to turn it into the issue that it is in this generation, and the biblical texts were a couple of millennia too early for this. Thus the entry on "Abortion" in *The Oxford Companion to the Bible* begins with this simple statement:

Abortion as such is not discussed in the Bible.[1]

People have therefore been moved to rely on passages that (1) relate to abortion only remotely or (2) do not really relate to abortion at all. Ironically, people cite the Bible more frequently in present-day discussions of abortion than in arguments over pretty much any other controversial topic—with the possible exception of homosexuality. A quick Internet search of "Bible abortion" demonstrates the extent to which abortion opponents and abortion rights advocates pick and choose passages in biblical narrative and law to prove that divine decree supports their position on the legality and morality of abortion. You may find it curious (we do), but there is only one place in the entire Bible in which abortion is actually, unquestionably mentioned. It is not a law about abortion, nor is it a story about abortion. Neither most advocates of choice nor opponents of abortion tend to use this particular passage in support of their arguments either (though there are some who do). In fact, readers from both sides of the issue may very likely be surprised to see the nature of the treatment of abortion in this passage below.

Curiously, the relevant sections of the Bible come from the Bible's laws and from its poems. No prose. First, the laws:

Law

You shall not murder

People often cite the commandment against murder in the Ten Commandments as biblical grounds for opposing abortion. Rendered famously in the King James Version as "Thou shalt not *kill,*" it is possible to see why English readers have misunderstood it. If the Ten Commandments forbade killing outright, then one could argue that such killing would include the act of aborting a fetus. However, that is not what the commandment says. The rendering of the Hebrew word in that commandment as "kill" in the KJV and other translations is not correct. Like English, biblical Hebrew has a variety of words to describe the act of taking a life, and, also like English, biblical Hebrew has a different word for "kill" than for "murder." As we shall discuss in the chapter on capital punishment, the word in this commandment, Hebrew *rṣḥ,* means "murder," not "kill," in all of its occurrences in the Bible.[2] What the commandment forbids is intentional homicide. It refers to taking a human life with malice. It does not refer, for example, to human sacrifice, even though this was condemned in ancient Israel and would be reckoned as murder in most societies today. Human sacrifice is powerfully forbidden in the Torah, but by way of its own commandment, not by the Decalogue. The Decalogue commandment also apparently does not refer to mercy killing, killing in war, killing in self-defense, or killing an animal. We may find one or more of these to be terrible, and we may judge them to be deserving of punishment, but still they are not what is meant by this particular commandment. As in most law codes, ancient and modern, murder is distinguished from manslaughter and other kinds of killing—both by the use of the two distinct terms, *rṣḥ* for murder and *mwt* for killing, and by these laws that reflect a distinction.

The distinction is both linguistic and legal. People sometimes say that this point of translation is controversial, but really there is no basis for controversy at all. Words have meanings, sometimes clear, sometimes not so clear. This case is clear. In Hebrew as in English and some other languages, killing is killing, and murder is murder. The commandment in the Decalogue is "You shall not murder." One can be against abortion or for it. One can have a strong conviction that abortion is murder or that it is not. But everyone should understand what this commandment means. It means that the covenant Decalogue that is depicted in the Bible between the people of Israel and the deity forbids murder and only murder. Other forms of killing are treated in other places in the Bible.

This means that if one regards abortion as a violation of that commandment, one must first argue that abortion is consistent with the thing that that commandment prohibits. One would have to make the case that abortion would fit with what was understood as murder in ancient Israel. Or one would have to make the case that abortion is properly within the range of meaning of the word *rṣḥ* (murder)—and that it is not more properly in the range of meaning of the word *mwt* (killing). Maybe one could make one of these cases, maybe not. We have to say that we know of no evidence from the Bible that such a case would be correct. But our point for now is only that this is the level on which one has to address the matter. One has to try to establish, through evidence and reason, that abortion is analogous to what is understood as murder in that famous commandment. One cannot just quote the commandment and stop there.

The fighters who strike a pregnant woman

People sometimes derive law about abortion from the biblical law in which people, in the course of a fight, strike a pregnant woman, and she has a miscarriage. Here is the text:

> And if people will fight, and they strike a pregnant woman, and her children go out, and there will not be an injury, he shall be penalized according to what the woman's husband will impose on him, and he

will give it by the judges. And if there will be an injury, then you shall give a life for a life, an eye for an eye, a tooth for a tooth, a hand for a hand, a foot for a foot, a burn for a burn, a wound for a wound, a hurt for a hurt.
(Exod 21:22–25)

Caution! The meaning of this law is unclear in several different ways, and learned scholars have questioned and debated its meaning over two millennia. Two men—or is it more than two? and are they necessarily men?—are fighting; and they cause a miscarriage—or is it a premature labor? and is it one or is it both/all of them who cause it?—by somehow striking the woman, and this results in injury or death to the woman—or is it to the baby? The law may mean: the woman loses the child, and the question is then whether there is any injury to the mother or not. Or it may mean: the child is born alive, and the question is then whether there is any injury to the child or not.

As we have seen in our discussion of homosexuality, viewing the Bible in the context of the ancient Near East is often valuable in understanding the biblical stance on such issues. In this case, the Law Code of Hammurabi, Middle Assyrian Law, and Hittite Law all contain similar tracts to what we see about the fighters striking a pregnant woman in Exodus 21. The Code of Hammurabi states that if a householder strikes the pregnant daughter of another householder and causes her "to drop that of her womb," he is to pay ten shekels of silver for the fetus. But if the woman dies, then the daughter of the perpetrator is to be put to death. The exception is if the woman is the daughter of a commoner or a slave, in which case the house-holder is simply to pay a fine for the death of the woman (and nothing for the fetus alone).[3] Hittite Law provides for monetary compensation in the same situation. The amount of the compensation depends on the status of the pregnant woman's father.[4] Middle Assyrian Law also describes the punishment of a man who causes a miscarriage. However, the laws there demand compensation for both the fetus and the mother. If the father of a household causes another man's wife to miscarry, then the man whose wife has miscarried is enjoined to cause the perpetrator's wife to miscarry in turn. In addition, the perpetrator is to give the victim a child from his own household. However, if the woman dies, then the perpetrator is to be put to death, in addition to a child from his household being given to the victim's household. If the woman miscarries but does not die, and her husband has no sons, then the perpetrator is executed; unless the fetus is female, in which case he only needs to give her a child from his household in recompense.[5] The details in each of these and in the biblical case vary, and the penalties in some of the ancient Near Eastern cases would strike most of us as repugnant. What is common to all of these similar cases, though, is that the question of injury is with regard to the mother, not to the miscarried infant. This probably suggests that the biblical law, too, is about the degree of harm to the mother after she loses the child, not about the degree of harm to the infant after being born alive. The law's severe consequences, in that case, are about the harm to a mother, not to a fetus. But all should acknowledge that this is, at most, probable but still not certain.

Moreover, this passage is not about abortion. It is about accidental miscarriage. It is about the unintended consequences of a fight. Involving miscarriage rather than abortion, and being about unintended consequences rather than about a procedure whose consequences are planned, this law is an extremely difficult precedent on which to base any view: either for abortion or against it. The goal at best, therefore, is not to get a direct ruling on abortion from it. Rather, people on both sides of abortion debates seek to find some basic principle in the case that might then apply to the question of abortion. That is a good approach. But the passage is just too uncertain even for that. It simply cannot be the basis for a definitive answer to such an important issue. William Propp's superb two-volume commentary on the book of Exodus includes a detailed treatment of this law's many uncertainties. A reading of those pages will show why no one should rely on this enigmatic passage to form a view on abortion.[6]

Jeremiah's wish

Whatever one makes of the commandment against murder or the case of the fighters who strike the pregnant woman, all should be able to agree that those cases are not originally, explicitly about abortion itself. They require interpretation and argument to prove whether they are relevant to abortion or not. They also require interpretation and argument to prove one side's claim or the other's. Therefore it comes as a surprise—at first—to many readers that the only explicit reference to abortion in the Hebrew Bible is rarely cited in debates. Also surprisingly, it occurs in poetry, in the book of a prophet, not in a story or a law. The prophet Jeremiah, in anguish, *wishes* that he had been aborted. Jeremiah, the saddest, most depressed, most anguished, most unbelieved of prophets, despite a good record of fulfilled predictions, finally outdoes even Moses, Elijah, and Jonah. Each of those three prophets finds his role as a prophet unbearable at times and, at some point, wishes for death. But Jeremiah does not wish or pray for death. He wishes that he had never had a life. He wishes that he had been stopped from ever coming out of the womb in the first place. He cries:

> Cursed be the day in which I was born.
> The day that my mother bore me: let it not be blessed.
> Cursed be the man who informed my father, saying,
> "A male child's been born to you," making him *glad*!
> And let that man be like the cities that YHWH overturned and didn't
>   regret.
> And let him hear crying in the morning and wailing at noontime.
> Because he didn't *kill me from the womb*,
> And my mother would be my tomb
> And her womb an eternal pregnancy.
> Why is this that I came out from the womb?
> To see suffering and agony
> And my days consumed in shame.
> (Jer 20:14–18)

This is our literal translation of the Hebrew (Masoretic) text. That text is clear and horrid. The Greek text, in place of "Because he didn't kill me from the womb," reads "Because he didn't kill me in the womb"—which makes the fact of abortion even more vivid.

Now, the passage likely is extreme hyperbole, and it is poetry, so one would be well advised to use caution when factoring it into any contemporary view on abortion. Moreover, the fact that Jeremiah wishes that someone had killed him at the womb does not mean that Jeremiah is favoring abortion any more than, when Moses and Elijah and Jonah wish for death, they are coming out in favor of death! Further, this wish may apply solely to Jeremiah himself and not be a position on whether all human lives—or any other human lives—would be better off aborted.

So one should surely not argue that this poem is in favor of abortion. Still, such a blatant reference to abortion—the only biblical reference so blatant—should be of some relevance to our question. In fact, we see three ways in which it sheds some useful light.

First, there is another passage in the book of Jeremiah that is very prominent in abortion discussions. It is the very first passage in the book, known as the inaugural vision of Jeremiah. Opponents of abortion often cite it. This verse frequently appears on signs in marches, on bumper stickers, and on Web sites. It is a passage that pictures God apparently addressing the prophet Jeremiah for the first time, and God says:

Before I formed you in the womb I knew you.
(Jer 1:5)

Abortion opponents understandably take this as proof that, in the Bible, a fetus is thought already to exist as a person from the very beginning. Now if ever there was a passage of poetry that needed to be taken with a wheelbarrowful of caution, it is this one. As we have seen in the preceding chapter, in biblical poetry it is important (and sometimes difficult) to distinguish when a poetic line is meant literally and when it is a metaphor. In the case of Ezekiel's imagery of Judah being stripped naked and humiliated in front of her enemies, for example, it is clear that the prophet is engaging in metaphor. In Jeremiah's poetic statement quoted here, it is more difficult to know if this passage is meant metaphorically or literally. It is not, after all, a view that we generally find elsewhere in the Hebrew Bible: that God knows people even before the sperm meets the egg, before they are even conceived. We do not even know if this line of poetry is meant to apply to Jeremiah alone as an extraordinary case, or to all human beings. One also cannot know if it implies that an abortion could undermine a divine plan, or if it rather means precisely the opposite: that Jeremiah's destiny was already divinely protected at conception from any possible harm that could come in his infancy—in which case the passage has nothing to do with abortion at all. Interpreting laws and principles out of poetry is always difficult, and this is a particularly difficult line of poetry, subject to multiple questions and interpretations, and the stakes are high.

There are thus many things that we cannot know for sure about this poem's meaning. One thing that we can know, though, is Jeremiah's own response to this revelation. His response is precisely the passage about Jeremiah's anguish that we quoted above: "Cursed be the man . . . because he didn't kill me from the womb, and my mother would be my tomb." God says, "Before I formed you in the womb I knew you." Jeremiah looks back at that and says: "I wish someone had killed me in that womb! I wish my mother would have been my tomb!" The already limited value of Jeremiah's inaugural vision in abortion debates is rendered even more equivocal by Jeremiah's wish. Whatever one makes of the inaugural vision and whatever one makes of the prophet's response, together they make too ambiguous a package to be a solid basis for an argument on so sensitive a matter as abortion.

The second way in which Jeremiah's wish may shed light on this matter is in regard to the relevance of the commandment about murder that we discussed above. The question there had to do with murder (Hebrew root *rṣḥ*) versus killing (Hebrew root *mwt*). Jeremiah is the one person in the Hebrew Bible to talk explicitly about abortion, and when he talks about abortion, he uses the term *môtĕtanî*, a form of the root *mwt*. This is the word that is not used in the Ten Commandments. In fact, this verb never means "murder" in the Bible. It is used for David's killing of Goliath in battle.[7] It is used by an Amalekite who claims to David that he killed King Saul at the king's own request.[8] In a psalm it refers to the just killing of the wicked.[9] Only in one psalm does it refer to ill-willed taking of life, and the nature of the act of killing is not identified in that poem.[10]

That is to say: the word that Jeremiah uses for abortion, the only word used in connection with abortion in the Bible, always refers to "killing" and never to "murder." Conversely, the word that is used in the Ten Commandments is the Hebrew root *rṣḥ*, which specifically means murder. The implications of this are serious: it means that the Ten Commandments cannot correctly be cited in support of present-day anti-abortion positions. It means that abortion does not constitute murder by the biblical definition. Now we realize that this will come as a disturbing surprise to many who oppose abortion. So we want to be clear about just what it establishes. One can still be opposed to abortion. One can still believe that it is wrong. After all, as we have seen, human sacrifice does not meet the definition of murder in the Ten Commandments either, but it is still forbidden elsewhere in the Bible. In Jeremiah's words, abortion is killing, not murder; but it is a kind of killing that one may still oppose.

What one cannot do, if our reading of these texts is correct, is to oppose it solely on the grounds of its being a violation of the Ten Commandments.

There is a third way in which Jeremiah's wish is relevant, but it is a broader and much more complex perspective. The larger question remains: whether Jeremiah's wish that he had never been born applies only to Jeremiah himself or if it sheds light on the nature and the value of human life generally—and what this implies for views of abortion. As it stands in the text, it certainly is a personal expression. But related passages in the Bible may broaden its implication. We turn to the Bible's wisdom literature, which, like prophecy, is written in poetry. In the wisdom books, visibly similar to Jeremiah, the Bible's most anguished man, Job, says:

> Let the day in which I was born perish,
> And the night one said, "A boy is conceived."
> (Job 3:3)

Job curses that night, saying:

> Because it didn't close the doors of my womb.
> (Job 3:10)

And, very close to Jeremiah, he says:

> Why didn't I die from the womb,
> Come out from the womb and expire!
> (Job 3:11)

To add the last piece of the parallel to Jeremiah, Job speaks of that never-been state thus:

> Like a concealed *nepel*, I wouldn't be,
> Like children who didn't see light.
> (Job 3:16)

The Hebrew word *nepel* may mean either an aborted fetus or a stillborn, so Jeremiah's wish remains the sole certain reference to abortion, but this passage that introduces the whole of Job's words provides another biblical picture of a human—an exceptional human—who judges the preemption of a life to be better than to have lived it. In the cases of Moses, Elijah, and Jonah, one could say that each seeks to die after having lived and functioned for some time. But the cases of Jeremiah and Job say that it would have been better to forgo the whole thing. A life could be too painful to have lived it. We advise students and friends, "Live your life so that when it comes to an end you can answer the question, 'Was the world better because you were here, or was it worse, or did it make no difference?'" The second and the third possible answers are each fearful in a different way. And the Bible gives us two of its most powerful figures being left with the answer that it would have been preferable not to have been here at all.

The depiction of a second biblical figure who expresses this view raises the possibility that the implications of Jeremiah's wish may be understood as more than idiosyncratic. And it is the speaker in the wisdom book of Ecclesiastes (Hebrew Qohelet) who connects this rejection of life to the human condition broadly, not just to an individual. Qohelet says:

> I saw all the oppressions that are done under the sun. . . .
> And I praised the dead who've already died
> more than the living who are still alive,
> And better than both of them is one who has not yet been,
> who hasn't seen the bad thing that is done under the sun.
> (Eccl 4:1–3)

And, then, giving the case of a long-lived and many-childed man who still ends his life unfulfilled and unburied, Qohelet says, "Better than he is a *nepel*!"[11]

The cautions still apply: just because Qohelet says that it is better to be a *nepel*, that does not mean that the author advocates causing a *nepel* by abortion. After all, this author also says that the day of death is better than the day of birth,[12] but that does not mean that he favors causing deaths by murder. But the implications of these Qohelet passages, together with the other passages we have considered, are significant. If an individual human's life is such that it is better to die before birth and not to live it, then what does this pessimistic (or tragic) philosophy imply for views on abortion?

Opposition to abortion is grounded in a belief—or a desire to believe—that a human life has value and has some meaning. The cases of Jeremiah and Job, broadened by the wisdom of Qohelet, question that belief. They still do not make it acceptable to take the life of a living breathing human being, because we have an explicit commandment against that. But we have no explicit commandment prohibiting abortion. These passages taken collectively, therefore, challenge the belief that every life has some inherent value that cannot be prevented from coming into existence.

When does life begin?

A broader factor to consider is how life is determined in the Bible. The usual biblical understanding is that life is judged in terms of respiration. For example, the creation of the first human is described as follows:

> YHWH God fashioned a human, dust from the ground, and blew into
> his nostrils the breath of life, and the human became a living being.
> (Gen 2:7)

In fact, in many places in Genesis the condition of being alive is contrasted with that of death by the same expression. In the flood account God is pictured as saying:

> And I, here: I'm bringing the flood, water on the earth, to destroy all
> flesh in which is the breath of life from under the skies.
> (Gen 6:17)

And the animals come

> by twos of all flesh in which was the breath of life
> (Gen 7:15)

And when the floodwaters come,

> Everything that had the breathing spirit of life in its nostrils, everything
> that was on the ground, died.
> (Gen 7:22)

The expression is used in texts that are traced to both the Priestly source and the J source in critical biblical scholarship.[13] Similarly, the word *breath* is in parallel with the word *life* in both Isaiah and Job.[14] The fact that it is not an expression limited to only one author or even just to prose or poetry increases the likelihood that having the breath of life was commonly understood in ancient Israel as an expression of being alive. Biblically, life comes with the first breath that a human draws. The words for spirit, soul, and living being in Hebrew all have root meanings that denote respiration. Hebrew *rûaḥ*, commonly translated as "spirit," also means wind/breath. (The Greek of this word in the Septuagint, *pneuma*, also has the range of both "spirit" and "breath.") Hebrew *nĕšāmāh*, commonly translated "soul," also has a root meaning of "to breathe." (In modern Hebrew this same root is used in the term for a respirator.) And Hebrew *nepeš*, commonly translated as "soul," "self," or "living being," has the meaning in Akkadian of "getting breath." In biblical terms, those who did not have the breath of life were not alive. If one were to draw an inference, then, from the biblical authors of when they thought life began, it would be difficult to make the argument that they thought it began at conception or at any point prior to the birth and drawing of the first breath.

We are not arguing that abortion is moral or that it should be legal. What we conclude, cautiously, is first that one cannot base opposition to it solely on the Bible. And, second, on the basis of the principles we have considered here, we would have to say that the weight of the biblical evidence is in the direction that abortion is not biblically forbidden. Do not misunderstand us. We are not taking a pro-abortion or pro-choice position here. We are saying as biblical scholars that there are not sufficient grounds to base a position against abortion on the Bible alone. One may be for or against abortion for various reasons: moral, ethical, biological, social, or religious. And the Bible may figure among the influences that persuade a person of one side or the other. But not the Bible alone. The crucial texts simply are not there.

Abortion in the ancient Near East

Are there more explicit texts anywhere in the ancient Near East? There are two different types of texts from the ancient Near East that refer to abortion: medical texts and legal texts.

The Ebers Papyrus from ancient Egypt is a medical text. It was written sometime between 1550 and 1500 BCE but copied from an earlier original.[15] And it contains prescriptions for medications designed to induce abortions. For example:

> To cause a woman to stop pregnancy in the first, second or third period
> [trimester]:
>> unripe fruit of acacia
>> colocynth
>> dates
>> triturate with 6/7th pint of honey; moisten a pessary of plant fiber and
>> place in the vagina.[16]

From Mesopotamia, we know of only one medical text that details a prescription for a medication designed to induce an abortion, or, as the text puts it, "to cause a pregnant woman to drop her fetus."[17] The prescription mixes beer, a lizard, and some unidentifiable plants to be taken by the woman with wine on an empty stomach. (The Egyptian concoction is at least more appetizing.)

These and similar texts indicate that there were known means of contraception and abortion in ancient Egypt and Mesopotamia.[18] The question remains as to how societies and governments and religious leaders felt about it. Was abortion socially sanctioned?

Middle Assyrian Law is the only ancient law code that prescribes a penalty for a woman who has a "miscarriage by her own act." In other words, the Middle Assyrian code actually contains a law against abortion:

> If a woman has had a miscarriage by her own act,
> when they have prosecuted her and convicted her, they shall
> impale her on stakes without burying her. If she died in
> having the miscarriage, they shall impale her on stakes
> without burying her. If someone hid that woman when she
> had the miscarriage [without] informing [the king]. . . .
> [tablet is damaged and unreadable here].[19]

This is noteworthy for the strict stance the Assyrian law took on the issue of abortion. There is no similar law in the Bible or anywhere else that we know of in the ancient Near East.[20]

But this law also highlights another aspect of abortion in the ancient world that does not figure into present-day discussions of the issue: the potential danger to the mother. Thanks to fairly recent technology, abortion now does not present nearly the dangers to the life of the mother that it would have in the ancient world—and is in fact employed in situations when her life may be endangered rather by the pregnancy. Miscarriages could be caused by physical abuse or by medicinal concoctions, whether accidentally or purposely, but such measures always involved a severe threat to the life of the mother, a threat that was taken seriously in all of the ancient law codes. In the Bible, it is only the loss of the mother's life that is compensated/ punished by the death of the one who caused the miscarriage.

It is possible, therefore, that the lack of discussion of abortion in the Bible and other ancient law codes (with the exception of the Middle Assyrian code) has to do with the relative rarity of inducing abortions in the ancient world, not because of any moral objection but, rather, due to the physical danger that abortions presented to the mother. We simply cannot know for sure.

Pregnancy and law

Why is this so difficult? Why are the biblical texts so complex and usually unhelpful? Why are societies so divided and their laws so uneven and sometimes seemingly arbitrary? There is one biblical case that is not about abortion but which may help us understand better what makes this so complex. It is the case of the suspected adulteress. We would have included it in the chapter on women's status below, but we are presenting it in the present chapter because of what it may reveal about abortion debates. In Hebrew it is called the case of the *sotah*, the woman who is suspected of having "gone astray." Here is the entire text:

> Any man whose wife will go astray and will make a breach of faith
> with him, and a man has lain with her—an intercourse of seed—and
> it has been hidden from her husband's eyes, and she has kept con-
> cealed, and she has been made impure, and there is no witness against
> her, and she has not been caught, and a spirit of jealousy has come
> over him, and he is jealous about his wife, and she has been made
> impure, or a spirit of jealousy has come over him, and he is jealous
> about his wife, and she has not been made impure:

Then the man shall bring his wife to the priest and shall bring her offering along with her: a tenth of an ephah of barley flour. He shall not pour oil on it and shall not put frankincense on it, because it is an offering about jealousies, an offering about being recalled: causing a crime to be recalled.

And the priest shall bring her forward and stand her in front of YHWH. And the priest shall take holy water in a clay container, and the priest shall take some of the dust that will be on the Tabernacle's floor and put it into the water. And the priest shall stand the woman in front of YHWH and loosen the hair of the woman's head and put the offering of bringing to mind on her hands; it is an offering of jealousies. And in the priest's hand shall be the bitter cursing water. And the priest shall have her swear, and he shall say to the woman: "If a man has not lain with you, and if you have not gone astray in impurity with someone in place of your husband, be cleared by this bitter cursing water. But you, if you have gone astray with someone in place of your husband and if you have been made impure, and if a man other than your husband has had his intercourse with you," then the priest shall have the woman swear a curse oath, and the priest shall say to the woman, "let YHWH make you a curse and an oath among your people when YHWH sets your thigh sagging and your womb swelling, and this cursing water will come in your insides, to swell the womb and make the thigh sag."

And the woman shall say, "Amen, amen."

And the priest shall write these curses in a scroll and rub them into the bitter water. And he shall have the woman drink the bitter cursing water, and the bitter cursing water will come into her. And the priest shall take the offering of jealousies from the woman's hand and elevate the offering in front of YHWH, and he shall bring her forward to the altar. And the priest shall take a fistful from the grain offering, a representative portion of it, and burn it to smoke at the altar, and after that he shall have the woman drink the water. When he has had her drink the water, then it will be, if she has been made impure and has made a breach of faith with her husband, when the bitter cursing water will come into her, and her womb will swell and her thigh will sag, then the woman will become a curse among her people. And if the woman has not been made impure, and she is pure, then she shall be cleared and shall conceive seed.

This is the instruction for jealousies, when a woman will go astray with someone in place of her husband and be made impure, or when a spirit of jealousy will come over a man and he will be jealous about his wife. And the priest shall stand the woman in front of YHWH and do all of this instruction to her. And the man shall be clear of a crime, and that woman shall bear her crime.

(Num 5:11–31)

It says in several different ways that there is no evidence or witness, so as to leave no doubt that this is a case of an unproven suspicion. So a special ritual is done, not as a legal procedure in front of a judge but as a religious procedure in front of a priest. The suspected woman drinks a mixture of water, dust from the Tabernacle, and ink from the words of a curse invoking the divine name, and she swears an oath. Then if her womb swells and her thigh sags (or drops, or falls) she will be a curse among her community. It reads as a strange law. And it raises all kinds of questions and problems:

Is this a trial by ordeal? There is no other case of trial by ordeal in the Bible.

Why is this only for an intercourse of seed—and not just any sex act? As we saw in the homosexuality chapter, "an intercourse of seed" is the phrase that is used for sex that could produce children.

Why is this used only for adultery? Why not use it for any other crime?

Why is this used only on a woman, not on a man who is suspected of adultery?

Adultery is punishable by death, as we shall see in the chapter on capital punishment. Why is this woman not executed if the ritual proves her guilty?

When it says at the end that the man shall be clear of a crime, which man does it mean: the husband or the lover?

How would this work? Drinking water with dust and ink in it does not make a person's womb swell or her thigh sag.

And, scholars being scholars, our colleagues over the centuries have raised more questions and problems: are the womb-swelling and thigh-sagging immediate, or do they happen over some unstated period of time? What exactly is meant by womb-swelling and thigh-sagging anyway?

Why is the water especially noted to be bitter? How does this case compare to other ancient Near Eastern laws? (In the laws of Hammurabi, if a woman is accused by her husband, she swears an oath. If she is accused by others—"if a finger has been pointed at a man's wife because of another man"—she jumps in the river.[21]) Is this law a composite of two separate texts?

Virtually all scholars who have ever worked on this case have struggled to understand what is going on here. Is this really a law that requires a miracle to take place in order to work? And, if the miracle did not in fact take place, what effect would that have on people's trust in the law and the priests? Some have said that the law's effect was psychological in one way or another: It might be to scare guilty women into confessing rather than face the ritual. It might be to traumatize the woman so much as to cause her to have a miscarriage—which would in effect be a psychologically induced abortion.[22] Some have tried to picture actual physical outcomes, such as infertility or deterioration of the sexual and reproductive organs. The ancient historian Josephus wrote that it could be edema.[23] Our friend the biblical scholar Tikva Frymer-Kensky, of blessed memory, suggested that the procedure may have produced the condition known in medicine as a prolapsed uterus, in which the uterus may descend or even protrude and expand (hence the womb-swelling and thigh-sagging).[24] She takes "thigh" to mean probably the sexual organs because of such expressions as "those who came out of Jacob's thigh"[25] and possibly the account of a servant's putting his hand under Abraham's thigh when taking an oath about Abraham's son Isaac's marriage.[26] We caution, however, that it is a long way from a euphemism for a man's progeny to an explicit term for a woman's genital organ.

Scholars have taken it to mean that the procedure will cause her to conceive seed if she is innocent. From this some scholars even derived the reverse: that the procedure causes sterility in her if she is guilty.[27] There was even a speculation that a woman might use this law to help her if she has been childless. She could leave half-smoked cigars and two martini glasses around the house to make her husband suspect her of adultery. So he takes her to the priest for this procedure. Since she has not in fact been unfaithful, the procedure finds her innocent and causes her to conceive a child! But all of this is overinterpretation of a phrase. When the text says that she will conceive seed, that need mean only that the cleared woman was not pregnant through adultery, so now she is free to become pregnant by her husband.

large part, why the case of the fighters who strike the pregnant woman is so uncertain to us. And this is, in large part, why we are so divided over abortion today. Putting it in terms of "pro-life" versus "pro-choice" means focusing more on the fetus ("pro-life") or more on the woman ("pro-choice"). Other formulations of the issue will, each in its particular way, still reflect the entanglement of the two lives. And it is nearly impossible—or perhaps utterly impossible—to reconcile these through law.

Conclusions

Societies allow for killing in a variety of circumstances: self-defense, war, mercy killing, execution, possibly to save other lives. The question is whether we are prepared to add abortion to that list as another case of permissible taking of life. There is no point in denying that it is a taking of life. It is. The question is whether it is one of the cases a society is willing to permit. Proponents of abortion have framed it in terms of choice. That concerns the legal issue of whether it is the state or the woman who makes the decision. But it still leaves us with the moral issue of what the decision should be. Choice is a valid matter for proponents and opponents of abortion to debate as a matter of what the law should be. But the legal matter of the right of choice does not release one from also debating the moral matter of what choice should be made. We have seen that abortion is something that cannot be reconciled through law alone. If we learn anything from the Bible's small treatment of this large matter, it is that abortion is not mentioned in the law but is mentioned as a question of human existence. Whichever position we take on abortion, the Bible prods us to elevate our thinking and our debates to that level.

THREE

Women's Status

There were (at least) two great revolutions in our species in the last century and a half. The first was the human community's rejection of slavery, and the second was the change in the status of women. We do not mean that slavery has vanished from our planet. It has not. But slavery is at least beaten in name. World forums denounce it. Laws forbid it. Societies that allow it to prevail have to lie: "Those children like working all day. Those people are free to leave. Those women choose to live that way." The difference between the nineteenth century and the twentieth was that in the nineteenth century slavery was still formally accepted. In the twentieth century it became indecent.

So with women. In the authors' own lifetimes we have seen changes in the language we use, changes in professions, changes in legal rights, in social opportunities, in economic opportunities, in sexual relations, in influence, in leadership, in roles in families. The present generation is probably the one that has seen the most change—and the most rapid change—in women's status in human history. As with slavery, the transformation is not yet complete. But practically all cultures must now address women's status. And even those who begrudge equal status to women are bound to come up with creative explanations and justifications: "Women's status is not lower; it's just different." "Our women prefer it this way." We have even heard a lecture defending women's controlled status in some Muslim societies by means of an analogy to slavery: "If you *choose* to be a slave, then you're not a slave."

We would answer: "Yes you are."

Where does the Bible fit into this? The arguments over what the Bible has to teach about women's status are curious. Some people say that the

Bible was enlightened for its time, a crucial step in an evolution (some would say a revolution) of women's status. Others say that males composed the Bible, that it was the product of patriarchal society, that it was the justification of such patriarchal society, and that it has been one of the best-known contributors to maintaining an inferior status of women.

Both groups are reading the same book.

Why do people understand the same evidence in such opposite ways? One reason is because it is the *Bible*. And people want to have the Bible on their side. But the main reason, we think, is that the Bible was one stage—an extremely important stage—in a process that took millennia. Let us suppose that it was, say, stage number sixteen in a process of transformation of women's status that took forty stages. We may criticize the Bible for being *only* at stage sixteen, or we may praise it for moving us *all the way* to stage sixteen. But such a debate is unlikely to produce very much. And it is likely to be downright tedious. We propose rather to look at the Bible's record in some key areas regarding women's status—and see what role those biblical steps played on this staircase.

In the Bible's first chapter, both man and woman are created in the image of God:

> God created the human in His image. He created it in the image of God; He created them male and female.
> (Gen 1:27)

In terms of equality of the sexes, one would think that that is pretty close to definitive. But then the Garden of Eden story comes two chapters later, in which God tells woman:

> Your desire will be for your man, and he'll dominate you.
> (Gen 3:16)

That looks pretty definitive as well. And this strange interspersing of sexual parity and male dominion continues through the rest of the text.

Women can be prophets, but all fifteen of the Bible's books of prophecy are about male prophets.

Women can be Nazirites, a kind of voluntary clergy, but only males can be priests.[1]

An upper-class woman has privileges above those of some lower-class men, but all the rulers are kings except for one case of a queen who usurps the throne—and is later killed![2]

Women can inherit property, but then special limits are imposed on them. (More on this below.)

Males dominate the family, but women are depicted as acquiring power and influence through good means and bad: through their sons, through sex, through wisdom, through strength of character, through nagging, through lies or trickery, through love.

The book starts and ends with a woman playing a determinative role: Eve and Esther.

A woman (Eve) is the first human to say the name of God.

Thus the scholars Carol Newsom and Sharon Ringe wrote of this two-sided dynamic in the Bible:

> Throughout the centuries, of course, the Bible has been invoked to justify women's subordination to men. But it has also played a role, sometimes in surprising ways, in empowering women.[3]

And:

> To read the Bible self-consciously as a woman is a complex experience, alternately painful and exhilarating.[4]

To talk about women in the Bible, we need to do more than praise Sarah and Rebekah and other biblical females. We attended a Bat Mitzvah at which the rabbi wanted to impress the feminist mother of the *bat mitzvah*, so he discussed *all* the major women of the Bible. It occurred to us at the time that he had showed just the opposite of what he had intended: if you can cover all the Bible's major women in one sermon, then that is no great tribute to women.

So how are we to address this in a way that is fair? In the first place, it means respecting the text itself. As with our treatment of homosexuality, we need to study each of the main kinds of biblical texts in its own way: poetry, prose, and law. And, second, we must look at the world that produced those texts, which means both ancient Israel and the other cultures of that world of the ancient Near East.

In the case of homosexuality, we were able to look at the prominent cases in the three types of texts: prose, poetry, and law. But in the matter of women's status it is impossible: there are too many stories, too much poetry, and too many laws. So we shall have to choose good examples and also look at the big picture through perspectives of history, anthropology, religion, literature, psychology, and archaeology.

The thing is: women are not just one of the main subjects of the Bible, one of the top ten. They are less favored than men, but they are as *integral* to the entire Bible as are men, from beginning to end, from Eve to Esther. The very first chapter of the Bible is about the creation of both men and women. The end of the Hebrew Bible is about a woman who can do what no man can do: save all the Jews in the Persian Empire—which is virtually every Jew on earth.

So let us look at some texts of poetry, prose, and law, and then we shall look at the context in the world of the ancient Near East in which these works were created.

Poetry

The two most prominent American biblical scholars—and we would say the two greatest—of the last generation were Frank Moore Cross and David Noel Freedman. Cross built a center at Harvard where he produced over a hundred doctoral students who went on to careers in the field as professors all over North America. Freedman, at the time of his death, had the second longest entry in *Who's Who in the World*. Professor Cross was the teacher of Richard Elliott Friedman at Harvard. Professor Freedman was the senior colleague, collaborator, and friend of Shawna Dolansky and Richard Elliott Friedman at the University of California. Our dear friend Noel Freedman died during the writing of this book, in April of 2008. Freedman and Cross had themselves been the students of the great scholar of the previous generation, William Foxwell Albright, at Johns Hopkins University. Albright allowed his two brilliant students to write two joint dissertations together instead of one each. That is something that almost never happens in any university in any subject. But it must have been the right decision because both dissertations became extremely important works in the field. One of them was *Studies in Ancient Yahwistic Poetry*. In it, Cross and Freedman treated four poems (plus two were added in the Introduction). They made the case that these were the oldest compositions in the Bible. They based this early dating on spelling (orthography), contents, setting, language, and new knowledge from inscriptions that had been discovered. They wrote it in 1947–48, just as the Dead Sea scrolls were discovered, and evidence from the scrolls further persuaded Cross and Freedman of the correctness of their conclusions. Their dissertation was published as a book in 1975 and republished in 1997. Other scholars have challenged various parts of it over the years, but we believe that its evidence has held up well. Noel Freedman wrote in 1997:

> I am as firmly convinced today as I was forty-five years ago that early poems really are early. While it is true that many, perhaps most, serious scholars date this poetry across the whole spectrum of Israelite history, from premonarchic to postexilic, I believe that the whole corpus belongs to the earliest period of Israel's national existence, and that the poems were composed between the twelfth and tenth–ninth centuries B.C.E. I have encountered neither compelling evidence nor convincing argument to the contrary, or to make me think otherwise.[5]

We mention this bit of history of scholarship because it sets the stage for two important texts in the Bible: the Song of Miriam and the Song of Deborah. Noel Freedman always spoke of them as the two oldest compositions in the Bible. Some people follow the conclusions of critical scholarship, while others believe the traditional Jewish and Christian doctrines about the origins of the texts in the Bible. But, for both the believer and the critic, when it comes to establishing by evidence that biblical texts really are of great antiquity, these two poems stand out. That is why we are beginning this chapter with the poetry. And, as our starting point in this chapter on women's status in the Bible, we note: if Cross and Freedman are right, then the two oldest things in the Bible are associated with women. One is sung by a woman. The other is *about* a woman.

This may mean that women were the composers and singers of songs back in the days when Israel first formed as a people in the land. As a matter of fact, we intend to show that it means much more than that. For now, though, we just recognize that it means that women in ancient Israel, from its earliest stage, were not just wives of patriarchs, appendages, property, or baby makers.[6] How significant were their roles? Here is the case of Deborah:

The Song of Deborah

The Song of Deborah is found in Judges 5. It celebrates a victory of Israelite tribes in a battle against a Canaanite army. It says that things were bad until Deborah arose.

> Until you arose, Deborah,
> you arose, mother of Israel.
> (Judg 5:7)

Israelite tribes follow her and a man named Barak to fight the battle. The song pictures more than just a coalition of a few tribes. It names ten of the tribes of Israel.[7] This is the first text known to us in which Israel is pictured as a united people in the land. Before this, Israel's origins historically are unknown; and in the Bible's account the people are in Egypt, not Canaan, prior to this. The time is the twelfth century BCE. This is the period when we first have archaeological evidence of the existence of the people of Israel, and it is the period of the events in this oldest text in the Bible. As the biblical historian Baruch Halpern wrote, "For the period before Deborah, the time of Israel's formation, the evidence is utterly circumstantial—insubstantial."[8] That is: *the first time in which we find Israel as a people existing in its land, it is led by a woman.*

There are many candidates for the title of "most underappreciated person in the Bible," but Deborah must come first. (That rabbi who spoke about the Bible's great women in one sermon did not include Deborah.) When people are asked to name the great women of the Hebrew Bible, they very commonly begin with Sarah, Rebekah, Leah, and Rachel.[9] They are indeed important, but they are all known in the first place as wives. The qualities for which they are praised occur in the stories of Genesis in connection with their husbands (and sons). Even for biblical women who are thought of more for their own significant roles, like Ruth and Esther, their stories start off with their marriages and then develop from there. Deborah, however, stands out as a leader, as the first leader of Israel in the land. The song does not even mention a husband or father or son.

Even more, the song identifies Deborah, the founding leader of Israel, by that phrase "mother of (or: in) Israel." Biblical commentators have long treated this notation as a touching sidelight. Isn't that nice: she was a great leader and judge, and she was also a good mom. She made the best chicken soup in Beth El. But, as Halpern was the first to point out, "mother of Israel" is more likely to be comparable to calling George Washington the father of the United States. An *'ummâ* (a "mother's house") is a political unit, reflecting kinship.[10] Halpern noted that the Song of Deborah reflects four of such *'ummôt*; that is, four political regions. He concluded: "Deborah is 'the mother of Israel,' all of it. She is the woman who united the four regions into full-brother unity, into a single *'ummâ*."[11]

The reason why people have taken the verse to mean she was a good mother rather than a founding figure is a matter of a technical point of Hebrew grammar. The phrase in Hebrew is *'ēm běyiśrā'ēl* (Judg 5:7). The particle *bě* in that word is a preposition that usually means "in." So translators usually have taken it to mean "mother in Israel." But prepositions are extremely fluid in Hebrew and are possibly the hardest words to translate, much as new speakers of English find it hard to master the use of them: "I live *in* the house, *by* the store, *near* the street, *at* the corner *of* the block." Halpern observed that "of" is the meaning of the particle *be* elsewhere in the Song of Deborah:

> In Judg 5:15, *śāray beyiśśākār* is translated by nearly everyone as "the princes *of* Issachar."
> In Judg 5:24, *nāšîm bā'ōhel* can mean "women *of* the tent" as well as "women *in* the tent."
> In another poem, *hārê baggilbō'a* is commonly translated "mountains *of* Gilboa."[12]

This meaning is a characteristic of early Hebrew poetry. Later the particle *be* does not have this meaning, so readers have misunderstood it. Instead of being the Mother of Israel, Deborah is taken to be a nice mom. Danna Nolan Fewell, trying to work with this image, wrote in *The Women's Bible Commentary* that "Her relationship to Israel has public dimensions, both religious and judicial, but it is not without its familial dimensions as well. Later she will be called a 'mother in Israel,' and in the context of this story one might well envision a Spartan mother who goads her children to fight."[13] That is a stirring image, but Deborah's significance surpasses it by a factor of thousands.

Another layer: The story of Deborah is written in prose. The prose account was written after the song, but then it was placed ahead of it. So now the story appears in Judges 4, and the Song of Deborah comes in Judges 5. So practically everyone who has ever read the song has seen it in the light of the story that precedes it. But that confuses the issue somewhat. First, the singer of the song is not identified in the song itself. The prose introduction that precedes the song says that Deborah and Barak sing it. That seems possible but strange since the song addresses Deborah ("Until you arose, Deborah"). Making Deborah a singer as well as a leader does not necessarily reduce her status. It may even enhance it. But the prose does even more. It calls her a woman of *lappîdôt*. In Hebrew, as in other languages such as German and French, the word that means "woman" is also the word for "wife." The word *lappîdôt* means something like flames or flashes. So the phrase (Hebrew *'ēšet lappîdôt*) may mean that she was a "woman of flashes"—meaning what? Or it may mean that she was the wife of someone named Lappidot. Some have gone so far as to say that Barak is Lappidot. Why? Because *Barak* in Hebrew means "lightning," and *lappîdôt* means "flashes." But that is a very long stretch, not to mention that the word *lappîdôt* is a feminine plural in Hebrew, so it is possible but unlikely to be a man's name. The inclination to turn Deborah into Mrs. Barak may be yet another case of identifying a biblical woman in terms of her husband—precisely in the case of the most independently significant woman in the Hebrew Bible.[14]

The Song of Miriam

Now turning to the Song of Miriam, there is nothing of particular significance in terms of women's status in the words of the song. It is rather the fact of the song itself that is worth noting here. When the song is first presented in the text, the narration says, "Then Moses and the children of Israel sang this song."[15] Then the whole song follows in Exodus 15. But then the song is introduced a second time in these words:

> Miriam, the prophetess, Aaron's sister, took a drum in her hand, and all the women went out behind her with drums and with dances. And Miriam sang to them:

Sing to YHWH for He *triumphed*!
Horse and its rider He cast in the sea.
(Ex 15:20–21)

Both Miriam and Deborah are identified as prophetesses. That is important because prophets in the Hebrew Bible usually speak in poetry—or
in mixtures of poetry and prose. In the Hebrew Bible, history is written
in prose; prophecy is written in poetry. This further fits with the idea
that these two women are thought by some to be the composers of these
poetic songs.

The identification of Miriam as Aaron's sister here does not necessarily
mean that she has no standing on her own. This is simply the first time
that she is mentioned by name in the text, so it tells us who she is,
connecting her to a known person. People naturally ask why she is not
identified as *Moses's* sister. Various possible answers have been proposed in
traditional scholarship, which follows the belief that the whole of the first
five books of the Bible was written by one person, Moses. In the critical
scholarship of the last two centuries, however, scholars have assembled
evidence that the five books come from several separate sources. In the two
earliest sources (known as E and J) Aaron and Miriam are never identified
as Moses's brother and sister. Only a later source claims that Aaron is the
(older) brother of Moses.[16] People who know their Bible stories will ask:
what about when Moses's sister watches over him as he floats down the
Nile as a baby in Exodus 2? But that story never names the sister. In that
early source (J), the name Miriam does not occur, and there is no reason to
think that it refers to Miriam.

A Woman of Substance

A treatment of the role of the Bible's poetry with regard to women's status
must include one of the Bible's most famous passages, traditionally known
as "A Woman of Valor." It does not appear to be about any particular individual woman. It is rather presented as a picture of the qualities that a
certain kind of woman brings. There is a Jewish custom that a man is
supposed to sing this to his wife every Friday evening as the sabbath begins.
It is in the book of Proverbs, which is one of the three books of wisdom
literature in the Hebrew Bible. (The other two are Job and Ecclesiastes.)

We take the Hebrew to mean "a woman of substance." "Woman of valor" is more poetic but not really accurate, and therefore it is misleading. The term *substance* is more consistent with other occurrences of this word in the Bible, and it conveys better that this is about a person of intrinsic worth, a substantial person in her own right. The poem conveys by the end that she thus brings benefit to her children and to her husband through her qualities. Here is the complete text:

A woman of substance who will find?
Her worth: far above jewels.

Her husband's heart trusts in her,
and he won't lack profit;
she pays him back good and not bad
all the days of her life.

She seeks wool and flax
and works with her hands willingly.

She's like merchant ships;
she brings her bread from far.

And she gets up while it's still night
and sets [order] for her house
and instruction for her maids.

She considers a field and gets it,
she plants a vineyard with the fruit of her hands.

She clothes her body with power
and strengthens her arms.

She tastes that her product is good.
Her lamp won't go out at night.

She puts out her arms to the loom,
and her hands hold the spindle.

She opens her hand to the poor
and puts out her arms to the needy.

She won't fear for her house from snow,
for all her house is dressed in scarlet.

She makes herself coverings,
her clothing is linen and blue.

Her husband is known in the gates
when he sits with the land's elders.

She makes and sells a wrap
and gives a garment to a Canaanite.

Her clothing is strength and beauty,
and she laughs at the future day.

She opens her mouth with wisdom,
and the teaching of kindness is on her tongue.

She watches out for her house's ways,
and she won't eat the bread of idleness.

Her children get up and make her happy;
her husband: he praises her:
"Lots of daughters have produced substance,
and you: you've surpassed them all."

Grace is a lie, and beauty is a wisp.
A woman of the fear of God: she will be praised.
Give her from the fruit of her hands,
and let her deeds praise her in the gates.
(Prov 31:10-31)

This poem is not picturing some ideal that all women should try to
be. Its "woman of substance" is more specific than that: she is a married

woman from a household with property and respect in the community. The things for which it praises her are: she is reliable, hardworking, organized, versatile, kind, wise, and reverent. It rejects physical appearance. "Beauty is a wisp." Rather, the things that she accomplishes are what establish her standing: "let her deeds praise her." Even if we take the most limited view of its applicability, it indicates that there were at least some in that ancient society who valued qualities of strength and ability and independence in a woman. Once this poem became a part of the Bible it played a role, to whatever extent, encouraging respect for such qualities.

More bitter than death: woman

But, for balance, if we look at "A Woman of Substance" as a positive source of wisdom by a biblical writer, then we should also look at another passage in the Bible's wisdom books that many of us, male and female, would find downright offensive. It comes from the book of Ecclesiastes, called *Qohelet* in Hebrew. Here is the passage:

> And I find more bitter than death:
> woman,
> that she is traps
> and her heart is nets,
> her hands are manacles.
> One who is good before God
> will escape from her,
> while a sinner will be caught by her.
> See this I've found,
> said Qohelet,
> one by one, to find a total,
> what my soul still looked for,
> and I haven't found.
> A man: I've found one out of a thousand.
> And a woman: I've not found in all of these.
> (Eccl 7:26–28)

That is not exactly a feminist tract. We might say that this is the view of one individual biblical author, as is the passage about a woman of substance, and that the Bible thus collects differing views from persons in that age. After all, the Bible includes the story of a betraying woman, Delilah, as well as a noble woman, Deborah, in the book of Judges. Still, telling prose stories of wicked women is different from including such a hostile characterization of *all* women—and setting it in, of all places, a book that is presented as wisdom.[17]

Scholars question whether Qohelet is the name of the person who speaks in the book or if it is a title, possibly meaning the preacher, the speaker, or the convener. The word *Qohelet* is strange because it has the form of a feminine noun, yet Qohelet is identified in the book as a king, and the word takes masculine verbs—except once. The one exception is in the middle of this passage. The English "said Qohelet" hides this because in English verbs do not look different between masculine and feminine. But in Hebrew the way to say "said Qohelet" is:

'āmar qōhelet[18]

Our text does not say that. Rather, it uses the feminine verb:

'āměrāh qōhelet

It is as if the speaker is now a woman. Some scholars have thought it was a scribal mistake, possibly as a result of a confusion over the feminine form of the word *Qohelet*.[19] But we scholars of the Bible should not be too quick to conclude that we are smarter than the authors and scribes of the Bible. After all, the scribes got their verbs right in every other case in the book. We suggest that it is more likely that placing the feminine verb here, and only here, was intentional. The whole book is written in the masculine, but when something nasty is said about women it is suddenly said in a feminine voice. It is, most probably, a *joke*. It may be the sort of joke that still contains a snide message. Or it may be a joke that mocks men who hold such views of women by putting their thoughts into a woman's voice. It is hard to say. Interpreting jokes that are over two millennia old is difficult. Just look at the footnotes on editions of plays by Aristophanes.

One might ask, would any writer in any period do such a thing? Actually, there is a remarkable parallel in world literature. In Nietzsche's *Thus Spoke Zarathustra*, Zarathustra concludes a speech about women with "a little truth" that he hides in his cloak. He reveals it to be: *"Du gehst zu Frauen? Vergiss die Peitsche nicht!"* Translation: "You're going to women? Don't forget the whip!" Most readers have surely found that to be at least as harsh as the passage in Ecclesiastes. But recently we observed that, just months before Nietzsche wrote those words, he posed for a comic photograph together with a woman, Lou Salome, and a man, Paul Ree. In the photograph, the two men pretend to be horses pulling a wagon, while the woman sits in the wagon holding a whip! So when Zarathustra says, "You're going to women? Don't forget the whip," who is holding the whip?! It is likely that Nietzsche meant it as an ironic joke.[20] And one more point: it is a woman who gives this little truth to Zarathustra. So the parallel to Ecclesiastes is even more intriguing. At minimum, understanding this curious biblical passage as having been meant as humor might soften its edge, and it may even reverse its message. And, after all, somehow we must explain the fact that elsewhere in Ecclesiastes women are regarded as something good.[21] This increases the likelihood that this strange passage was in fact meant as a joke and not as the real, serious view of the author—or else it might have been someone's mischievous addition to the book after its author was long gone.

Now, to broaden the array of roles of women that the Bible reflects, let us turn to prose.

Prose

It is not a small point that the Bible's story *starts* with the matter of the sexes. The Bible begins with two accounts of the creation. In the critical scholarship of recent centuries scholars have identified the sources from which these two stories come.[22] Two authors, separated by at least decades, and possibly centuries, wrote them, and an editor later set them side by side at the beginning of the Bible's story. Orthodox Jews and fundamentalist Christians believe rather that the two accounts come from a single author: Moses. Where both traditional and critical readers can agree is that both accounts feature the relationship of the sexes as something that must be identified as crucial at the very beginning. On any view, religious or nonreligious, everything that will follow in the Bible's story of humankind must be based on this relationship, no less than the formation of the earth, water, and sky; no less than the existence of plants and animals. It is not at

all obvious that a history has to begin with a discussion of the sexes' relationship. Most histories do not. But, in the Bible, this most essential fact
about the human species underlies everything that will happen.

A remarkable development takes place. As we saw at the beginning of
this chapter, men and women are created equal in the first account of
creation. The text says:

> And God created the human in His image. He created it in the image
> of God; He created them male and female.
> (Gen 1:27)

The second account is different. It pictures God creating a man first,
then plants, then animals, and then a woman last. Some might take this
fact—that woman is created later than man—as showing women to be
lower: created only as a companion for men. We have heard the opposite
claim made as well, that woman, being created last, is thus the pinnacle of
the creation! (There is a joke: Why did God create a man first? Answer:
practice!) We do not need to take a side in this matter. The two views
together convey the point that order does not prove significance one way
or the other. To put it another way: So woman is created second. So what?
That does not make her lower or less important.

More relevant to the question of woman's significance in the Bible is
the fact that woman is created, according to the Hebrew, as an *'ēzer
kĕnegĕdô*.[23] Interpreters have long taken this phrase to mean a suitable
helper, or a help appropriate for him. In the King James translation it is "an
help meet" (not a help*mate*!). This is another case in which knowledge of
the range of meaning of the original Hebrew is crucial. The Hebrew word
that is taken to mean "help" there actually has two meanings. Besides
"help," it also means "strength."[24] In that case, the meaning of *'ēzer kĕnegĕdô*
in Genesis is "a strength corresponding to him." That is rather different
from a helper. It sounds more like the woman in "Woman of Substance,"
more like Deborah. But even in a more universal way it conveys an idea of
woman as a person of comparable worth to the male. It also seems more
consistent with the picture in the first creation account, in which the deity
creates both man and woman in the divine image.

We should add, though, that even if we understand the word to mean
"helper" rather than "strength," we may still be misconstruing the text if

we take the word "helper" to mean someone lower—as if all women are supposed to be the administrative assistants of all men. On the contrary, a helper is not necessarily lower. It can even be higher, as when a parent helps a child. In fact the word *'ēzer* in the Bible is often used to characterize God Himself, as being the help in whom humans can trust.[25] In cases like these, it is a relational term, designating a beneficial association. So whether *'ēzer* means helper or strength, one cannot be sure that the author meant to portray women as being somehow lesser than men. And one cannot use this text to support a claim that, biblically, women are supposed to be subordinate to men.

Let us return to the point about the order in this second creation account. The text reports that first God fashions an *'ādām*. The Hebrew word *'ādām* (from which we get the English name Adam) means a human being (or humanity). It does not mean a man in the sense of a male. At various places in the Bible it can mean just males or both male and female humans. In a later step, God makes a woman. She is called *'iššāh*, which is the standard Hebrew word for woman. It is only at this point that, for the first time, the *'ādām* is referred to as an *'îš*, which is the standard Hebrew word for a man. One might say: there is no man until there is a woman, no sexual distinction until there is more than one of the species. After all, sexual identification does not mean anything so long as there is only one of something.

On the relationship of the words *'îš* and *'iššāh*: the text says that the man declares,

> This will be called "woman" [*'iššāh*], for this one was taken from "man" [*'îš*].
> (Gen 2:23)

The particle *-āh* at the end of a word in Hebrew is the feminine ending. So this wording makes it sound as if *'iššāh* is a kind of female *'îš*. As a matter of fact, though, *'iššāh* in Hebrew does not derive from the word *'îš*. People easily make that mistake because the words happen to look similar. But the word *'iššāh* developed from an earlier form *'inšāh*. It corresponds to another Hebrew word for a man, *'enōš*. Their common root is *'nš*. The word *'îš*, on the other hand, has a different root, *'yš*. Whatever this story means, it does not mean that a woman is a female version of a man.

Eden

And another thing worth noting: in their state of innocence before eating the forbidden fruit, the man and the woman are equal to each other in their position, authority, and status. The story at this point does not distinguish them in terms of rank.

But then in the Bible's third chapter everything changes. Near the end of the story in that chapter, men get dominion. Here is the text:

> And the snake was slier than every animal of the field that YHWH God had made, and he said to the woman, "Has God indeed said you may not eat from any tree of the garden?"
>
> And the woman said to the snake, "We may eat from the fruit of the trees of the garden. But from the fruit of the tree that is within the garden God has said, 'You shall not eat from it, and you shall not touch it, or else you'll die.'"
>
> And the snake said to the woman, "You won't die! Because God knows that in the day you eat from it your eyes will be opened, and you'll be like God—knowing good and bad." And the woman saw that the tree was good for eating and that it was an attraction to the eyes, and the tree was desirable to bring about understanding, and she took some of its fruit, and she ate, and gave to her man with her as well, and he ate. And the eyes of the two of them were opened, and they knew that they were naked. And they picked fig leaves and made loincloths for themselves.
>
> And they heard the sound of YHWH God walking in the garden in the wind of the day, and the human and his woman hid from YHWH God among the garden's trees. And YHWH God called the human and said to him, "Where are you?"
>
> And he said, "I heard the sound of you in the garden and was afraid because I was naked, and I hid."
>
> And He said, "Who told you that you were naked? Have you eaten from the tree from which I commanded you not to eat?"
>
> And the human said, "The *woman*[!], whom *you* placed with me[!], *she* gave me from the tree, and I ate."
>
> And YHWH God said to the woman, "What is this that you've done?"
>
> And the woman said, "The snake tricked me, and I ate."

And YHWH God said to the snake, "Because you did this, you are cursed out of every domestic animal and every animal of the field, you'll go on your belly, and you'll eat dust all the days of your life. And I'll put enmity between you and the woman and between your seed and her seed. He'll strike you at the head, and you'll strike him at the heel."

To the woman He said, "I'll make your suffering and your labor pain great. You'll have children in pain. And your desire will be for your man, and *he'll dominate you.*"

And to the human He said, "Because you listened to your woman's voice and ate from the tree about which I commanded you saying, 'You shall not eat from it,' the ground is cursed on your account. You'll eat from it with suffering all the days of your life. And it will grow thorn and thistle at you, and you'll eat the field's vegetation. By the sweat of your nostrils you'll eat bread until you go back to the ground, because you were taken from it; because you are dust and you'll go back to dust."

And the human called his woman "Eve," because she was mother of all living.

And YHWH God made skin garments for the human and his woman and dressed them.

And YHWH God said, "Here, the human has become like one of us, to know good and bad. And now, in case he'll put out his hand and take from the tree of life as well, and eat and live forever:" And YHWH God put him out of the garden of Eden, to work the ground from which he was taken. And He expelled the human, and He had the cherubs and the flame of a revolving sword reside at the east of the garden of Eden to watch over the way to the tree of life.

(Genesis 3)

It is a remarkable story—phenomenal in accomplishing so much in so few lines. We could spend a whole book in explaining, interpreting, and appreciating it by itself. But we shall limit ourselves to the aspects that most shed light on our particular concern in this chapter.

As we said at the end of our first chapter, this is a story that depicts the origin of several facts of life that the author observed in the world:

—Why snakes do not have legs.
—Why humans and snakes are hostile to one another.

—Why women have labor pain.

—Why men dominate women.

—Why men have to work the ground to get food from it.

—Why plants have thorns.

—Why people wear clothes (and experience embarrassment about nudity).

—Why people die.

These stories of origins are called etiologies. There are at least these eight etiologies in this story; some would count more. One thing that they all have in common is that they are all bad. The story comes to explain how the world came to include such bad things. Among these the story tells us why men dominate women. The author is not saying that this *ought* to be the case. In fact in the original creation and state of nature in the garden of Eden, it is explicitly *not* the case. But now, outside the garden, even though childbirth will be painful, women will still desire men, and men will dominate women. But take note: it is an etiology, not a prescription. Every one of these etiologies is something negative in our life experience. That goes for male domination of women just like everything else in the group. The text is not approving of it, recommending it, requiring it, or commanding it—any more than it is approving of death, thorns, or labor pains. There is no changing the fact that this story comes out with men dominating women. There is no point in trying to translate that away, interpret it away, theologize it away, or rationalize it. But one also cannot justify an interpretation that says that this is the way things are *supposed* to be. It is an injustice to the text (and to women!) (and to men!) to interpret this to mean that the Bible commands men to dominate women, or expects men to dominate women, or commands or expects women to accept submission to men.[26]

Later Christian interpretations came to describe the serpent as the devil, and Eve as his agent, first falling under his evil sway and then tempting her trusting husband to primordial sin. But none of that is actually in the text. There is no such being as the devil in the Hebrew Bible.[27] The snake is pictured as just that: the ancestor of the snakes, as the man and woman are the ancestors of humans. The woman does not tempt her husband, sexually or otherwise. It just says:

She took some of its fruit, and she ate, and gave to her man with her as well, and he ate.

No trick, no sex, no seduction, no description at all. Indeed, since it says "gave to her man *with her*," it may even suggest that the man is present for the whole exchange with the snake too. That is not clear. If the author of this story had wanted to blame her, to castigate her, to portray the man as an innocent victim of feminine wiles, the author certainly could have. But the story does not do this.[28]

Patriarchs and matriarchs

Biblical studies of women often try (desperately) to build a lot on limited stories and characters. In the stories that follow Eden in Genesis, we learn almost nothing of the women of the flood generation. We do not get even the names of Mrs. Noah or his sons' wives. There is little on Sarah or Hagar, less on Rebekah, even less on Rachel, and still less on Leah. Abraham's third woman, Keturah, is practically unknown, another of the most underappreciated figures in the Hebrew Bible. She and Abraham have six sons together! (Try this test: ask people, even people who know their Bible pretty well, who is the father of Midian, the ancestor of the Midianites? Very few will know. The answer is Abraham. Midian is one of the sons of Abraham and Keturah.[29]) Bilhah and Zilpah are the patriarch Jacob's concubines, who mother four of the twelve tribes of Israel, but they fare about the same as Keturah. So let us look at some of the relevant narratives, recognizing the relatively small quantity but with an eye to the specific roles and actions that the texts ascribe to the women of the foundational generations.

If Eve is the protagonist who moves humanity out of Eden and out of a state of nature to the (higher? more labor-intensive?) world of culture through her desire for divine knowledge, her granddaughters and great-granddaughters certainly continue the trend of being movers. In fact, given the explicitly patriarchal world depicted in Genesis, in which men are granted blessings and birthrights to pass on to their sons, and women aspire to produce those sons, the power, authority, and agency of women in some of the narratives are actually impressive.

Abraham is the crucial first patriarch, the one to hear God's voice and with whom God will establish His covenant. His wife Sarah[30] is introduced in the very first mention of her as being infertile and childless.[31] In the following chapter she is part of the group whom Abraham leads to

Canaan. When famine in Canaan causes Abraham to move his household to Egypt, he addresses Sarah for the first time in the text: "Here, I know that you're a beautiful woman. And it will be when the Egyptians see you that they'll say, 'This is his wife,' and they'll kill me and keep you alive. Say you're my sister so it will be good for me on your account and I'll stay alive because of you." Many have attempted to explain Abraham's actions in this story, some in his favor, some harshly critical.[32] Our point for now, though, is that Sarah is still not depicted as speaking in this strange drama, in which Abraham is rewarded with wealth as Sarah is taken into Pharaoh's harem. Plagues in Pharaoh's household indicate to him that he has done something wrong, and he sends Sarah and Abraham away. Sarah has still not spoken a word in the narrative. She will be silent for another four chapters, and when she speaks it will be to say to Abraham, "Here, YHWH has held me back from giving birth. Come to my maid. Maybe I'll get 'childed' through her."[33] In her first words in the story, she is proposing surrogate motherhood. Because Hagar is Sarah's maid and has no status as wife, if she bears a child to Abraham it will be counted as Sarah's child. Sarah's grandson Jacob's wives Rachel and Leah will both do this as well. They give their maids to Jacob explicitly for the purpose of producing children who will count as their own.[34]

Other stories indicate that there are other options available to Abraham in order to get sons: why does he not simply marry a second wife or acquire a concubine on his own rather than take Sarah's maid? He can certainly afford one. Later on God will tell Abraham that His covenant will be passed down specifically through a child issuing from Sarah.[35] But in these earlier chapters, Abraham does not yet know this. The interesting thing is that it is not Abraham who raises the point about Sarah's being childless. Sarah raises it, and Sarah says what to do about it. The problem is not presented as *Abraham's* childlessness but as *Sarah's* childlessness. Indeed, the first mention of Sarah's infertility appears in the biblical source known in critical scholarship as P, and this passage about Sarah bringing it up is in the source known as J. So both sources present it as a Sarah matter; they do not present it as being about Abraham's covenant or his need for an heir. (The only reason why people connect it to Abraham at all is that he mentions his childlessness to God in Genesis 15, though that text does not mention wives, concubines, or solutions at all—and it is from a disputed, uncertain source.) And so the answer to the question of whether there are other options open to him is that there are in fact no other options that solve this problem—*Sarah's* problem. His marrying a second wife would be a far worse thing for Sarah. And his acquiring a concubine other than Hagar is no solution either. Rather, it appears that it has to be the wife who gives her maid to her husband in these stories, not the husband who just takes his wife's maid. Thus Rachel and Leah also give their maids to their husband, Jacob. Jacob, like Abraham, does not take them of his own accord.

So Sarah asks Abraham to take her maid, "And Abram listened to Sarai's voice." Despite her intentions, though, the surrogate motherhood does not work out. When Hagar sees that she is pregnant, "her mistress was lowered in her eyes." Sarah unhappily complains to Abraham. Again, Abraham's response is surprising in the ancient Near Eastern patriarchal context of the story. He responds to Sarah by giving her complete authority over the situation: "'Here, your maid is in your hand. Do to her whatever is good in your eyes.' And Sarai degraded her, and she fled from her."[36] The text does not tell us why, but the implication may be that, in this story, Sarah's happiness is more important to Abraham than the continuity of his own lineage.

An angel convinces Hagar to return to Abraham's household, and she gives birth to Ishmael. We hear of no more interactions between Hagar and Sarah. It seems that Abraham's lineage is secure. But Genesis 17 has the deity reiterate His covenant with Abraham and now adds a new twist: "Sarai, your wife: you shall not call her name Sarai, because her name is Sarah. And I'll bless her, and I'll also give you a son from her. And I'll bless her, and she'll become nations. Kings of peoples will be from her." Abraham's response is incredulous laughter; after all, he is a hundred years old, and Sarah is ninety. And then he asks God, "If only Ishmael will live before you."[37] Why is Ishmael, son of Hagar, not to be his heir?

God does not tell him why not. Instead, God insists that Sarah will give birth to Abraham's heir. And she does, and as a result Isaac, and not Ishmael, will be the second Patriarch.

People tend to focus on the "patriarchs" in these stories. After all, are they not the ones with the power? They are certainly the ones to whom God will speak, the ones with whom God will covenant, the ones whom He will bless with prosperity and continuity of lineage. But this story suggests very strongly that it is not only the patriarchs who are important. Their wives and mothers are part of God's concern as well. If the point of the story were that Abraham needed a son through whom the divine covenant would continue, Ishmael would have been fine. But the deity wants the covenant to continue in a different line. To God, there seems to be nothing wrong with Ishmael (who will also be blessed) and nothing inherently better about Isaac as a person (after all, he is not even born yet). The issue is the future patriarch's mother. God insists that "I shall establish my covenant with Isaac, *whom Sarah will bear for you* at this appointed time in the next year."[38] She is important to Abraham, important enough that he gives her autonomy and authority in his household, and she is important to the text, which emphasizes that God wants Sarah's biological son, and not the son of her maid, to be the second patriarch and receive the deity's covenant.

Why Sarah? There are several possible answers: we saw that when Abraham asks her to pass herself off as his sister to save him, she obeys unquestioningly—as Abraham obeyed God when God told him to leave his home and go to Canaan, or as Abraham will when God commands him to offer Isaac as a sacrifice. And she comes from the same family as Abraham; perhaps the issue is as simple as kinship. Maybe, for the author, because Hagar is Egyptian she will not do as the biological mother of an Israelite patriarch. Whatever the reason, Sarah is important. She is important to Abraham and to God and His covenant with their descendants, the people of Israel.

And so Isaac becomes the second patriarch. His wife Rebekah will be even more important in determining succession: not only will the third patriarch be her son, but *she herself* will determine which son will inherit the covenant with God. God will not be visibly involved in the decision as He was with Sarah and Isaac. In fact, Rebekah's intervention contradicts and overrides Isaac's own choice of heir.

When Rebekah becomes pregnant with twins and feels them struggling inside her, she seeks an oracle from the deity. And the text reports that God responds to her; He has not yet spoken to Isaac but addresses Rebekah directly. He explains:

> Two nations are in your womb
> and two peoples will be dispersed from your insides
> and one people will be mightier than the other people
> and the older the younger will serve.
> (Gen 25:23)

People usually miss the ambiguity of this oracle. Since readers know that the story ends with Jacob, the younger twin, receiving dominion over his older brother, Esau, they usually read this oracle as predicting this circumstance. Understood this way, when Rebekah manipulates Jacob's deception of Isaac to usurp Esau's blessing (see below), readers have traditionally understood that Rebekah is simply fulfilling God's will according to the oracle she received when she was pregnant.

But, as David Noel Freedman first observed to us, this is not what the Hebrew says. In Hebrew the verb can come before or after the subject. The oracle can therefore mean *either*: "the elder will serve the younger," *or* "the elder, the younger will serve."[39] It can have two opposite meanings, and so the person who receives it may hear it either way. Rebekah favors her younger son, Jacob, and so it comes as no surprise that she hears the former meaning. She will take action to ensure that her favorite, Jacob, will be the next patriarch.

But in the context of her society, Rebekah cannot simply go to Isaac and discuss Jacob's merits over coffee. Isaac has his heart set on Esau, a hunter, a man of the outdoors, and, after all, the one who emerged first from his mother's womb. By expectation, the firstborn Esau should receive his father's preeminent blessing.

This does not stop Rebekah from taking matters into her own hands. She just has to find a way to do it. When Isaac sends Esau to hunt and cook a special meal for him so that he might confer his dying blessing on his firstborn, Rebekah sees her chance. Taking advantage of her husband's blindness, Rebekah prepares food and provides Jacob with clothing of Esau's that would fool Isaac into thinking Jacob is Esau. Even further, when Jacob worries that a discovery of his deception would lead to his being cursed instead of blessed by Isaac, Rebekah assumes the outcome of any curse onto herself ("Let your curse be on me, my son; just listen to my voice"[40]). This relieves Jacob of the responsibility for his actions; if he is caught, Rebekah will be the one who will suffer. It also credits Rebekah with determining—through her own deception and scheming—who the next patriarch will be.

This is no small matter. When the ruse is successful, Jacob keeps the blessing of the preeminent son. Isaac cannot undo it. As he explains to a distraught and disenfranchised Esau, "Here I've made him your superior, and I've given all his brothers as servants, and I've endowed him with grain and wine. And for you: where, what, will I do, my son?"[41]

Esau plots to kill his brother for what he has done. Once again, Rebekah intervenes. She tells Jacob to flee for his life to her brother Laban's household and to stay there until she has determined that it is safe for him to return. She also complains to Isaac about Esau's Hittite wives. She tells him, "If Jacob takes a wife . . . like these daughters of the land, why do I have a life!"[42] And Isaac tells Jacob to go to his mother's family to find a wife from Laban's household.[43]

To call these the "stories of the patriarchs" is partly right, but it misses the crucial importance of the matriarchs. God determines the succession of Isaac rather than Ishmael. But in the next generation *Rebekah herself* determines the succession of Jacob over Esau. Through Rebekah's actions Jacob becomes the third patriarch, father of the twelve tribes of Israel.

In Israel's patriarchal society, women are portrayed as having few rights relative to men. This is a society depicted as patrilocal (women move away from their families into the households of their husbands) and patrilineal (descent is traced through the father). Women themselves do not generally own property. Men can have numerous wives and concubines; women must be exclusively monogamous. A woman must be obedient to her husband— even if it means becoming another man's wife to save her husband's life. Yet the authors of these stories in Genesis—who, after all, consider themselves descendants of Jacob—repeatedly show the agency of women in pivotal roles. Why would the author not have made Jacob act on his own bold initiative? Or why not have Esau disqualify himself from consideration through disgraceful actions (as Reuben does later by sleeping with his father's concubine and thereby losing his own rights as firstborn son)? For whatever reason, the author portrays Rebekah as the unlikely heroine, not Jacob as hero or Esau as villain. Like Sarah before her, Rebekah as matriarch is just as important literarily—and therefore historically, since these stories are intended to explain the author's own ancestry—as is Isaac as patriarch.

Rebekah's story is even more remarkable than Sarah's. In this story, the author does not have God intervene at all in Rebekah's actions; the deity allows her to determine the meaning of His oracle for herself. And then God *confirms her choice* by covenanting with Jacob after he receives Isaac's blessing through Rebekah's manipulations.

What is going on here? If these stories come out of a man's world, why are they depicting women with these powers? Why include stories about women outsmarting men? We shall consider at least one answer near the end of this chapter.

The Two Tamars

There are two stories that are usually left out of Sunday school studies because of their very explicit sexual subject matter. They each involve a woman named Tamar, and in each case an event that starts out small ends up having tremendous consequences for the destiny of the Jews. Each case starts out as a family story but ends up having consequences for a nation. This family-to-nation connection is an essential aspect of the Bible. Five times it declares the crucial message that the patriarchs' descendants are to be a "blessing to all the earth." The first and fifth time, it says that they will be a blessing to "all the *families* of the earth." The three middle times, it says that they will be a blessing to "all the *nations* of the earth." Thus:

> "all the families of the earth will be blessed through you."
> (Gen 12:3)

> "all the nations of the earth will be blessed through him."
> (Gen 18:17–18)

> "all the nations of the earth will be blessed through your seed."
> (Gen 22:16–18)

> "all the nations of the earth will be blessed through your seed."
> (Gen 26:2–4)

> "all the families on the earth will be blessed through you and through your seed."
> (Gen 28:10–14)

Note also that the blessing is given to the male leaders, the patriarchs, alone, not stated to the women of these founding generations. But the blessing is formulated in terms of whole families and whole nations, not just through the males. It does not say something like "all the *sons* of the earth." It speaks of families and nations, which include both men and women. Again the Bible stands on the line of transition between favoring males and recognizing both males and females. And in the stories of the two Tamars, likewise, the structure and the power are in the men's hands, but the two women's roles are the energy via which the events spiral. It is in families that women may be most effective, even in a world in which they do not yet exercise power through government over nations. And it is in these family settings that the two Tamars play their roles.

The First Tamar: "She's more right than I"

A story in Genesis 38 tells about Judah, one of Jacob's twelve sons, the one from whom the country Judah and its people the Jews derive their name. Judah has three sons. The first one, named Er, marries Tamar, but he dies before they have had any sons. Judah directs his second son, named Onan, to perform levirate marriage with the widow Tamar to "raise seed for your brother." (We referred to this part of the story in our discussion of "onanism" in the last chapter.) In levirate marriage, the first son to be born is regarded as the son of the deceased man. So when Onan and Tamar would have a son, the boy would be called "So-and-so the son of Er" even though he would be biologically the son of Onan.[44] Onan does not much like this idea, so "when he came to his brother's wife he spent on the ground so as not to give seed for his brother."[45] God does not approve. Onan is struck dead.

We would expect that Judah would now have his third son, named Shelah, perform levirate marriage with Tamar. But all that Judah knows is: everybody who marries this woman dies. So Judah, fearful of Tamar, sends her back to her father's house as a widow, claiming that this is just "until my son Shelah grows up." Tamar is now in a real predicament. Judah has promised her to Shelah, which means she is betrothed and cannot marry anyone else. But, as time passes and Judah does not follow through on his promise, Tamar waits in her father's house, biological clock ticking.

Finally she decides to take matters into her own hands. Dressing as a prostitute with her face veiled, Tamar attracts Judah on his way to sheep-shearing. She demands his seal, his cord, and his staff as pledges against the goat kid he has promised to bring as payment on his return. He has sex with her and continues on his way. But when his friend returns to collect the seal, cord, and staff in exchange for the goat kid, the prostitute is gone. Three months later, Judah is informed that "Your daughter-in-law Tamar has whored, and, here, she's pregnant by whoring as well." Judah's response: "Bring her out and let her be burned." After all, she has committed adultery. But Tamar shows Judah the seal, cord, and staff of the man who impregnated her, and he declares, "She's more right than I am, because of the fact that I didn't give her to my son Shelah." Providentially, Tamar is proved right as well: she is rewarded for her subterfuge with twins, one of whom will be the ancestor of King David himself.

In a patriarchal society, a woman cannot simply dictate or impose her choices and preferences. But the women of Genesis manage to work within their capacity as women, within their secondary social status, to get what they want, to outwit their men, and—if you see a providential plan unfolding in the narrative—to carry out God's will in the process. This is known as dual causation, referring to stories in which human hands and the hand of God both function in such a way that it is difficult to say how much each force is at work. Thus in this story it is a man's world. Men decide who marries whom. Sons count for preservation of a man's name; daughters do not. Sons count for inheritance. They count for establishing lineage. But a woman is depicted as able to accomplish destiny-changing things through cleverness, deception, and sex. Men are the guns, but women are the triggers—and sometimes the targets. Read on.

The Second Tamar: A rape in the royal house of David

Fast-forward a few centuries. It is ten generations later, and Judah and Tamar's descendant David is the king of Israel. David has many wives and concubines, and so he has children who are half brothers and half sisters to one another. His eldest son, the heir apparent to his throne, is Amnon. His third son is Absalom. Absalom has a beautiful sister named Tamar. Tamar and Absalom have the same mother, so Tamar is a full sister to Absalom. She is a half sister to Amnon. And he loves her.

Amnon pretends to be ill and asks his father, King David, to send Tamar to care for him. In an exceptionally crafted scene of literary tension, Tamar cooks for him while we wait to see what he will do. Finally he pounces, ignores her pleas, and rapes her. Immediately after he has taken her, his love transforms to hate. He has her thrown out. She cries to her brother Absalom. And he kills his brother Amnon.[46]

We have heard it claimed that Tamar in this story is more savvy than one would think at first sight, that she is in fact attempting to make things play out a certain way in terms of the customs of the time. We see no justification for this in the text. She is a victim. It is one of the worst stories of rape in world literature, as the man, once he gets what he wanted, turns his infatuation to disgust. Tamar begs him, saying that his ejecting her disdainfully is even worse than the rape. But he will not hear it as he rather tells his servant, "Send *this one* away from me outside! And lock the door behind her!" He will not even say her name. And "lock the door"?! Is he afraid she wants to come back in?

People puzzle over Tamar's words at the start of Amnon's attack. As he takes hold of her and says, "Come, lie with me, my sister," she says:

> Don't, my brother! Don't degrade me. Because such a thing isn't done in Israel. Don't do this foolhardy thing. And I, where would I bear my disgrace? And you'll be like one of the fools in Israel. And now, speak to the king, because he won't hold me back from you.
> (2 Sam 13:12–14)

In the last sentence she apparently tells Amnon that their father, King David, would be willing to give her to Amnon as a wife. It has been suggested that this is evidence that she should be understood to have planned this situation—or at least to be taking advantage of it—to get a marriage to the heir apparent to the throne. But that is a great deal to derive from these words. The full context looks rather like she is throwing out everything that she can think of to stop him: reminding him that they are siblings ("Don't, my brother"), mercy ("Don't degrade me"), it is immoral in their culture ("such a thing isn't done in Israel"), pity ("where would I bear my disgrace?"), his own degradation ("you'll be like one of the fools in Israel"), and finally she says that he can get her permanently from their father. In context that last line looks more like desperation than manipulation. It appears that she is trying anything (six different things) to get him off of her. There was a case in the United States of a woman who pleaded with a rapist at least to use a condom. He did, and his defense in court was to claim that this was proof that she consented. The jury rejected that argument. What a woman says in the middle of a rape is not evidence of intent. We can hardly infer anything about her intent or about her society's rules from what she is depicted as saying in that horrible moment.

As in biblical law (see below), so in biblical narrative, the Bible does not tolerate rape. The narrative conveys sympathy for Tamar. It tells that she puts ashes on her head, tears her clothing, and goes on screaming. Her brother Absalom tells her to keep quiet: and "Don't set your heart on this thing." That sounds unfeeling, but it turns out that Absalom is just biding his time and that he in fact "hated Amnon over the fact that he had degraded Tamar, his sister." And so both Tamars are victims, but their compensations for their sufferings are quite different. The first Tamar achieves something through her own plans and actions. The second is avenged by a man. Situations vary. The strengths and weaknesses of individual women vary. Each story conveys a different aspect of the place of women in a patriarchal setting.

So we have stories of two Tamars. Both are stories about events in a family, but both change the destiny of nations. The first Tamar's experience results in the birth of the royal line of David, the line that produces the messiah. The second Tamar's experience results in a crucial change in the succession to this line's throne. The elimination of Amnon from the succession is the first step that culminates in the throne passing instead to another of David's sons: King Solomon.

Dinah

The biblical narrative visibly and directly connects the nation's destiny to situations involving men's attraction to women. Another episode that does this comes between the stories of the matriarchs (Sarah, Rebekah, Leah, Rachel) and the story of the first Tamar. It is the story of Dinah, the daughter of Leah and Jacob.[47] Most readers think that it, too, is about a rape. Some Bibles even add a heading over it, giving it the title "The Rape of Dinah." Strangely, remarkably, however, it is actually uncertain whether there is a rape in the story or not. In the narrative, a man named Shechem, the prince of the Canaanite (Hivite) city of Shechem (his father the king gave his son and his city the same name), has sexual relations with Dinah. Unlike Amnon, though, after the sex Shechem's "soul clung to Dinah, Jacob's daughter, and he loved the girl and spoke on the girl's heart." He and his father the king ask her family for her hand in marriage. Her brothers deceive them, insisting that the only way that their family and the Shechemites can live together and intermarry is if the Shechemite men all become circumcised. The Shechemites agree to this; but, when they are all hurting from the surgeries, Dinah's brothers Simeon and Levi come and kill every male. Their father, Jacob, criticizes his sons for what they have done, but they answer: "Shall he treat our sister like a prostitute?"

So, does Shechem rape Dinah, or is it some other sexual offense that upsets her brothers? The text says:

> And he took her and lay with her and degraded her.
> (Gen 34:2).

These words are what lead interpreters generally to see a rape here. These same three words ("took, lay, degraded") occur in the Amnon and Tamar story as well. These words, however, do not denote rape. The first term, to "take" a woman, is used elsewhere in the Hebrew Bible to refer to marriage! The second word (literally "to lay") is commonly used to refer to sex, but it does not imply sex by force. The third word (to "degrade") is the most negative. The same word is used elsewhere for what the Egyptians do to the Israelites by enslaving them and for the way that Sarah treats her maid Hagar.[48] It comes closest to involving rape in the story of the raped concubine to which we referred in the first chapter.[49] Most notably, the latter two terms, "lay" and "degrade," both occur in a law in Deuteronomy that we shall discuss in the section on law below.[50] Both terms appear there in a case that is explicitly ruled not to be a rape. So the word is sometimes used in connection with rape, and sometimes in situations that do not involve rape, and sometimes in situations that do not even involve sex.[51] In the case of Tamar and Amnon, we have no doubt that it is a rape because the text adds "he took hold of her," and explicitly informs us that Amnon ignores her pleas when she says, "Don't!" But precisely these elements that make it clear that it is a rape in Tamar's story are missing from the Dinah story. Interpreters have been too quick to see a rape here. It may be a rape. It may not. We cannot tell from the wording of the text. In recent years other scholars besides ourselves have come to note this uncertainty.[52] Whether it is by force or with consent, though, her brothers are outraged, and the justification they give for their violent response is that one cannot treat their sister that way.

Whether it is a rape is in doubt. What should not be in doubt is the biblical view of rape: it is horrid. It is decried in the Bible's stories. It is not tolerated in the Bible's laws (see below). Some may claim that this is just because it is an offense against the woman's father. We do not see sufficient grounds for this claim in either the stories or the laws. The rape story of Tamar is not concerned that this is an offense against David. The story is told sympathetically to *her*.

What different scholars see in this story sheds light on the nature of biblical scholarship itself. The biblical scholar Susanne Scholz discusses a range of scholarship that responds to the Dinah story in a variety of ways. She says that most interpreters do not acknowledge the rape as the central event in Genesis 34. She concludes: "They have to take the rape seriously and express their clear disapproval of the rapist. At stake are the ethics of biblical studies in a culture that has often used the Bible to support injustice and discrimination."[53] Even though we (Dolansky and Friedman) do not see evidence that it is clearly a rape in the story in Genesis 34, we still agree, of course, that it is bad to use the Bible to support injustice and discrimination. And we agree that interpreters who thought that it is rape yet did not acknowledge this rape's centrality in the story fell short in their task. In the end, a study of the Bible's value and impact for present issues is a study not only of the Bible itself but also of the way people have interpreted and misinterpreted it, for better and for worse.

David and Bathsheba

Amnon rapes Tamar. Absalom kills Amnon. Absalom later rebels against his father, David, and is killed. What causes these and all the other terrible things that happen in the portrait of this unhappy royal family? The narrative traces their root to King David's misdeeds over a woman: Bathsheba. Dual causation!

The book of 2 Samuel, in which all of this takes place, is also known as the Court History of David. It is especially about succession. Its central question is: who will be the successor of King David? As it turns out, that is a question that depends on women. We have already begun to see this in the story of the second Tamar. But it starts with Bathsheba. And it begins on a roof:

> And it was at evening time, and David got up from his bed and walked
> on the roof of the king's house and saw a woman washing from the roof,
> and the woman was very good looking.
> (2 Sam 11:2)

The setting fits with the excavations of the City of David in which we participated. The city stands on a steep hillside, with the best housing, which presumably included the king's residence, located at the highest elevation.[54] So the king could look down from his roof at the homes below. He has the very good-looking Bathsheba brought to him, and he impregnates her. There is a problem: she is married—to one of David's soldiers! David arranges her husband's death in battle, and he marries Bathsheba. But "the thing that David had done was bad in YHWH's eyes."[55] The prophet Nathan comes with condemnation and pronounces a double curse on David's house: first, "The sword won't ever turn away from your house," and second, "I'll take your women before your eyes and give them to your fellow man, and he'll lie with your women in the eyes of this sun! Because *you* did it in secret, but *I'll* do this thing in front of all Israel and in front of the sun."[56] And it all comes true. The rape of Tamar and the fratricide of Amnon are only the beginning. Absalom is killed when his rebellion fails. And there will be one more fratricide. And what of the curse that another man will take David's women publicly? His own son Absalom is the man. When he seeks to replace his father on the throne, Absalom sleeps with ten of David's concubines. And just to make sure that we get the ironic connection back to David's act with Bathsheba and Nathan's curse, the text reports: "they pitched a tent for Absalom on the *roof,* and Absalom came to his father's concubines before all Israel's eyes."[57] And in case we miss the mention of the roof there, the narrative later reports that David learns that a messenger is coming with the news of his son Absalom's death from a lookout on a roof.[58] And these are the only mentions of a roof in the book of 2 Samuel.

The history of misinterpretation of this episode is almost as interesting as the episode itself. Some commentators have pictured Bathsheba as a seductress, or even as a harlot.[59] And part of the backup for this claim is that Bathsheba chooses to wash up on her roof where she can be seen from the palace above. Talk about a misunderstanding! They have taken the words "saw a woman washing from the roof" to mean that *Bathsheba* goes up to her roof to wash. It is rather David who is walking on the roof and David who sees her washing *from* the roof. Nothing in this text suggests a subtle plan of seduction by Bathsheba. On the contrary, Nathan's prophecy explicitly condemns only David and does not blame Bathsheba for anything.

Bathsheba and Abishag

Our starting point in this discussion was that the Bible depicts a male political structure but at the same time casts women in roles that change the course of the nation. Women do not figure in every single story, but there is no telling the David story without Bathsheba, and no telling the story of King Ahab without Jezebel. In particular we should look at the account of the last days of David to sum up this point. David is old and is said to be unable to "get warm."[60] So they bring him Abishag, the most beautiful woman they can find in all Israel. But "the king did not know her." You know what that means. And the very next sentence of the story says that Adonijah, David's next oldest son, "promoted himself, saying, 'I'll rule.'" In the ancient Near East, when a king could no longer be sexually potent, his throne was in jeopardy. Near Eastern kings say about themselves "my scepter was straight." When Absalom challenges his father's rule, he takes ten of his father's women. And now Adonijah claims the throne when his father cannot know a woman.

Enter Bathsheba. Literally. She comes into the room where, the text notes, "Abishag, the Shunammite, was serving the king." So there is David in the room with two women: Abishag, the woman who is now his greatest failure, and Bathsheba, the woman who was his greatest conquest. At this point, one imagines, Bathsheba can ask for just about anything, and the answer will be yes. She says that David once promised her that her son Solomon would be his successor. (We do not know from the text if this is true.) Then Nathan enters—the prophet who had condemned David for the Bathsheba affair—and he echoes what Bathsheba has just said. The answer is yes, and David makes Solomon the king.

After David's death, Adonijah comes to Bathsheba and accepts that his younger brother Solomon has won. He just asks for one thing: Abishag. Bathsheba conveys his request to her son Solomon, to which Solomon replies:

> And why do you ask for Abishag . . . for Adonijah? Ask for the *kingdom*
> for him—because he's my brother who's older than I.
> (1 Kgs 2:22)

And he has Adonijah executed. What just happened there? In seeking to have the woman with whom David could not perform, Adonijah is making a potential claim on the throne. Thus what starts with Bathsheba ends with

Bathsheba and Abishag. It is a man's world—but, not so fast, dear reader. It is complex. Subtle, artistic, nuanced, realistic, savvy great literature is like that.

We hardly need to be told that there is a tight connection between sex and politics. Half the clergy in the United States made sermons about David and Bathsheba when an American president acknowledged an affair that very nearly brought down his presidency. And Europeans, who have much more experience with monarchy than Americans do, should find no surprise in this biblical sequence of events at all.[61]

And people ask if the Bible is still relevant.

Law

We have seen cases in biblical poetry and prose in which there is a male-favored framework but in which women rise in status and power. This dynamic between the social framework and the individual case is likely to have contributed to the fact that people have two opposite views of women's status in the Bible. The same situation prevails in the Bible's sections on law.

Property rights

Here is a particularly useful example of the way the Bible involves both an advance and a restriction of women's rights. Step one: sons, not daughters, inherit property from their fathers. Step two: what happens if a man has just daughters, no sons? This is not uncommon. This case arises in an episode that takes place in the very first generation after the laws are established at Sinai. In Numbers 27, a man named Zelophehad has five daughters and no sons. When he dies, his daughters plead their case that they should inherit his property. On one hand, they are making an important claim for women's rights, but, on the other hand, they word their case in terms of their father, not themselves. They say:

> Why should our father's name be subtracted from among his family because
> he didn't have a son? Give us a possession among our father's brothers.
> (Num 27:4)

In biblical law, land in Israel is unalienable. Every fiftieth year is called the Jubilee, at which time all land goes back to the original owners. Even if a man loses his land through sale or foreclosure, the loss is for a maximum of forty-nine years, and then it must be returned to him. If he has died, it goes to his sons. If they have died, it goes to his grandsons. But, Zelophehad's daughters say, if their father's land would pass to his brothers, then the land that would have continued in his name would now be in the name of his brothers and their descendants instead. Moses takes their case to God, and God Himself declares, "Zelophehad's daughters speak right." So, for a reason that has to do with male rights, women acquire a significant female right. Thus this matter stands in a middle ground on a scale that extends from patriarchy to women's liberation. Still, it establishes an important precedent. Males dominate in matters of property, but there can be situations in which females precede males. In inheritance, daughters come before their father's brothers.

But the matter does not end there. It is in the nature of law that new decisions will also generate new, unforeseen complications (as our generation has learned a thousand times). The case in Numbers 27 establishes this female right of inheritance, but nine chapters later a problem surfaces. Step 3: Zelophehad comes from the Israelite tribe of Manasseh. In Numbers 36, this tribe's heads come with a case of their own. If Zelophehad's daughters marry men from one of the other Israelite tribes, and then if they have sons, then those sons will be members of their fathers' tribes. (In the Bible, one's identity as an Israelite, a Jew, a priest, or a member of a tribe goes by one's father, not by the mother, 100 percent of the time. The practice of establishing Jewish identity by the mother, which is currently practiced by Orthodox and Conservative Jews, began only in the post-biblical period.) That is, if a daughter of Zelophehad, who comes from Manasseh, marries a man who comes from the tribe of Benjamin, then their son will be a man of Benjamin. Now, in that case, Zelophehad's land, which was part of Manasseh, would now become part of Benjamin instead. The heads of Manasseh are not prepared to give up territory so easily, and the possible ramifications for the nation are tremendous, potentially wreaking havoc with all the tribes' boundaries. This time God says, according to Moses, that the heads of Manasseh "speak right." So what is the solution to this dilemma? The law remains that women precede their uncles for inheritance, but this stipulation is added: they have to marry men from their own tribe.

The LORD giveth, and the LORD taketh away.

Adultery

Let us take another example. Both men and women are forbidden to commit adultery.[62] The man and the woman who do this both have the same penalty (execution).[63] So far, so fair. But what changes all this is the fact of polygamy. As we saw in the chapter on homosexuality, polygamy has potentially enormous implications. There are few more striking differences between the biblical world and our own. In a world in which polygamy is permissible, the definition of adultery is: sex between a man and a married woman. It does not apply to sex between married men and single women. A married man may have other wives, he may have concubines, girlfriends, dates, or go to prostitutes. So, again, individual laws may provide for equal standing of females within a framework that overall favors the interests of males.

The law on adultery goes further, giving a case in which the judgment for a woman may even be better than that for a man. Following the law about the equal penalty for male and female adulterers, the very next verses treat the case of sex between a man and a woman who is betrothed to another man.[64] If the sex takes place in a city, then both the man and the woman are regarded as guilty and are executed. If, however, it takes place out in a field, then only the man is punished. The woman is not regarded as guilty, and she suffers no punishment. The principle is: if it happened where people would hear if the woman called for help, then they are both guilty. But if it happened where no one would hear if the woman called for help, then there is a presumption in the woman's favor. It is presumed that she called for help but was not heard, and the case is regarded as a rape. Here is the text:

> If it will be that a virgin young woman will be betrothed to a man, and a man will find her in the city and lie with her, then you shall take the two of them to that city's gate and stone them with stones so they die: the young woman on account of the fact that she did not cry out in the city, and the man on account of the fact that he degraded his neighbor's wife. So you shall burn away what is bad from among you.
>
> But if the man will find the betrothed young woman in the field, and the man will take hold of her and lie with her, then only the man who lay with her shall die, but you shall not do a thing to the young

woman. The young woman does not have a sin deserving death, because, just as a man would get up against his neighbor and murder him: this case is like that; because he found her in the field, the betrothed young woman cried out, and there was no one to save her.
(Deut 22:23–27)

The woman here is automatically regarded as a victim, comparable to the victim of a murder. From the law's point of view, she had no control in the matter. Some might claim that the law is not primarily concerned with the woman; rather, the issue is the offense against the man to whom she is betrothed, or possibly against her father. But there is no basis for this claim here in the words of the text. On the contrary, the wording seems focused on the situation of the woman herself. The treatment of this case in the second paragraph does not even mention her father or the man to whom she is betrothed.

Laws from Israel's neighbors confirm this focus on the woman. The Code of Hammurabi (seventeenth century BCE) stipulates that an adulterous couple caught in the act are to be bound and thrown into the water.[65] But when a man *rapes* a betrothed virgin (her lack of consent is indicated in the law by the fact that the rapist is said to have "bound" her), he is to be put to death and the girl is to be declared innocent.[66] Hittite law (1650–1200 BCE) is similar in its wording to the law in Deuteronomy: if the sex occurs "in the mountains," then the man is guilty and sentenced to death, and the woman is presumed innocent. But if the adultery happens indoors, then the sentence for the woman is death; no mention is made of the man; here the focus is exclusively on the woman. And if the woman's husband catches them in the act, he is empowered to kill them both.[67] This last provision is an important difference from the law in the Bible. It is common in other ancient Near Eastern law codes to allow the husband the power of life and death over his wife. No similar laws exist anywhere in the Hebrew Bible.

Compare the Assyrian Law Code (1114–1076 BCE), the one that is closest in time period to the biblical laws. Like the Hittite Code and Deuteronomy 22, provision is made that a woman's lack of consent means that only the male adulterer (rapist) is executed. But if she is found in his house, then she is presumed to have consented, and both are executed. Likewise, if the adultery takes place "at an inn or in the street," both can be executed at the discretion of the woman's husband; whatever he decrees as punishment for his wife must also be enforced on the male accomplice.[68] With one exception: if the male adulterer did not know that the woman with whom he was sleeping was married, he is exempt from punishment. Only the wife must suffer whatever punishment her husband decides to inflict.[69]

The biblical law is unequivocal; unless the woman is presumed innocent by the fact that the adulterous sex takes place outside of the city, both parties are executed. There are two important differences from other ancient Near Eastern laws here: first, there is no exception for a man who pleads ignorance of the woman's marital status; and, second, the husband has no say in the punishment. He can neither mitigate it nor carry it out himself. Why are these differences important? Because it seems that the law in the Bible has entirely removed a husband's authority to inflict punishments on his wife. The Middle Assyrian Laws state explicitly that a man can, at his own discretion, pull out his wife's hair and mutilate or twist her ears if he feels she deserves it.[70] There are no comparable biblical laws.

A captured woman in war

Similarly in a case in the chapter that precedes this, there is a law that provides for male prerogatives yet includes an element of sensitivity to a woman.

> When you'll go out to war against your enemies, and YHWH, your God, will put him in your hand, and you'll take prisoners from him, and you'll see among the prisoners a woman with a beautiful figure, and you'll be attracted to her and take her for yourself as a wife, then you shall bring her into your house, and she shall shave her head and do her nails and take away her prisoner's garment from on her. And she shall live in your house and shall mourn her father and her mother a month of days. And after that you may come to her and marry her, and she shall become your wife. And it will be, if you don't desire her then you shall let her go on her own, and you shall not *sell* her for money. You shall not get profit through her, because you degraded her.[71]
> (Deut 21:10–14)

It is a fact of war that men on a victorious side rape women on the side that they have defeated. Even laws and conventions that forbid this have not eradicated it. This law prohibits the rape of captured women and apparently seeks to curtail it not by forbidding it outright. Rather, it tells the man in the heat of the moment that he must take the woman home, let her mourn, wait a month, and then may marry her. If, after all this, the man does not want her anymore, then he must let her go. (Middle Assyrian Law makes no similar provisions. It simply states that, if a man wishes to marry a captured woman, then all he needs to do is declare in the presence of five witnesses that she is his wife.[72]) So the overall structure in biblical law remains in favor of male prerogatives. After all, the text does not suggest that the woman has any say in whether to be married to this man. But the law still is framed so as to save her from the rape, and it is sensitive to what she has suffered even in this situation, so it forbids the man to degrade her further or use her situation for his own profit.

And note: he cannot *sell* her. We italicized it in the English because it is expressed as an emphatic in the original Hebrew: *mākōr lō' timkĕrennāh*. In Biblical Hebrew, one makes emphasis by placing the infinitive before the verb; literally: "selling you shall not sell." This strong wording absolutely, positively commands the man that he cannot sell her. This is evidence against the claim that women are property in biblical law. People commonly assert this, but no one ever lays out the evidence for this claim. You can sell property. You cannot sell a woman, not even one who is captured in war.

A slave woman designated for marriage

Now there is one circumstance in which one *can* sell a woman: one can sell a slave woman. This is true, but one can sell a slave man as well. The issue there is slavery, not gender.[73] There is, nonetheless, a law that we should note, a law that is specifically about a slave woman; and it is another case of a law covering a male prerogative while including an element of sensitivity to a woman's situation. Namely, one may not sell a slave woman who has been rejected as a wife. On one hand, the context of the law is that a man might sell his daughter to another, which we could argue would be the one case in which a woman might be treated like property, namely, that a man's children (male and female?) are his property. On the other hand, the law establishes that this daughter is not to be treated the same as the slaves. The man who acquires her may (1) marry her, in which case he must provide her food, clothing, and hygiene forever, or (2) designate her for marriage to his son, in which case he must treat her as any daughter, or (3) let her go free. So the woman is not free; she is subject to her father's power and can be placed in an arranged marriage. But she is not exactly sold in the same way as property either. Her father is receiving a bride-price for giving her over to marriage. Here is the text:

> If a man will sell his daughter as a maid, she shall not go out as the slaves go out. If she is bad in the eyes of her master who has designated her for himself, then he shall let her be redeemed. He shall not dominate so as to sell her to a foreign people in his betrayal of her. And if he will designate her for his son, he shall treat her according to the manner of daughters. If he will take another for himself, he shall not subtract from her food, her apparel, and her hygiene. And if he will not do these three for her, then she shall go out free. There is no money.[74]
> (Ex 21:7–11)

There is one phrase in that law that we should not let go by quickly. It says, "He shall not dominate" (v. 18). This is the first occurrence of the word *dominate* in the book of Exodus. Back in Genesis, it is one of the consequences imposed on women for the woman's part in the events in the garden of Eden. There it says that woman's desire will be to man, and "he'll dominate you."[75] This law in Exodus is thus striking in the context of the Bible's first story, for now it says, "he shall *not* dominate . . ." That is, the male dominion that is divinely bestowed in Genesis is not absolute. It is subject to subsequent limitation. It does not mean that a man can do anything he wants to his mate. This law does not do away with the male framework of Genesis, but, in affirming that a woman has certain rights, even in the one situation in which she can be sold, it chips away at the notion of male domination of female as originally formulated. Apparently the LORD can also taketh away and then giveth back.[76]

Similarly, polygamy was a male prerogative in the world that produced the Bible, but this biblical law is sensitive to a woman's situation in such a marriage, and it protects each wife. The law says that if a man takes a second wife, he cannot diminish the basic needs of his first wife. A husband is obligated to provide food, clothing, and the necessary cosmetics for her hygiene and appearance. (There are two other common interpretations of the word *'ōnātāh*, which we translated here as "her hygiene." The first is "shelter," which is a possibility if the word *'ōnātāh* is cognate to Hebrew *mā'ōn*, "dwelling." The second, a traditional Jewish view, is that this refers to sex, but there is no evidence in support of this. The comparative evidence from other cultures of the ancient Near East favors hygiene/cosmetics.[77])

Rape

The Bible's laws, like its prose stories, do not tolerate rape. We have seen this in the cases of the betrothed woman and the female captive in war. But what of a case of rape of an unmarried, unbetrothed woman? The law is that the man "shall give the young woman's father fifty weights of silver, and she shall be his for a wife. Because he degraded her, he shall not be able to let her go, all his days."[78] Fifty weights of silver is a substantial sum, and loss of the right ever to divorce her is a substantial penalty imposed on the man. But, still, in most cultures of our own time we would hardly approve of this woman's having to be married to the man who raped her! The problem is partly the result of the brevity of biblical laws. This law states the penalties that can be imposed on the rapist. It does not say that the woman's father or the woman herself has to accept the marriage. It may mean that the choice of marriage is in the father's hands, not in the hands of the man who raped the woman. The father retains his rights; the rapist loses his: both his right to choose to marry and his right to divorce.

Interestingly, Middle Assyrian Law provides us with the same crime but a slightly different solution. If a man rapes another man's unmarried, virgin daughter, the father of that girl is to take the rapist's wife in recompense! In addition, as in the biblical law, he may choose to have the rapist marry his daughter, in which case the rapist must pay three times the usual bride-price, and he loses the right ever to divorce her. And, after payment is made, the father can choose to keep his daughter and marry her to someone else instead.[79] But if the alleged rapist swears that the woman freely consented, then her father is not to touch the man's wife, the man is to pay three times the standard bride-price, and the father may punish his daughter as he wishes.[80]

In Deuteronomy 21, the rapist's wife is not treated as compensation to the father of the raped woman. And the woman's consent is not an issue; at stake is her loss of status. And her father retains the ability to decide whether or not she must marry her rapist. We cannot know how much say the woman herself has because we have already seen a law above in which a father can make an arranged marriage for a daughter, so the daughter in this law may have no more or less say than in any other situation. (Even in a culture where fathers can make arranged marriages for their daughters, there may be the possibility of caring how the daughter feels about it. Thus in the story of the arranged marriage of Isaac and Rebekah in Genesis, her brother and her father negotiate the marriage, but then her brother and mother say, "We'll call the girl and ask her from her own mouth." And they call Rebekah and say to her, "Will you go with this man?" And she says, "I'll go."[81] Rebekah has at least some say there in the timing of her departure and possibly in the marriage itself.) So, again, the overall legal structure remains male while an individual law acts to protect a woman at least from the loss of status as a result of the rape within that male structure.

The loss of status is specifically related to the fact that the laws in that chapter of Deuteronomy refer to virgins. In addition to her suffering the rape itself and all the pain that follows it, the woman suffers the loss of the status that she had as a virgin. The law offers the only compensation that it can for that loss in that culture: marriage for her, monetary compensation for her father. The law does not say what the penalties are for rape of a woman who is not a virgin. It seems unlikely that the men or the women in ancient Israel thought that it was acceptable to rape a widow or a divorcée or a single woman who had had sex, but we simply do not know what the law would be at any period in that culture. We only know that the Bible's law codes do not include it.

Mothers and fathers

The biblical family is generally pictured in prose and in laws as patriarchal. We have seen laws and stories in which the father is the head of the household. Still, it is important to note how frequently the laws in this patriarchal structure speak of both the mother and the father in significant matters. The best-known case is the instruction among the Ten Commandments, to "Honor your father and your mother."[82] One might possibly say that the father still comes first here. That may or may not be significant, but, in any case, the Bible also gives the instruction: "You shall each fear his mother and his father."[83] There the mother comes first. People have commented about the reverse order in these two commandments since the medieval Bible commentators. The commentator Rashi observed it nine hundred years ago. He surmised that people are more likely to fear their father than their mother, so the law needed to put the command to fear the mother first; but people are more likely to honor their mother than their father, so the law needed to put the command to honor the father first. He might be psychologically correct or not, but his comment reflects that he did not think that this was a question of who is more important or who is head of the house. The presence of both orders in the law taught that, even in a patriarchal society, mothers are important, as are fathers.[84]

Other laws reflect this. The laws protecting parents are particularly harsh, and they are the same for mother as for father. One cannot strike one's mother or father: "And one who strikes his father and his mother shall be *put to death*."[85] One cannot curse one's mother or father: "Any man who will curse his father and his mother shall be *put to death*. He has cursed his father and his mother: his blood is on him!"[86] One cannot disrespect one's mother or father: "Cursed be one who disrespects one's father and his mother."[87] The law of the rebellious child particularly emphasizes the role of both parents, over and over:

> When a man will have a stubborn and rebellious son, not listening *to his father's voice and his mother's voice*, and *they* will discipline him, but he will not listen to *them*, then *his father and his mother* shall take hold of him and bring him out to his city's elders and to the gate of his place. And *they* shall say to his city's elders, 'This son of *ours* is stubborn and rebellious, he doesn't listen to *our* voice, a glutton, and a drunk.' And all his city's people shall batter him with stones so he dies.
> (Deut 21:18–21)

Mother and father both figure when the case calls for protection of their child as well. If a man levels a charge at his wife that she had been represented to be a virgin at the time of their marriage but then did not prove to be a virgin in fact, the law says:

> Then the young woman's *father and her mother* shall take and bring out the signs of the young woman's virginity to the city's elders at the gate.
> (Deut 22:15)

We do not know all the cultural factors involved here. The signs in question may be the sheet or garments from the wedding night bearing the blood that proves the bride's virginity. The practice may have been to keep these things with the bride's mother because of men's discomfort with their daughters' intimate matters. After all, this was a culture that forbade sex during menstruation.[88] Whatever the reason, though, the fact is that both mother and father are named in the law. So: both in defending parents from their children and in parents defending their children from others, the mother's legal standing is parallel to the father's.

We should note, by the way, that this is a law that penalizes a man for bringing "a bad name on a virgin of Israel."[89] This in itself has two edges with regard to women's status. On one hand, it stands in defense of a woman from a husband who has "asserted words of abuse"[90] about her virginity. On the other hand, it reflects a world where some substantial proportion of men demands virginity in a wife (but not in themselves), which in other times and cultures is regarded as a blatantly male chauvinist attitude. Also, the penalty on the man if his claim of non-virginity is proved false is:

> That city's elders shall take the man and discipline him. And they shall fine him a hundred weights of silver and give it to the young woman's father because he brought out a bad name on a virgin of Israel. And she shall be his for a wife: he shall not be able to let her go, all his days. (Deut 22:18–19)

On the one hand, the man is penalized. On the other hand, the penalty is not exactly every woman's dream. He pays a (large) sum of money to her father, and he is never allowed to divorce her. That may mean a lifetime guarantee of security for her, but it may also mean that she is bound in marriage forever with a man who tried to disgrace her. It is unclear if she can ever seek a divorce herself. It is commonly thought that men could divorce their wives but wives could not divorce their husbands in biblical times, but the text never actually says that.[91] If wives could in fact seek a divorce, then this law gives a woman a significant benefit over her husband, who now has lost his right to divorce her. If wives could not seek a divorce, then the overall structure favors males, but this law still establishes that circumstances exist in which men can forfeit their legal advantages.

It is in fact curious that the Hebrew Bible's laws say so little about marriage and divorce. Religions commonly function in a significant way around life's four crucial psychological moments, namely: birth, puberty, marriage, and death. Often people who are otherwise not religious will call the priest or rabbi or minister when a baby is born, or when there is going to be a wedding, or when a child reaches the age of Bar or Bat Mitzvah or confirmation, or, especially, when someone dies. Yet there is practically nothing in the Hebrew Bible about the ceremonies surrounding these things. There is the fact of circumcision for males, but even in that matter there is nothing about the procedure or the ceremony. There is nothing about how to perform ceremonies of betrothal or weddings or funerals. Bar (and Bat) Mitzvah is not mentioned at all. The only law concerning divorce is a requirement that if a man divorces a woman and writes her a divorce document, and if she then marries someone else, if the second husband dies or divorces her, she cannot go back and remarry the first husband, ever.[92] That is interesting itself, but our concern for now is just to recognize that it is difficult to judge several biblical laws in terms of women's status when we lack information about some basic practices in that ancient culture.[93]

To return to the matter of virginity in marriage, we should be clear that premarital sex is not prohibited anywhere in the Hebrew Bible. Women who are not virgins are free to marry. In biblical law, there is only one man who must marry a virgin, and that man is the High Priest of Israel.[94] That law still places a value on a certain male attitude toward virgins, but it applies to no one but that high priest. Not even the king need marry a virgin, and in fact there are stories that reflect this attitude, notably King David's marriages to Bathsheba and Abigail.

Witches

One law that really does seem to single out women is this one:

You shall not let a witch live.
(Ex 22:17)

The Hebrew term for a witch there is a feminine noun (*mekassepah*). Now males are pictured as practicing magic in the Bible as well. The case of the Egyptian magicians in the exodus story comes to mind. They can turn sticks into snakes and water into blood and can produce frogs.[95] (They are not very good at getting rid of lice or boils.[96]) The cognate term in the Semitic language Akkadian (spoken in Assyria and Babylonia) is *kišpu/ kaššāpu*, meaning "sorcerer" or "magician." "Sorceress" would in fact be a better English translation of Hebrew *mĕkaššēpāh* because it is the feminine of *sorcerer*, making the profession itself seem less specialized by gender than the word *witch* implies in English. We use the word *witch* in this discussion because that is the word that English readers have read, and so this technical point of translation came to have an impact on women's situation at some famous moments in history.

In Deuteronomy the law is framed in the masculine and forbids Israelites from practicing magic.[97] The masculine term in the context there (which addresses all of the people) presumably forbids both men and women from doing this. So the question is: why does the law in Exodus prescribe execution only for a female (*mĕkaššēpāh*) and not for a male (*mĕkaššēp*)? The answer may lie in a textual problem. The Greek text (the Septuagint) does not have the feminine noun here. It has a masculine plural. This would refer to both males and females. Our friend Professor William Propp, whom we believe to be the preeminent scholar of the book of Exodus, prefers the Hebrew reading of the feminine on the grounds that it is the shorter and more difficult reading. (There is a guideline in textual criticism that goes: it is precisely the text that makes less sense that is more likely to be the original—*lectio difficilior praeferenda est*—because scribes tend to try to soften difficulties, not create them.) He suggests that the Greek translators (and some other texts) may have made the change precisely because they were bothered by the text that only forbade females and not males as well. Still we should take into account that, in the Hebrew text, this is the only occurrence of the feminine, that is, the only occurrence of the word *witch/sorceress* in the entire Hebrew Bible. We lean toward the masculine plural reading, in which case this verse sheds no light at all on women's status in the Bible. Alternatively, at most, we would say that the reading is uncertain with regard to gender, in which case we still cannot establish anything on this subject confidently. Readers might prefer a more exotic answer to the question of why females are singled out in this verse. But we are reminded that our teacher Frank Moore Cross used to say, "The most banal answer is usually the correct one."[98]

As it happens, the biblical woman who is most commonly known as a witch is, in fact, not one. She appears in the biblical story of King Saul at En-dor.[99] Saul goes to En-dor (now better known for its use as the name of a moon where the *Star Wars* films culminate) to consult with a woman who can communicate with dead spirits. She raises the spirit of the prophet Samuel, who is as harsh with Saul as he was in life. He tells Saul that he will die in battle the next day. People often refer to this woman as "the witch of En-dor." In fact, though, the word *witch* does not occur in this story. Rather, she is specifically described as a medium, not a witch. She is said to be a woman who can produce an *'ôb*. We have written elsewhere about this Hebrew term, and we noted that the term *'ôb* is particularly ambiguous because it is found in a variety of contexts.[100] But its meaning of "a spirit" fits the context in this story. She produces Samuel's spirit. That is all she does. People who claim to be able to do this today are not called witches; neither are they called that in the Bible. And the biblical law explicitly notes that such people can be "a man or a woman."[101] There is no specifically female issue here, and there is no witch at En-dor.

Women are not property

To return to an earlier point: women are not property. The only humans who are property are slaves.[102] Wives cannot be sold. They can influence a family's affairs (or a nation's). They can own property. Some laws are written in their favor. These are not just differences from property; they are essential differences, definitional differences. We do not think that the culture that gave us a commandment to honor mothers as well as fathers, and "woman of substance," and all those family stories in Genesis (where wives never appear as property), plus all the comparable family stories in 2 Samuel, plus the limitation on wives in the Law of the King, plus even the line in Ecclesiastes about women being bad ("more bitter than death"; women are pictured there as dangerous and powerful), plus the requirement that the mother as well as the father bring the rebellious son to court, feels like a culture in which women are commonly viewed as property.[103]

As we saw in the case of the suspected adulteress (the *śoṭah*) in chapter 2, a husband's unproven suspicions about his wife's fidelity are up to God to deal with. Men cannot simply take matters into their own hands as they might with their cattle or slaves.[104]

Overinterpreted texts

In interpreting biblical law, one walks a tightrope in linguistics. Scholars have to be cautious in reading each text's words with precision. And, at the same time, they have to guard against being so concerned with precision that they take each tiny twist of language to imply more than is actually there. For example, in a summary statement about following the laws, Moses tells the people of Israel of the benefits of keeping these judgments. He says:

> And it will be because you'll listen to these judgments and observe and do them that YHWH, your God, will keep the covenant and kindness for you that he swore to your fathers. And He'll love you and bless you and multiply you and bless the fruit of *your womb* and the fruit of your land: your grain and your wine and your oil, your cattle's offspring and your flock's young, on the land that He swore to your fathers to give to you. You'll be more blessed than all the peoples. There won't be an infertile male or female among you or among your animals.
> (Deut 7:12–14)

People have narrowed in on the words *your womb*. The word for "your" is masculine singular. Some took this to mean that the passage is speaking to each individual man and is saying that he owns his wife's womb. In fact, though, the whole list of blessings in this section is in masculine singular. That is what is used for mixed groups in languages that are inflected for gender. The masculine singular in this verse is just consistent with the whole section, which is explicitly addressing the entire people. We may address the much broader question of using the masculine for a group in so many languages, but that is a separate matter from this particular word in this particular verse. In context, it says nothing to suggest that the author of this biblical law thought that men own their wives' wombs.

A similarly overprecise reading sometimes occurs when interpreters look at the account of the giving of the Ten Commandments at Mount Sinai. The text says: He [Moses] said to the *people* . . . "Don't go close to a woman." (Ex 19:15). Some have taken this to mean that a command to "the people" means just the men. One commentator went so far as to say, on the basis of this, that women may not have participated in the Sinai covenant at all.[105] The text may indeed reflect a male chauvinism, but it is more probably the chauvinism of language that we have already seen elsewhere. It does not necessarily mean that the women in this story are not present or participating. It may just reflect the way a male author formulates a command about sex. On the contrary, the text has referred many times to "the people" prior to this in the story where it must include the women as well.[106] It would make no sense now to use it for the first time referring to just the men without an explicit pointer to that at the beginning of the verse.

Similarly one could read the command in the Decalogue not to covet "your neighbor's wife" as suggesting that the Ten Commandments are directed only to men. But, as we emphasized above, one of the biggest differences between biblical times and our own is: the biblical world had polygamy. Men can have multiple wives, or they can even have women in addition to their wives. In that world a woman would not be commanded not to covet her neighbor's husband. She is *allowed* to be with her neighbor's husband (as long as she herself is not married). The inequality of the sexes is in the fact of polygamy. But that is not grounds for imagining that the Ten Commandments—which are the Sinai covenant—are given only to men. As in the linguistic matters, this reflects a male-dominated society, but it does not mean that women were excluded from the covenant.

On the other hand

The result of examining many of these cases is that we come to see the laws in a different way than one would think on first reading. These biblical laws, like most biblical laws, are frequently more nuanced, less blatantly sexist, than readers have imagined. One might get the impression that we have been deliberately trying to soften the Bible's rough edges. So we want to emphasize: biblical laws truly are more nuanced than you would think. They truly are more balanced on matters of gender than people think. But, still, there are plenty of areas in which the laws favor men, serve men, and preserve men's economic, political, and religious control of the society. There are cases of bride-price being paid. There is polygamy. The laws of the priests include the rule that only a man can be one. The Law of the King does not allow for Israel's monarch to be a queen. After all, it forbids the king to have a lot of *wives*.[107] In fact the word *queen* never occurs in the laws or in *any* text in the Hebrew Bible about Israel. It occurs only in reference to a couple of other lands: to the Queen of Sheba and to Esther when she becomes queen of the Persian Empire.

The law on women's vows, too, leaves little room for nuance.[108] If a woman makes a vow, her father can cancel it. Once she marries, this power passes from her father to her husband. If her husband hears her make a vow that he does not wish her to keep, he can cancel it. The nullification of women's vows is a male prerogative.

Yet even here the gender message is mixed. Fathers can cancel their daughters' vows. Husbands can cancel their wives' vows. But, by accepting this power over the women they also accept a huge responsibility. The law says:

> And if she vowed or made a restriction on herself by an oath at her husband's house, and her husband heard it and kept quiet to her—he did not hold her back—then all her vows shall stand, and every restriction that she made on herself shall stand. But if her husband nullified them on the day he heard all that came out of her lips for her vows and for restricting herself, it shall not stand. *Her husband had nullified them, and YHWH will forgive her.* Every vow and every oath of restriction to degrade oneself: her husband shall make it stand, and her husband shall nullify it. And if her husband will keep quiet in regard to her from that day to the next, then he has made all her vows and all her restrictions that are on her stand. He has made them stand because he kept quiet to her on the day he heard it. And if he will nullify them after he has heard them, then *he shall bear her crime.*
> (Num 30:11–16)

See especially the lines that we have italicized. If a man nullifies his wife's oath, then God does not hold the woman responsible; if she does not keep to her oath, she is forgiven. And if a man does not nullify his wife's oath until a day after he heard her make it, then he himself bears the crime for her. His wife does not. The expression "to bear a crime" in the Bible refers to cases that are between a human and God, not punishable by human courts. So here it means that the deity holds the husband, not the wife, responsible. So, once again, we have a case that explicitly empowers males over females, though it at least contains an element of fairness to women in such a situation.

God as male

Through all of the biblical texts—poetry, prose, and law—the visible, unignorable fact is that God is pictured as male. It was more than the elephant in the room. It was the God in their cosmos. In later stages of religion, many people—from ordinary folk to theologians—came to regard God as beyond sex, as neither male nor female. But we must acknowledge that all of the signs indicate that biblical Israel conceived of God as male. The terms for God in the Hebrew Bible are all masculine words. The Hebrew word that became most associated with a feminine aspect of deity in later Judaism is *Shechinah*, but this word does not occur in the Hebrew Bible. The name of God, YHWH (most probably pronounced Yahweh), is as masculine a name as Robert or Richard. (If it were feminine, it would be Tahweh.) God is pictured as a father but not as a mother, as a king but never as a queen, as a husband but not as a wife.

This is a matter in which the ancient Near Eastern context is particularly important. Everyone around the ancient Israelites had both male and female deities—on all three neighboring continents, from Babylonia and Persia on the east to Egypt toward the south to Greece toward the north, including all the nearby peoples: the Phoenicians, Arameans, Philistines, Moab, and Edom. This made the depictions of God as male that much more significant. Those depictions had a context, and in that ancient Near Eastern context deities were either male or female.

The ancient Israelites themselves were at least as uncertain about relating this to monotheism as people in subsequent ages, for there were times when they conceived of their God as having a female consort. Thus the prophet Jeremiah criticizes the people for including "the Queen of the skies" (either the goddess Astarte or the goddess Asherah) in their worship.[109] And an inscription (graffiti, actually) that was excavated at Quntillet Ajrud refers to "YHWH and His Asherah."[110] The book of 2 Kings reports that the worship of Asherah took place alongside the worship of Yahweh at or near the Temple in Jerusalem.[111] According to that text King Josiah of Judah removed the Asherah elements from there.

Archaeological evidence: Small figures of females are extremely common finds, but in all the excavations in Israel so far very few male figures have ever been found. And one of them, which we uncovered in the City of David excavations of biblical Jerusalem under the direction of our friend Yigal Shiloh, was clearly not Israelite. It is uncircumcised. That is, female figures often escaped the ban on statues, but male figures did not—not because they were Baal or Dagon figures but because they could be YHWH! So in ancient Israel and Judah, we have found this plethora of female (and some animal) figures but an extreme paucity of male figurines. If we did not have the biblical text to describe the (ideal) religion of ancient Israel as centered on the worship of one male God alone, it would be logical to conclude—by analogy with contemporary cultures and with modern ethnographical accounts—that ancient Israel focused its worship on goddess figures! Now, in fact, the figurines may well have represented the goddesses whom the people worshiped as the consort of the male God of Israel.[112] Or they may have represented female worshipers in search of fertility.[113] The authors of this book disagree on this point. Dolansky has argued that the assumption that they have anything to do with fertility should itself be questioned, but she still thinks it possible that they are goddess figures.[114] Friedman is persuaded that they may be nothing other than dolls. In that case, for the answer to why there are so many females and so few males, just go into a toy store and see how many more Barbies there are than Kens!

Women authors?

We have seen that women can be judges, poets, prophets, Nazirites, and property owners. There is one other area of the biblical world in which women may have participated, namely, as authors. Biblical scholars have raised this possibility—but rarely. We have already noted that a woman may have composed the Song of Miriam, which is likely the oldest thing in the Bible. Scholars have sometimes said that a woman may have composed the poetry of the Song of Songs.[115] This is speculation, not something derived from the text. The text begins: "The Song of Songs that was Solomon's" or "that was to Solomon" or "that Solomon had." The meaning of the Hebrew is uncertain, so some have thought that this means that the text was purporting to have been written by Solomon, but those introductory words could also mean that the book was dedicated to Solomon, and there are other possibilities as well. Sometimes even scholars have to say, "I don't know." (It doesn't hurt much after the first couple of times. Actually, we scholars usually say, "*We* don't know"—thus graciously sharing the ignorance with our colleagues.)

All of the biblical law codes appear to come from priests. Since the priesthood is always pictured as exclusively male, it is extremely unlikely that a female could have been an author of any of these.

So biblical poetry may have been written by women, and biblical law almost certainly was not. But what of the Bible's prose? One of the authors of this book (Friedman) suggested in *Who Wrote the Bible?* the possibility that a woman was the author of one of the earliest prose portions of the Bible, the source text known in critical Bible scholarship as J. This source contained many of the most famous stories in the Bible, including several that we have discussed in this chapter—the second creation account, the garden of Eden, Dinah, the first Tamar—and much more.[116] This idea was not presented there as something extraordinary. Biblical scholars had always addressed questions of whether the Bible's authors were priests or laypersons, upper or lower class, from the northern or the southern kingdom, or from one century or another. It just seemed natural that we should also consider such an essential question as whether the author was a man or a woman. Friedman observed that most of the authors of the first five books of the Bible were almost certainly male. In those books, the evidence in the texts known in critical scholarship as E, P, and D indicates that they were composed by priests. We refer to both the laws and the stories in these sources. The source known as J, however, was different. Friedman wrote:

> The case is much harder to judge with regard to J. Originating at—or at least reflecting the interests of—the Judean court, it came from a circle in which both men and women had a certain status. That is, even in a male-led society, women of the noble class may have had more power, privileges, and education than males of a lower class. The possibility of J's being by a woman is thus much more likely than with E. More important, the J stories are, on the whole, much more concerned with women and much more sensitive to women than are the E stories. There is really nothing in E to compare with the J story of Tamar in Genesis 38. It is not just that the woman Tamar figures in an important way in the story. It is that the story is sympathetic to a wrong done to this woman, it focuses on her plan to combat the injustice, and it concludes with the man in the story (Judah) acknowledging her rights and his own fault.

This does not make the author a woman. But it does mean that we cannot by any means be quick to think of this author as a man. The weight of the evidence is still that the scribal profession in ancient Israel was male, true, but that does not exclude the possibility that a woman might have composed a work that came to be loved and valued in that land.[117]

Indeed, the biblical scholar Jo Ann Hackett wrote that, even in societies where men are in control, an upper-class woman is more likely to be literate than a lower-class man.[118] Others followed Friedman in this matter.[119] In a later book, Friedman made the case that this text known in critical Bible scholarship as J was just one part of a much larger collection of texts that are now embedded through the biblical books of Joshua, Judges, 1 and 2 Samuel, and the first two chapters of the book of 1 Kings. When separated, these texts read as a continuous story. If this is correct, then this is the first lengthy work of prose known on earth.[120] At the time that he was doing this research, Friedman was unaware that another scholar, Hannelis Schulte, had worked on this same material, and she had arrived at nearly the same finding.[121] When two scholars independently arrive at the same result, that does not automatically make it right, but that is an encouraging reinforcement to the evidence itself. There is no long work of prose—either fiction or history—known anywhere on earth prior to the texts that Schulte and Friedman treated. So, if Schulte and Friedman are correct, then this is the work of the first great writer.[122] Friedman called this work *In the Day*, following the custom of naming ancient Near Eastern works after their opening words, and he again raised the possibility that its writer was a woman. The possibility that women wrote portions of the Bible, then, is not just a bone thrown to women readers today. It is well within reason that a woman could have been an author of portions of the Bible—and not just any portions but, rather, the Bible's longest prose source, the world's first great literary work of prose.

The poetry that is the oldest work in the Bible (the Song of Miriam and the Song of Deborah) and the work that is the oldest prose in the world (*In the Day*) may come from women. This is just a speculation, but, at minimum, it is a corrective to writers from all sorts of backgrounds who have asserted that the Bible's writers were all male.

Respected scholars like our friend the archaeologist Lawrence Stager and Philip King wrote:

> The Bible was written and compiled by males who had no special interest in women's roles.[123]

Both halves of that statement are partly true but overstated. A very large part of the Bible may well have been written by one or more women; and both the female and the male writers spent more time and space on males, true, but they were very much interested in women's roles. The biblical scholar Susan Ackerman was a bit more cautious in her wording. She did not declare unequivocally, as Stager and King did, that women did not write these things. She stated it rather in terms of what we presently can know for sure:

> Among the challenges facing those who would reconstruct the lives of women in ancient Israel is the fact that, *as far as we know*, none of our primary textual sources, either the Hebrew Bible or the extra-biblical texts, is authored by women.[124]

So the question remains open. What we wish to establish for now is that (1) it is incorrect to claim without evidence that women did not write any of the Bible and (2) women may have written significant portions of the Bible's poetry and prose but probably not its laws.

This may even be part of the answer to the question that we left open in the section on the patriarchs and matriarchs above: why do the works that came out of a man's world include stories of women wielding such power? One answer may be that the majority of the stories that we considered above come from that great prose collection that Schulte and Friedman saw as a unity, and a woman may have been the author of that collection. This would include the stories we discussed of Sarah, Rebekah, Rachel and Leah, Dinah, both Tamars, Bathsheba, and Abishag. They would also include the stories of Rahab, Delilah, Abigail, and more. In fairness, we should recognize that this work also contains the Eden story, in which the first woman is told, "Your desire will be for your man, and he'll dominate you." Maybe we can picture a woman writing these words in that world; maybe not. After all, as we said above, the writer is just describing (not prescribing) the world that she or he really saw. Now that the proposal of *In the Day* is on the table, what is needed is an analysis of the unusually manifest place of women in it.

Sexual politics, feminist scholarship, and the Bible

The impact of feminism on politics, economics, society, and academia over the last century has been remarkable. Although feminists may lament the slow progress of that impact, the extent of it across every aspect of twenty-first-century consciousness is undeniable. Particularly in modern scholarship, the presence of feminist research has revitalized disciplines from biology to history, from archaeology to literary criticism, by forcing the recognition of gender both as a distinct mode of experience and also as a system subject to analysis.[125] But in no discipline has it proved more contentious than in the study of religion.

This is because there is much more than academic debates at stake: at the heart of the feminist study of religion is its application to lived religion. The birth of feminist religious studies is inextricably intertwined with the advent of feminist theology, and both are tied directly to the women's suffrage movement in the nineteenth century. The major leaders of the National Woman Suffrage Association, Matilda Joslyn Gage, Elizabeth Cady Stanton, and Susan B. Anthony, were themselves deeply divided on the issue of the origins of patriarchy.

Gage saw patriarchy as a creation of the Bible's authors, who imposed male domination, war, and violence on a preexisting peaceful matriarchal civilization. She was therefore deeply suspicious of Christianity, which she saw as a mainstay for women's oppression. She argued that historically, as long as the feminine was recognized as "a component and superior part of divinity," civilizations remained just, peaceful, and highly cultured. In *Woman, Church, and State* (1893), Gage related the feminine principle and its worship to spirituality and intelligent wisdom, whereas masculinity was related to force, violence, sexual promiscuity, and materialism. In her view, the key to the fall from high feminine to low masculine societies came about through Judaism and the continuation of its religious viewpoint in Christianity. She observed that patterns of violence, wars, the subjugation of women, and the sexual and physical violation of women have continued throughout the history of Christianity, declaring that Christianity has been

Women's Status | 121

"of little value to civilization." (For Gage, Jews are uniquely "gross," violent, and materialist, and Christianity inherits this from the Jews.) So for Gage, the great revolution being brought about in women's suffrage was not limited to winning the vote; its deepest meaning was the rebellion of women against the oppression of the Christian Church.[126]

Starting from the same premise of original matriarchy (an idea that was very much in vogue in nineteenth-century anthropology and classical studies but has since been rejected by a number of anthropologists, archaeologists, and historians—including most feminist scholars[127]), Elizabeth Cady Stanton went in a slightly different direction from Gage. In her commentary on Genesis 3 in *The Women's Bible*, Stanton expressed her belief that a long period of female rule—85,000 years—had preceded the advent of patriarchy. Only in the barbarian era did males "seize the reins of government," imposing a patriarchal system of rule.[128]

Although her view was too radical for many of her more conservative Christian constituents, Stanton's commentary on the Bible was designed to show that the flaws of patriarchy were human in origin, not divine. She interpreted and commented on the Bible from this premise, ultimately demonstrating to many that, despite the claims of Gage, true Christianity was not incompatible with the goals of feminism, although institutionalized Christianity had become so. In her comments on Genesis 1, Stanton described God as androgynous, containing both male and female elements, and "thus, the Old Testament, 'in the beginning,' proclaims the simultaneous creation of man and woman, the eternity and equality of sex." The patriarchal elements of the text and its subsequent interpretation effecting the subordination of women in society were human productions. This is why, she explained, there were two creation accounts: dissatisfied with the equality thus accorded to women in the divine scheme in Genesis 1, "some wily writer, seeing the perfect equality of man and woman in the first chapter, felt it important for the dignity and dominion of man to effect woman's subordination in some way," and thus penned the story of the Garden of Eden.[129]

Gage's and Stanton's reflections on the Bible still underlie the major controversies of both feminist theology and feminist religious studies. Feminist theology has had to grapple with the problem of asserting equal rights for women in the context of a received Jewish and Christian biblical tradition that they perceived as irreparably sexist and patriarchal. This has meant that feminist theologians have had either to leave their traditions in search of entirely new spiritualities that are more empowering to them as women or to attempt to reform their traditions from within by often radical revision and reinterpretation of those traditions.[130] Feminist religious studies, on the other hand, have devoted enormous effort to exposing the inherent "patriarchy" and "androcentrism" of the biblical authors' worldview.

Such analyses of the Bible risk judging the ancient world by current standards—seeing stage sixteen from our perspective here at stage forty. Now, there is no question that ancient Israelite society was patrilineal (as exemplified in the many genealogies in the Bible); and upon marriage women likely left the homes of their birth and joined their husbands' families. Gender relations in the ancient Near East, reflected in the Bible, were such that men were at an advantage when it came to legal rights, formal positions in society, and performing valued and prominent activities in the community. But it does not follow from this that women were subservient, inferior, oppressed, or enslaved in that world. Both the archaeological record and the biblical texts that we have seen give us a much more complex picture of gender relations, power, and authority in ancient Israel.[131] In fact, despite the thousands of cuneiform tablets from Mesopotamia and papyri from Egypt, the Bible gives us more stories about women and insights into the importance of women in ancient Israel than we have from any other ancient society contemporary with Israel.

These analyses also take biblical patriarchy as *prescriptive*. Some scholars mistakenly declare that the Bible, as a text produced in a patriarchal context, not only *describes* the inferior position of women but actively *advocates* the oppression of women.[132] But we have not seen evidence of this in the poetry, prose, or legal texts that we have considered here. We may not make friends or influence people by arriving at this conclusion here, but we think that the textual evidence is contrary to the views at both ends of this spectrum. At one end are those who cite the Bible to justify subservience of women. They say that this is what the Bible prescribes. At the other end are those who criticize the Bible for prescribing it. From our view, the burden of proof remains to be met by both. They need to show meticulously by proof from the text and archaeology that the Bible was not just describing the world at its time—and that it is rather prescribing such a world for all time.

Patriarchy and male monotheism

Since the time of Matilda Joslyn Gage and Elizabeth Cady Stanton, it has become fashionable among possibly well-meaning but uninformed scholars from other fields to blame the Israelites for creating patriarchy. There are different versions of this myth, but the gist is that, prior to the advent of Israelite religion, civilizations enjoyed peaceful matriarchies focused on goddess worship. Then the patriarchal women-hating Israelites came along, destroyed the peaceful matriarchies, and implemented a religion focused on one male god. By its very nature, this monotheism was oppressive to women, and it forever after changed the nature of society from being peaceful, egalitarian, and female-revering to a warlike, misogynist culture in which goddesses were dead.[133]

Not only is there no actual archaeological evidence that there were ever goddess-worshiping matriarchies in prehistoric times, but there is no documentary evidence from historic cultures that the act of worshiping goddesses predisposed societies to treat their women better.[134] All of the ancient civilizations contemporary with biblical Israel worshiped goddesses, and all were just as patriarchal. In fact, in her *In the Wake of the Goddesses*, our friend the late Tikva Frymer-Kensky used accounts of myth and ritual dating back to the early days of Sumer, Assyria, and Greece to show the opposite: although polytheism did accord females an important role, the strict division between male and female actually served to keep women in a subordinate position. The goddesses were progressively marginalized as they were progressively relegated to home and hearth, while male gods took over as patrons of wisdom and learning. The Bible, on the other hand, advocated a more egalitarian view of human nature in which women were not considered to be inherently inferior.

Viewed from our age's perspective, the Bible's patriarchy certainly seems to subordinate women in ways that most people we know today would not tolerate. But within its ancient context, some of these "patriarchal" laws show an advance in women's rights. Even though people have used the critical line in the Eden story describing the dominion of man over woman consistently for millennia to justify the subordination of women, the Bible offers a much more well-rounded and complex view of women than we might expect from a patriarchal society. Women are important, valued, crucial members of society: they are wives and mothers but also leaders. They are both vulnerable and powerful. These varied images of women, along with the emphasis in the Hebrew Bible on one law for all (as compared with the hierarchies and double standards written into other ancient Near Eastern law codes, where crimes and punishments varied depending on one's social status and rank) helped pave the way for advances in women's rights that we are realizing in the Western world in our own time.

The bottom line

We have looked at texts of prose, poetry, and law. The books of the prophets, which are mostly poetry but combine all three of these kinds of texts, usually figure less in discussions of gender. As we said at the beginning, all fifteen books of the prophets are named for men. The situation in those books in regard to women's status, however, is not so different from the other books: man's world, women are crucial. Isaiah marries and gives their children names that reflect prophecies symbolically. Hosea marries a prostitute, they have offspring, and he prophetically names them. Jeremiah is told by God not to marry. Ezekiel is told by God, "I shall take away the delight of your eyes," and then his wife dies. We cannot cover all that we want in this one chapter. In the case of homosexuality or abortion, we can at least cover the main passages and some major treatments of them in a chapter. But the matter of gender is vastly more to cover. Half the people in the world are, after all, women. And the scholarly literature on this is a mountain. There are whole books and a huge number of articles even on individual persons and stories we have treated here: Dinah, Eve, Sarah. But we hope that you will agree that we have at least covered enough texts, of enough kinds, to begin to form some picture of the mixed, complex, good-and-bad status of women in the Hebrew Bible. If we did not want to know both good and bad, after all, we should not have eaten from that tree.

So we do not mean to paint some fake picture in which women's status in the Bible is equal and okay, and we also would not condemn the Bible as a woman-hating treatise. We seek instead to understand the complexities of a male-ordered society in which women are valued and sometimes powerful members. We read the poems and stories and laws as, at least partly, reflections of life in the ancient world, a world in which men *and* women were placed in definite gender-defined roles, and each had limits on their freedoms to self-determination. That is why people who are all reading the same book have seen that book in such opposite ways: because both ways are really there, in the text and in the world that produced it.

Understanding the status of women in biblical society is not just an exercise in academic curiosity. As with the issue of homosexuality, what the Bible has to say about women still directly informs the social practices of many religious Jews and Christians today. Some look at the biblical stance on gender and claim that God endorses a patriarchal society in which the male is head of his household and women are created to be submissive and to bear and care for children.[135] However, from what we have observed here, the Bible's depictions of women in narrative and poetry are *descriptive*, not *prescriptive*. The biblical authors are describing the situation they found rather than advocating an unchangeable divine order of things. Whether one concludes that the Bible leans more toward patriarchy or more toward equality, whether it was good or bad for women, we feel certain at least in the conclusion that one cannot *use* the Bible to justify treating women with a lower status than men.

In the Bible's picture, women are created with equal worth to men, but men come to have superior status to them through a variety of mechanisms. That is not just a Bible story. That is really what happened on this planet. Where do we go from here? The Bible opens various doors that point to an eventual return to balance between women and men. And that, too, is not just a Bible story. That is what is happening in our age.

FOUR

Capital Punishment

A t the time that we are writing this, countries are divided on whether execution is an acceptable human practice. Industrialized countries with widespread education and advanced institutions of higher learning disagree about this. Internally as well, individuals and groups and religious denominations within these countries debate this: whether it is just, whether it is humane, whether it is deserved, whether it deters others from committing crimes. What could one learn from the Bible that might be helpful in judging this?

Once again we need to look at the Bible's different genres. The law codes are the obvious first place to look. Biblical poetry has hardly anything about it, but the prose adds some impressive stories and information to the laws.

Law

The Bible places such a high value on human life, yet its law codes allow execution. Indeed, they do more than just allow it. They call for execution for many offenses that would not be capital crimes in the United States or Europe or in many other nations in this century. There are more than twenty-five of these capital offenses in the Bible. They are of two kinds: (1) crimes of a social nature, mostly involving either taking life or sexual matters; and (2) crimes of a religious nature. They are:

Social:

    Murder (Exod 21:12–14; Lev 24:17)
    Ownership of a dangerous animal that kills a human (Exod 21:28–32)

Kidnapping a person to sell as a slave (Exod 21:16; Deut 24:7)

Striking one's parents (Exod 21:15)

Cursing one's parents (Exod 21:17; Lev 20:9)

A rebellious child (Deut 21:18–21)

Rape of a betrothed virgin (Deut 22:25)

Adultery—both are executed (Lev 20:10; Deut 22:22)

Sex with one's father's wife—both are executed (Lev 20:11)

Sex with one's son's wife—both are executed (Lev 20:12)

Male homosexuality (Lev 18:22, 20:13)

Sex with a mother and daughter—all three are executed (Lev 20:14)

Sex with an animal (Exod 22:18; Lev 20:15–16)

Sexual misbehavior by a priest's daughter (Lev 21:9)

Religious:

Sacrificing one's children (Lev 20:2)

Working on the sabbath (Exod 31:15; 35:2)

Desecrating the sabbath (Exod 31:14)

Entering the Tabernacle if one is not a Levite (Num 1:51; 3:10, 38; 18:7)

Profaning the divine name (Lev 24:16)

Taking *ḥerem* (Deut 7:26; cf. 13:18)

Sorcery (witch) (Exod 22:17)

Consulting a medium (*'ôb* or *yidĕ'ōnî*) (Lev 20:27)

Pagan worship (Deut 17:2–5) or inciting others to engage in it (Deut 13:7–11)

Sacrificing to other gods: "shall be completely destroyed (*ḥrm*)" (Exod 22:19)

Prophet who says to follow other gods (Deut 13:2–6)

False prophecy (Deut 18:20)

The two groups—social and religious—partly overlap. Sacrificing children involves taking lives just as murder does, but it is also a religious act. Sexual misbehavior by a priest's daughter involves an offense against the realm of the sacred just as the religious laws do, but it is also comparable to the other forbidden sexual activities among the social laws. Also, there is a final, overarching offense that covers both social and religious laws. It is: presumptuously disregarding the decision of higher authorities in "a case that is too hard for you" (Deut 17:12).

These categories—social and religious—are just our own, to help us give a sense of these laws. They are not found in the Bible itself, which mixes these laws in various groups. As we noted earlier, we humans are basically symmetrical, with bicameral brains, and we have a natural tendency to group things, usually into two kinds, to understand them better. There is a saying that there are two kinds of people: those who divide people into two kinds and those who don't. So if you find a way of categorizing these cases in a way that is more meaningful to you, feel free.

Meanwhile, some specific points about some of these cases are important.

Murder

First is the matter of execution for murder. As in most law codes, from ancient to modern, the Bible distinguishes between murder and manslaughter. The distinction in the law in Exodus is absolutely explicit. One who takes a life by accident, without scheming to do it, is not executed. This is manslaughter, not murder. For manslaughter, the biblical law provides cities of refuge, places where the manslayer can go and be protected from the dead person's relatives (the "blood avenger").[1] These cities serve mainly as protection, not punishment. They are towns, not prisons. They would prevent back-and-forth vendettas from developing between the families of the manslayer and the victim. And how long must the manslayer stay there in the city of refuge?

> He shall live in his city of refuge until the high priest's death.
> (Num 35:28)

After that, he is free to leave, and the blood avenger is no longer free to kill him (or her).

Now why should the high priest's death change anything? The father of critical biblical scholarship in the late nineteenth century, the German scholar Julius Wellhausen, asked: why the high priest and not the king? Wellhausen's answer was that this text was written during the period when the Jews' country was under the power of the Persian Empire. There were no more Jewish kings at that time, so the authors made the law about the high priest.[2] Wellhausen's idea was logical, but it was not correct. First, evidence has mounted in the last few decades that this law does not come from the Persian period after all. It is much earlier. Many, perhaps most, scholars still follow the Persian dating, but the language in that source (known as the Priestly source, or P for short) comes from a much earlier period of Hebrew. This and other evidence indicate that this law comes from a time when Judah was still an independent country and had kings.[3] Traditional believers still understand the text to come from Moses himself, which would be even earlier. So, either by critical or traditional dating, we need to find some other reason why the manslayer's fate depends on the high priest's death.

A second development that has called Wellhausen's view into question is the increased recognition of the tremendous importance of anthropology in studying the Bible. In Wellhausen's day, history was the queen science of our field. In the 1970s and 1980s, literary studies made a particularly big impact on our studies. In the 1990s and 2000s anthropology, the study of human cultures, increased in impact. The reason that getting out of the city of refuge depended on the high priest's death is not because, historically, there was no king. The reason is much more probably because, culturally, the high priest is connected with *atonement*. In the intriguing biblical law of the scapegoat, we see a ceremony in which all the people's sins are symbolically placed on a goat, which is driven away.[4] Thus, all of their sins are atoned for. And this ceremony is associated with the holiday known as the Day of Atonement (*Yom Kippur*). Now, only the high priest can perform this ritual of the scapegoat. Specifically, he is described as: "the priest *whom one will anoint*."[5] Compare the wording of the law of the manslayer in the city of refuge: he must stay there, specifically, "until the death of the high priest *whom one anointed*." The distinguished scholar Moshe Greenberg recognized this connection as well. He wrote: "The sole personage whose religious-cultic importance might endow his death with expiatory value for the people at large is the high priest."[6]

What this means is that a human's death, when caused by another human, requires some sort of expiation. The community has to do *something*. It may be execution. It may be an atonement through the high priest. But it cannot be left unresolved. Thus there is this amazing law about what to do when a corpse is found and no one knows who took its life or what the circumstances were:

> If a corpse will be found in the land that YHWH, your God, is giving you to take possession of it, fallen in the field, unknown who struck him, then your elders and your judges shall go out and measure to the cities that are around the corpse. And it will be, the closest city to the corpse: that city's elders shall take a heifer that has not been worked with, that has not pulled in a yoke. And that city's elders shall take the heifer down to a strongly flowing wadi that would not be worked with and would not be seeded, and they shall break the heifer's neck there in the wadi. And the priests, sons of Levi, shall go over, because YHWH, your God, chose them to serve Him and to bless in YHWH's name, and every dispute and every injury shall be by their word. And all of that city's elders, who are close to the corpse, shall wash their hands over the heifer whose neck was broken in the wadi. And they shall testify, and they shall say, "Our hands did not spill this blood, and our eyes did not see it. Grant atonement for your people Israel, whom you redeemed, YHWH, and don't impute innocent blood among your people Israel." And for them the blood will be atoned for. So you shall burn away the innocent blood from among you when you will do what is right in YHWH's eyes.
>
> (Deut 21:1–9)

Few biblical laws are stranger to contemporary eyes than this one. The ceremony does not sound like something that people would perform if a body were found today halfway between Hartford and New Haven. But it is consistent with what we have seen so far in the biblical treatment. Its bottom line is: "the blood will be atoned for." A person's life has been taken. Something must be done.

So the Bible has capital punishment for murder but not for manslaughter. And it has one more category, which lies halfway between these two: causing a death by negligence. This is expressed in the classic case of the goring ox. In contemporary law it is sometimes called the "two bite rule." If your dog bites someone once, you are not responsible; if it happens a second time, you are responsible, since you were aware of the problem and failed to deal with it. In biblical law, it is an ox, not a dog, and it is a case in which it gores someone to death. If an ox does this, its owner is not responsible; but if it is an ox with a known history of goring, and then it gores someone to death, then the owner is to be executed.[7] Now the interesting difference in this case is that "if a ransom will be set on him, then he shall give everything that will be set on him for the redemption of his life." That is, the owner can save himself from execution if he pays a penalty, however high. So in certain cases there can be something other than execution or expiation for the loss of a human life.[8] There is even a difference based on who the human is who was gored. There is no difference if it is a male or a female, but there is a difference if it is a slave, in which case there can be payment rather than execution. (As we saw in the chapter on women's status, this is another case establishing that slaves are property, but women are not property.)

We should emphasize that we are not referring to the commandment against murder in the Ten Commandments (the Decalogue) here. The Decalogue does not state penalties for violating commandments. It simply states, "Thou shalt not . . ." Penalties appear elsewhere in the Bible.[9] One cannot know just from reading the Decalogue that murder is punishable by execution. The Ten Commandments are not all punishable by execution, after all. There is no execution for stealing, for example. Moshe Greenberg emphasized especially "the remarkable leniency with which property offenses are dealt with in biblical law. No crime against property is punished with death."[10] This was actually a dramatic step in law. Other law codes of the ancient Near East had capital punishment for property crimes, including theft, breaking into a house, or unlawfully entering a house at night.[11] The Bible never uses capital punishment for theft or any other property crimes.

To complete this discussion, we shall have to look at some remarkable episodes when we come to the Bible's prose below, but for now we have begun to try to understand the biblical treatment of the taking of human life.

The other cases of social crimes punishable by execution do not involve the loss of a victim's life. They concern offenses against parents, forbidden sex, and kidnapping. A common element is that they all involve persons, not property. Again, biblical law rejected the use of capital punishment for property crimes.[12]

Crossing boundaries

The second kind of offenses that include the death penalty are what we have called broadly religious offenses. All involve crossing some boundary. The boundary may be in time or space.

Space: one can be executed for entering the Tabernacle if one is not a Levite. The Tabernacle is the sacred tent housing the ark containing the tablets of the Ten Commandments in the narrative of the people's journey from Egypt in the wilderness generation. We have argued elsewhere that the Tabernacle later was housed inside the first Jerusalem Temple.[13] Other scholars have held the view that the Temple was only a symbolic representation of the Tabernacle but did not actually house a historical Tabernacle. Either way, the law would mean that no one could enter the Temple but a priest—on penalty of death. The law of ḥerem likewise protects sacred space. Ḥerem is total destruction, which is applied in biblical law and prose only to the Amalekites and to Canaanite sites in the region that became Israel, most famously Jericho. In the wars with these opponents, Israelites are not permitted to profit from the war. They cannot take spoils, slaves, or livestock. An Israelite who takes some object of ḥerem and keeps it is subject to capital punishment. This is the closest that any biblical law comes to execution for a crime involving property. But the point is precisely that it is not just property. It is property that has been dedicated to God. If one steals candlesticks from one's neighbor, one must return them and pay a monetary penalty. If one steals candlesticks from a house in Jericho, one is executed. The issue is the sacred boundary, not the property itself.

Time: the institution of the sabbath is notable in that it takes a twenty-four-hour unit of time and declares it to be holy just as a building or an object can be holy. Violating this boundary of time, just like violating a boundary of space, can result in execution. In our experience, one of the hardest aspects of the Bible for people of recent generations to grasp is this notion of sacred zones. Ritual, zones that are holy or secular, pure or impure, are less common in present religion, especially Western religions, than in the biblical era. Violation of these things is dangerous and frightening in that world. It is different from crimes that are connected with morality, such as theft or murder or adultery. One may enter the Tabernacle for good reasons or bad: to put out a fire, to help the priest, whatever. It does not matter. No matter what one's intention is, if he or she enters the Tabernacle there is an execution. This is the opposite of the social laws, where intention has a great deal to do with it, as we saw in the case of murder versus manslaughter. The taking of the victim's life is determined to be a murder or not, depending on whether the person's motive was malicious or not.

Thus the law against human sacrifice is separate from the commandment against murder. The crime of human sacrifice is both a taking of life and a horrible violation of the sacred. It does not matter if the intention of the person doing the sacrifice is not malicious—if, for example, he thinks that he is giving up his child as a gift to God. He has crossed a sacred line, and the penalty is execution.[14]

Seeking a channel to any supernatural power other than the deity, or going through any channel other than the sanctioned priesthood, is also punishable by execution. Thus turning to sorcery or communicating with the dead are in this category. It is not that the Bible regards these things as fake. The Bible regularly treats them as real, as things that really work.[15] Ancient Israel believed in magic. To them, these practices work, but they are forbidden. And the ultimate boundary, of course, is turning to other gods. We should note, though, that it is an uncrossable boundary only for a Jew or Israelite. The law says nothing against other people practicing their own religions. Pagans are free to be pagans. It is Israelites who are prohibited from betraying their own religion.

Those are the laws. Before we can relate them to the contemporary debate over capital punishment, we must look at biblical stories that involve executions.

Prose

The Bible's first chapter narrates creation of humans in the divine image. We truly do not know what this means. Does it mean that Genesis 1 conceives of a God with a face and hands, who looks like humans? Or is its conception that humans have consciousness like God? Or that they can think like God? Or any one of a hundred other readings that people have proposed? What we can say at minimum is that the author of this creation account conceived of humans as participating in the divine in some crucial way, in a way that is part of the very structure of a human being, male or female, in a way that a cat or a bird does not. It is perfectly understandable that some people use this as a point against capital punishment, feeling that, if humans are in the divine image, then if we execute a human we are destroying something that is a reflection of God. *But:* this point is hard to maintain when eight chapters later the text says:

> One who sheds a human's blood: by a human his blood will be shed, because He made the human in the image of God.
> (Gen 9:6)

So the Bible itself puts forward its depiction of creation in the divine image as the basis for expecting a murderer to be killed. So this would seem to be a mandate for capital punishment, at least in a case of murder.[16] *But:* consider the context of that verse. In the verse that comes right before it, the deity says:

> I shall inquire for your blood, for your lives. I shall inquire for it from the hand of every animal and from the hand of a human. I shall inquire for a human's life from the hand of each man for his brother.
> (Gen 9:5)

It says, "*I* shall inquire." It says it three times. So this may mean that capital punishment for murder is in God's hands, not human hands. Even when it says, "by a human his blood will be shed," it may mean that God will bring this about through the course of human events. It need not necessarily mean that a human court is supposed to decide it. More broadly, the context here is a covenant between the deity and Noah. It takes place after the flood, when everyone on earth except Noah and his family have died. The covenant therefore is understood to be between God and all of humankind, who are all Noah's descendants. All of the laws about capital punishment that we have seen above are part of a different covenant, the covenant between God and Israel. Those laws apply only to the people of Israel.[17] The Noahic covenant is of singular importance for those who appeal to the Bible as a basis for humankind in general to practice capital punishment, because only the Noahic covenant is presented as something that applies to everybody and not just to Israel. And so we must be cautious in interpreting this passage (as with every other passage we have seen) because the passage is unclear about whether it means that the death penalty for murder is for God or for human authorities to carry out.

And it applies the death penalty only to murder, not to any of the other twenty-four offenses we saw, which apply only in the Israelite covenant.

Cain

The taking of human life comes up again in the first story after the humans leave the garden of Eden. Their son Cain kills his brother, Abel. We might imagine Cain's defense to be, "How could I know that I wasn't supposed to kill him? You never told us not to!" But in this story God precludes such a defense, telling Cain:

> What have you done? The sound! Your brother's blood is crying to me from the ground![18]
> (Gen 4:10)

God then condemns Cain to a life of nomadism. Now, this story is from an early stage in the Bible's narrative, at which the Bible depicts a world in which the deity is personally involved in human affairs: walking in the garden, directly questioning them about their behavior, personally rewarding and punishing them, personally making their clothes. This divine administration changes for most of the rest of the Bible, where humans administer most matters of justice themselves. So the question with regard to capital punishment in this stage of the Bible's narrative is: what should we make of the fact that God does not execute Cain? There are so many possible explanations of this that it is difficult even to have a preference, let alone to get to the bottom of it.

1. In the Bible, there is a difference between divine and human punishment. For example, the text declares that the deity reckons sins of parents on their children to the fourth generation; but it also instructs human courts that children are not to die for their parents' sins. These are not contradictory. The implication is that divine justice works differently from human justice (or at least *appears* to work differently from human justice) because the deity can look into human hearts and comprehend complicated developments through generations, which humans cannot do. In this picture, God may be more compassionate than humans in some cases and more strict in others. A human court might execute Cain. But in the divine mind there can be a reason not to do it.

2. More specifically, Num 35:33 says that the land on which blood has been spilled can have no expiation except by the blood of the one who spilled it, but the case of Cain seems to go against this. Even if God's punishment is different, the fact remains that the blood on the land in this case does not have expiation through the blood of the one who spilled it. Perhaps the difference is that the law in Numbers refers specifically to the land of Israel, after the people of the covenant settle there, not to the whole earth and all peoples, so this standard does not apply to Cain's case. Or, in the terms of critical biblical scholarship, perhaps this is an issue of authorship. In critical biblical scholarship, this story is part of the source known as J. Possibly the author of this J story saw things differently than the author of the principle in Num 35:33, which comes from the source known as P.

3. In this source, executing Cain could have ended the species. In J the only two sons whom Adam and Eve have are Cain and Abel. (In the source called P they have a son named Seth, and there is no Cain or Abel.) So if God executes Cain for killing Abel, there would be no humans left unless the author would have chosen to write in another son. There is in fact a similar case later in the Bible. In 2 Samuel, Absalom kills his brother Amnon over the matter of their sister Tamar, which we discussed in the last chapter. In that story their father, David, does not want to forgive Absalom, so Absalom is forced to flee the country. But then a woman known as "the wise woman of Tekoa" comes to David with a story that she has made up. She claims that she had two sons and that one of her sons killed the other. Now, she says, her son will be executed for the murder, but this will leave her with no sons. David therefore commutes her son's execution. He then realizes that the case is really about his own sons, and he pardons Absalom.[19] Executing Cain likewise would leave Adam and Eve childless, and it also could mean the end of humankind.

4. Perhaps this is not a murder but a manslaughter. The text gives no details about the killing. It simply reports: "And it was while they were in the field, and Cain rose against Abel his brother and killed him."[20] We usually understand Cain's motive to be that he is upset because Abel's sacrifice was preferred to his own, but the text never actually says that this is the reason for the killing. What's more, it never says what the circumstances are either. Is it done in the heat of the moment? Is it premeditated? Is it a plan to hurt his brother that goes too far? In the absence of any of the

information that would enable readers to make such a judgment, we cannot say whether it is murder or manslaughter. What we do know is that the story recounts God putting some sort of mark on Cain so that no one will kill him. This sounds more like the cities of refuge in subsequent biblical law, which protect the manslayer from those who would seek revenge. This may indicate that we should understand the fratricide to be a manslaughter, not a murder.

5. We have seen it argued that Cain's killing of Abel is a crime of passion and that crimes of passion do not receive capital punishment in the Bible. However, none of this is true. There is no indication in the text that it is a crime of passion. As we have just noted, there is nothing at all about the motive or circumstances. And there is no such principle that crimes of passion do not get the death penalty in the Bible.

6. Perhaps this is a great lesson about mercy, teaching that humans are instructed initially in their law codes to have execution but ultimately are to aspire to be as merciful as God.

Human performance of justice

When we come to the stories of humans carrying out justice, the motives and/or circumstances are clearer. In Leviticus there is a brief episode of a man who curses the name of God. The text explains that this happens in the course of a quarrel during Israel's travels through the Sinai wilderness.[21] This case leads to the law listed above: "one who profanes YHWH's name shall be *put to death*." In Numbers there is another episode from the wilderness journey of a man who collects wood on the sabbath. Like the cursing man in Leviticus, this wood-collecting man is placed under watch while YHWH is consulted. Then the divine decision comes, and he is executed.[22] The circumstances of this story are interesting because the law about working on the sabbath had already been given twice:

> Just: you shall observe my sabbaths, because it is a sign between me and you through your generations: to know that I, YHWH, make you holy. And you shall observe the sabbath, because it is a holy thing to you. One who desecrates it shall be *put to death*. Because anyone who does work in it: that person will be cut off from among his people. Six days work shall be done, and in the seventh day is a sabbath, a ceasing, a holy

thing to YHWH. Anyone who does work in the sabbath day shall be *put to death*. And the children of Israel shall observe the sabbath, to make the sabbath through their generations, an eternal covenant. Between me and the children of Israel it is a sign forever, because for six days YHWH made the skies and the earth, and in the seventh day He ceased and was refreshed.
(Exod 31:12–17)

Six days work shall be done, and in the seventh day you shall have a holy thing, a sabbath, a ceasing to YHWH. Anyone who does work in it shall be put to death. You shall not burn a fire in all of your homes on the sabbath day.
(Exod 35:2–3)

The commandment to put a sabbath violator to death is so explicit that one might well ask: why put this fellow under watch and ask God what to do? The answer may be that the details are not so clear. The law says that one who *desecrates* the sabbath shall be put to death, but it does not say what constitutes desecration: is it the act of working? Or is it some ritual violation such as an improper sacrifice or use of incense? The law says not to burn a fire in one's home on the sabbath. This is actually the only specific act that the law identifies as a violation of the sabbath. But the text does not say that this act is punishable by death. It only says that one is forbidden to do it. The law says that working on the sabbath day is punishable by death, but it does not specify what acts constitute work.[23] So, since this story is the first reported case of breaking the sabbath in the Bible, the people in the story are not certain if this man is guilty or not. Was his collection of wood considered work? Was it for the purpose of making a fire? What this story establishes, therefore, at minimum is that, in a matter involving capital punishment, the community must proceed with great caution. There must be a judgment of the person, the situation, the act, and the law. Whatever side one takes in the debate over capital punishment, and whatever one thinks of bringing in the Bible in this matter, all should agree at least to this principle that is found in the Bible: that taking a human life is a tremendous thing, so if a society uses capital punishment, there must be careful, deliberate inquiry, to avoid an error that cannot be undone.

The next story that involves capital punishment is a story of violation of *ḥerem*. In the book of Joshua, when the Israelites destroy Jericho, a man named Achan takes some of the forbidden property and hides them in his tent. When the Israelites confront the next battle, at the city of Ai, they are defeated, and the deity reveals to Joshua that the defeat is because someone stole from the *ḥerem*. They conduct a lottery, and it should come as no surprise that the lot falls on Achan. He admits his offense and points Joshua to the contraband in his tent. The people then stone him, then burn him, then heap stones over the spot.[24] The extra-difficult line of the text there in Joshua 7 is verse 25, which *may* mean that his family and animals are killed as well. It is uncertain. The text mixes singular and plural pronouns, and it reads differently from the Masoretic Hebrew in the Greek, the Syriac, and the Vulgate (Latin) texts. So there is the possibility that Achan alone is executed or that his family and even his animals are executed as well. Why would they suffer when only Achan committed the act? Because this is a ritual crime, not a social or ethical crime; and, as we have learned, in ritual offenses intention does not matter. Living in the tent where the objects of *ḥerem* were hidden, the family are infected, so to speak, by them. As Greenberg puts it, "This is not a case, then, of vicarious or collective punishment pure and simple, but a case of collective contagion of a taboo status."[25]

Two royal episodes fit with this picture. One is a case of assassination of a king of Judah, King Joash. The biblical historians report that when Joash's son Amaziah comes to the throne he has the two assassins executed. But the historians especially add that King Amaziah does not execute their sons "according to what was written in the book of the torah of Moses that YHWH commanded, saying, 'Fathers shall not be put to death for sons, and sons shall not be put to death for fathers. They shall each be put to death through his own sin.'"[26] This report in the histories is quoting a law in Deuteronomy that instructs human courts not to penalize children for their parents' crimes.[27]

The other episode concerns Saul, the first king of Israel. After Saul's death, the Gibeonites, who are one of the Canaanite peoples, come to Saul's successor, King David, and they complain that Saul had tried to massacre them. This is a tremendous offense because the Israelites had sworn an oath in their God's name to have peace with the Gibeonites.[28] To break an oath that is made in YHWH's name is a violation of one of the

Ten Commandments, which forbids taking YHWH's name in vain. This commandment does not mean that one cannot say things such as "God damn it" as people often think. It rather means the very thing that Saul is said to have done: to violate an oath in which one has explicitly invoked the divine name YHWH. The Gibeonites demand the execution of Saul's sons, and King David turns the sons over to them for hanging. Now there are several possible explanations of this. One explanation is cynical and political: David is willing to grant the Gibeonites' request because it means the removal of Saul's sons, every one of whom is a potential challenger to David for the throne. A second possible explanation is that the issue here is that Saul's offense is a ritual crime, breaking an oath made in God's name, and, as we have seen, in ritual crimes the standard is different from usual human justice. The problem with this explanation, though, is that this normally occurs in stories of miraculous interventions by God Himself, not in reports of human history such as this one, where God is not portrayed as telling David what to do. So this case is left uncertain. All we can say is that the standard is different in this ritual case from the non-ritual case of the assassination of King Joash.

Execution or prison

We have looked at laws and prose and have seen the offenses that involve capital punishment in the Bible. This has provided the specifics of what we said at the beginning of this chapter, namely, that there are far more capital offenses in the Bible than in many countries today—even countries where people cite the Bible as support for having capital punishment. So the question is: Why? Why does the Bible use capital punishment for so many crimes? Is it that the culture that produced the Bible valued human life less? We have seen evidence to the contrary: creation in the divine image, never using capital punishment for property crimes. The reason may be a more banal one, and, as we observed earlier, the most banal explanation is quite likely to be the right one. The most likely reason why the Bible has execution for so many crimes is that there were no prisons. Archaeologically, we have never found evidence of prisons in ancient Israel. And the Bible's prose narratives speak of no institution that is comparable to present-day prisons. And the Bible's laws never call for imprisonment for any crime.

In biblical narrative, both Joseph and the prophet Jeremiah are confined, but they are placed in special places for prisoners of the king. These places are not buildings that are constructed for the punishment of people in general for crimes.[29] In Jeremiah's case, the text specifies that he was put in a place of confinement (*bêt hā'ēsûr*) in a scribe's house that had been made into a *bêt hakkele'*, a "place of restraint" or "withholding."[30] King Ahab, likewise, has the prophet Micaiah held in a *bêt hakkele'*. The king says they are to keep Micaiah in this place until the king returns from a battle. It is explicitly a temporary holding situation, not an imprisonment, and it is specifically for a king's confinement of an individual opponent.[31] It is reminiscent of what is done to the man collecting wood on the sabbath that we discussed above: he is placed under watch (Hebrew *mišmār*) temporarily while waiting for judgment. The man who curses the name of God likewise is placed under watch (*mišmār*) temporarily while waiting for judgment.

At one point, the king of Judah takes Jeremiah out of that house where he was confined and instead moves him to an enclosure for watching (Hebrew *ḥăṣar hammattārāh*).[32] This term *mattārāh* appears to have a similar meaning to *mišmār*. Their root meanings are about the same: "to watch," "to guard." At another point, Jeremiah is placed in a *mahĕpeket*, which is usually understood to be some sort of stocks but not a prison.[33] Similarly, there is a report that a king of Israel, Asa, is angry at a seer named Hanani and sets him in a *bêt hammahĕpeket*. This phrase was translated "a prison house" in older English translations (King James Version and the old Jewish Publication Society translation) but is understood as "stocks" in more current translations (Revised English Bible and the New Jewish Publication Society translation, as well as the standard dictionary in the field, the BDB).[34]

The book of Ezra takes place during the era in which the Jews were under the power of the Persian Empire. Artaxerxes, the Persian monarch, gives Ezra the power to appoint judges so that the "law of your God" will be enforced, "whether for death, whether for banishment, whether for confiscation of possessions and for imprisonment (Aramaic *'ĕsûrîn*)."[35] But the text never suggests that Ezra utilized any of these. On the contrary, he has "the law of your God," the Torah, read publicly and exhorts the people to follow that. And the Torah contains no laws that impose imprisonment.[36]

As for biblical Israel's cultural context, the legal historian of the ancient world Raymond Westbrook wrote that imprisonment is "not generally used as punishment in the Ancient Near Eastern legal systems."[37] Edward M. Peters, writing in *The Oxford History of the Prison*, speaks of prisons in Egypt and Mesopotamia but gives no actual texts from those cultures referring to such things. What he describes, rather, is usually forced labor as punishment for crimes. This tells us nothing about where the forced laborers resided. One need not be imprisoned to do forced labor, and in fact the biblical account in Exodus depicts the Egyptian enslavement of the Israelites as precisely this: the Israelites are forced to do labor for the Egyptians but still live in their own homes and have animals and possessions. Other cases referred to by Peters are temporary confinements such as holding a prisoner while waiting for judgment.[38]

Consistent with this is the biblical story of the Philistines' treatment of the Israelite hero Samson. When they capture him they gouge his eyes, bind him in fetters, and make him do mill work in a *bêt hā'ăsûrîm*, which we generally translate as a "prison house" but is more specifically some kind of place of forced labor.[39] Similar is the Bible's description of the Babylonians' treatment of Zedekiah, King of Judah, when they capture him. They blind him, bind him in fetters, and, according to the Greek text of the Hebrew Bible, keep him in a mill house.[40] On the other hand, the Bible's accounts of the Assyrians' treatment of the Israelite King Hoshea and of the Babylonians' treatment of the Judean Kings Jehoiachin and Jehoiakim all refer to a *bêt kele'*, which may be a jail.[41] It is possible, therefore, that the Jewish historians of Kings and Chronicles did have in mind a form of imprisonment being used in the Mesopotamian empires. Still, even in these reports of Mesopotamian incarceration, it is used only by kings for other kings whom they have captured.

Now if prison was not an option in biblical law, what other means of punishment were there?

1. Beating. This is rare and limited. It is permitted in certain disputes, and the court cannot have anyone struck more than forty times.[42]

2. Mutilation. There is only one clear instance in the laws:

> If people will fight together, a man and his brother, and the wife of one
> will come close to rescue her husband from the hand of the one striking

him, and she will put out her hand and take hold of his private parts, then you shall cut off her hand. Your eye shall not pity.
(Deut 25:11–12)

The harshness of this law has long surprised, distressed, and puzzled scholars and readers. They have proposed many possible reasons for it, and some have interpreted it not to be taken literally. Our purpose here is not to attempt to solve the question of the reason for the law. We just emphasize that it is such an extremely rare punishment for what was probably an extremely rare event.[43] It is not part of the standard punishments in biblical law.

Some would take the commonly quoted biblical phrase "an eye for an eye, a tooth for a tooth" to mean that a court would literally mutilate a person who has injured another. Others take it to mean rather that punishment cannot exceed a crime. There cannot, for example, be a life for an eye. The phrase occurs in two passages in the Bible's law codes, and in the first one it cannot be taken literally. It is a law about a case in which two people are fighting, and they strike a pregnant woman and cause her to go into labor. If there is an injury, then:

you shall give a life for a life, an eye for an eye, a tooth for a tooth, a hand for a hand, a foot for a foot, a burn for a burn, a wound for a wound, a hurt for a hurt.
(Exod 21:23–25)[44]

Now there is no burn in this case, and, if the injury refers to the infant and not to the woman, infants do not have teeth. It appears rather that this law is citing a legal principle, not prescribing a mutilation. To put it most cautiously, we simply do not know if "an eye for an eye" was meant literally in the biblical world or if any courts ever followed these laws. What we do know is that it was understood in the earliest post-biblical rabbinic law to mean monetary compensation: one paid the *value* of an eye that he or she had injured; one did not have one's own eye injured. And we also know that mutilation was prescribed for various crimes in other ancient Near Eastern cultures, while biblical law does not treat these crimes in that way: In the laws of Hammurabi these include cutting off a hand[45] or cutting off a slave's ear.[46] In the Hittite laws they may cut off the slave's nose and ears.[47] In the Middle Assyrian Laws, they may sever the finger or the lip of someone who touches or kisses another's wife,[48] and they may castrate an adulterer and cut off the nose of the adulteress.[49] This, too, may indicate that biblical law rejected mutilation as a standard, available legal penalty.

3. Sale into slavery. This is not done in biblical law. One's economic condition is not a punishment for crime.[50]

4. Banishment. An individual cannot be exiled from the country for any crime in the Bible. The legal texts do not prescribe it, and the prose and poetry do not report it. There is an account in which King Solomon sends the priest Abiathar away from Jerusalem to his town of Anathoth,[51] and Solomon restricts the rebel Shimei *to* Jerusalem, not permitting him to leave, on pain of death.[52] But the first case never says that Abiathar is not free to go anywhere in the country, including Jerusalem, and the second case is a keeping-in, not a throwing-out.

5. Vicarious punishment. If one rapes another man's wife, there is no delivering of the rapist's own wife for rape as a punishment. Likewise, there is no delivering of one's own children for slavery or execution as a punishment for one's crimes. Other ancient Near Eastern law codes used such punishments-by-substitution, but the Bible excluded it.[53]

6. Stocks. We mentioned above that the prophets Jeremiah and Hanani were put into a *mahĕpeket*, which may possibly mean stocks or some other form of holding structure. But we do not know if this was a common method of punishment or if it is something extraordinary that is done to these prophets. The Bible's law codes do not prescribe it for any offense.

7. Punishments in the hands of God. Certain legal sanctions are considered to be between the offender and God. Often the text will say, "He shall bear his crime" or "She shall bear her crime."[54] In another form, the law will say that the offender will be *nikrāt*. Usually translated as "cut off," the term's meaning is uncertain. It is usually expressed as one's being cut off from one's people.[55] It may mean some sort of geographical exile, but, as we said above, there is no case of this ever happening in the Bible's prose records. And the term can also refer to being cut off from before God,[56] which is unlikely to refer to something geographical. We might imagine that it means some sort of shunning by the community, but, again, there is no reference to a single case of such a thing. More probably it means the cutting off of a person's family line. It is a threat that a person will not have descendants, and so his name and family will be lost from among his people. This is not achieved by killing him or his children; it is understood to be in the deity's hands.

What all of this means is that there were really only two main options for human courts: fines or execution. The standard biblical fine for cheating or stealing is full restoration of the amount taken plus one fifth (plus a guilt offering as a sacrifice of atonement).[57] For any crime that seemingly called for more than paying a fine, in the absence of prisons, capital punishment was the only option. We cannot say what they would have done if they had had prisons. Would they have had fewer executions? Would they have had any executions? We truly do not know.

It is understandable that societies that do not have prisons are more likely to impose the death penalty. The point for our concern in this book is that one cannot just say that the Bible has execution and that this is therefore a support for using the death penalty in any country in our era. Countries today have other options. The most obvious is prison. Other options include community service and medical treatment for persons who are judged to be criminally insane. People in these countries are free to debate the merits of these alternatives as opposed to capital punishment. But the existence of execution in the Bible does not in itself constitute an argument.

Two more points may shed light on this. The first is the requirement of two witnesses. In biblical law, there must be two or more witnesses in a capital case. A court may not execute on the word of one witness alone.[58] The pressure on the witnesses is tremendous, moreover, because the law says:

The witnesses' hand shall be on him first to put him to death, and all the people's hand after that.
(Deut 17:7)

Take heed, witnesses! The witnesses themselves must participate in the execution. If you testify against someone in a capital case, then you must, very literally, cast the first stone. How differently might people see capital punishment today if present laws had this requirement. And even more powerful is the second half of that verse: "and all the people's hand after that." Everyone has to participate in the execution—the entire community. Stoning, after all, is understood to be performed by the community, not by just two or three people throwing rocks. Capital punishment really is a communal act. In the Bible's perspective, everyone must understand that he or she is part of the society that convicts, sentences, and executes under the law. In this perspective, if you say that you favor the death penalty, then you must walk the walk; you must be prepared to carry it out. This is not in itself an argument for or against capital punishment. It is a serious, sobering reminder of what is at stake. Capital punishment is not just an intellectual argument for debating tournaments and dinner parties. It is one of the most significant decisions a society makes. Especially in a democracy: the people choose the system of judges and trials, they participate in the juries, they determine whether their society will have capital punishment. Surely if they had to perform the executions themselves this would impact their opinions about the death penalty. But, even without this personal burden, they all can learn from this biblical standard that one must accept the responsibility of being part of a society that executes.

The second point that may shed additional light on this: People have occasionally suggested that the existence in the Bible of so many laws that prescribe execution does not necessarily mean that such executions really were carried out. The law codes, they suggest, may have served more to establish principles and to convey how serious some offenses were. This may or may not be correct. After all, this would be a hard thing to establish one way or the other through archaeology. What would we have to find to settle the question? The ruins of an ancient gallows with an inscription nearby saying what the hanged person's crime was? So there is really no evidence for this claim and very little evidence directly against it. One writer argued that "nowhere in the Old Testament is there a case in which what seem like prescriptions of the death penalty for various offenses were carried out by a criminal law system."[59] That was potentially a good approach because it tried to relate the laws to the accounts of events in the Bible's prose. However, it was not correct. We have seen several cases in which a capital offense is named in the law and an execution for that offense is carried out in the prose. Namely: Achan's execution for taking *ḥerem*; the execution of King Joash's assassins but not of their children; the execution of the man who collects wood on sabbath; and the execution of the man who blasphemes the divine name.

The case of the law of execution for sabbath violation is a bit different, however, because it calls for execution and for being cut off (*nikrāt*) as well. That is literally overkill. So this may possibly suggest that the purpose of the law's severe wording was to let people know that this new invention in human experience—the sabbath—was something tremendous, and perhaps it was to let them know that they should be afraid to cross its line. As we just noted, there is a story in the Bible's prose about a man who is executed for gathering wood on the sabbath, but this story may have been told precisely to convey the sabbath's importance, just like the wording of the law itself. It is a bit tricky because that story does not occur among other stories in a prose section of the Bible. It comes in a section of biblical law, and it serves precisely to tell of the original occasion of giving that particular law.

Also: The extreme strictness of the law of *ḥerem* and the story of Achan may also have had the function of conveying the seriousness of sacred matters. The present state of the evidence indicates that some of these situations never happened. The archaeological evidence has persuaded most archaeologists and critical biblical scholars that there was no Jericho event in the time of Joshua. No walls came tumbling down. No destruction of the Canaanites. If the archaeology is correct, and there was no *ḥerem* at Jericho and elsewhere, then what would be the purpose of the law? To warn, to teach.

So the question of what the Bible has to teach us about capital punishment therefore is not about whether the Bible allows executions. If it is correct that the reason for biblical capital punishment is that imprisonment was not yet an established means of dealing with felons, then everything is changed now that there are alternatives to execution. The more relevant biblical question may rather be about what the Bible has to say about justice. Opponents of capital punishment often point out that arguments based on deterrence are without any statistical basis: that there is no evidence that the fear of execution deters people from committing crimes. (We have heard the report that long ago in England an epidemic of theft became so severe that a law was established that pickpockets would be hanged publicly. But it turned out that the highest rate of picking pockets was at the hangings. Everybody was looking up!) And arguments based on saving the expense of keeping felons alive are morally reprehensible. The strongest arguments for capital punishment, we think, are not based on such "practical" considerations. They are based rather on appeals to justice. The Bible includes a fundamental command: "Justice justice you shall pursue."[60] There have been many interpretations of the repetition of the word *justice* in this verse, but at minimum it means that this is a crucial teaching. And, for the purpose of this book, it means that the Bible squarely points us to the central issue of capital punishment: the question of whether or not it is just. But this leaves us uncertain, because people are divided on whether execution is just. Proponents say that it is justice that someone who murders should lose his or her own life. Opponents say that execution is not just at all. And what shall we say about countries that use capital punishment even in cases that do not involve loss of a victim's life? So, if we cannot establish whether it is just or not, what are we to do?

Perhaps there is another, *underlying* issue that is even more central than justice. Perhaps it is: what we *are* if we execute. Does it mean that we are strong enough, wise enough, and noble enough to feel confidently that we are able to decide to take a human life? Or does it mean that we are small, frightened, and vengeful enough to band together for the purpose of taking a life of someone who threatens us or has broken our rules? If the former were so, then the debate over using capital punishment would take a different form. Both sides would frame their arguments differently. The case in favor of capital punishment in particular might be stronger. But it is not so. Few people would argue that our species has arrived at such a stage of wisdom, nobility, and confidence. The safest answer for now may well be that we cannot do execution until we arrive at a more advanced state of human civilization. It is a huge irony. Capital punishment may belong at the earliest and at the most advanced states of human development—but not in this middle period. This period may be our adolescence as a species. When we reach our species' maturity we may find that we are wise enough and strong enough to use capital punishment. Or we may find that at that stage we have no use for capital punishment. We may find better ways of dealing with matters of life and death.[61]

On this matter of human development, the Bible has a great deal to teach. The Bible's story traces the experience of humankind over several millennia. From Adam and Eve to Ezra and Esther, it pictures the human species as growing, learning, changing. It encourages this growth and allows for change in human law and behavior in the wake of such growth. It encourages going to those with expertise in the law, and it even regards this as so important that it includes it among the capital offenses! It encourages wisdom, dedicating three long, poetic books to it: Proverbs, Job, and Ecclesiastes. So perhaps the poetic books are more relevant to this chapter than we said at the beginning.

We therefore conclude that we are best advised to act with humility and—even for those who have thought this through and concluded that they favor capital punishment—to be extraordinarily hesitant to perform executions until we reach the kind of wisdom that the Bible encourages us to pursue.

FIVE

The Earth

The Bible did not have to begin with the creation of the world. It could have begun with Adam and Eve; it could have begun with the tower of Babylon, or with Abraham. But it begins with the creation of the earth and everything in it. So we should hardly consider it a great insight when we recognize that a book that opens with the creation of this world is concerned with the well-being of the whole earth.

In our age, the greatest threats to the earth's well-being since the flood have materialized. A revolution in technology has brought us extraordinary blessings—in medicine, in communication, in understanding the universe. But it has also brought threats to the existence of life on the earth: disappearance of animal and plant species, destruction of rain forests that affect the earth's atmosphere and that produce important medicines, nuclear facilities (both for weapons and for peaceful energy needs) passing into ever more untrustworthy hands, depletion of the earth's ozone layer, global warming, pollution of rivers and lakes and even the seas and even the sky and even space, plus the challenge of human overpopulation.

What might the Bible contribute, for better or for worse, to these matters? Now one might say that in the matter of overpopulation, for example, the Bible is the least likely source of guidance. After all, people's understanding of the Bible itself has contributed to the present condition. The first chapter in the Bible pictures God telling humans, "Be fruitful and multiply and fill the earth." Especially in Catholicism and Orthodox Judaism, this has been understood to instruct us to have many children. Similarly in matters of ecology, one might see the Bible as encouraging humans' right to abuse the earth because in that creation story in Genesis God declares when creating humans that they should "subdue the earth and dominate the fish of the sea and the birds of the skies and every animal that creeps on the earth." Some have taken this divine assignment of dominion over the earth to mean that humans have permission to use or abuse the earth and animal and plant life in any way they see fit.

On one level, these things are hardly an issue of liberal or conservative. They are questions of survival: the survival of our species—and other species with us. They are about our lives—and about the quality of our lives. But, even if we agree that we nearly all care about the destiny of our species and our planet, we still have disagreements among us about the specific threats, what their causes are, and what to do about them. In the United States, these things are at least partly political issues between left and right. So the question, as in the preceding chapters, is: how has the Bible contributed to people's views about this, and what wisdom does the Bible have to offer toward dealing with it now?

Be fruitful and multiply

Now the Bible does in fact say:

> Be fruitful and multiply and fill the earth.
> (Gen 1:28)

Scholars, clergy, and laypersons have often identified this verse as the first commandment in the Bible. We offer two different perspectives on this. The first is that this verse is not in fact a commandment at all. There are no other commandments in that chapter. Genesis 1 rather tells a story of why things are the way they are: Why is there light and darkness? Why do plants produce their own respective seeds? (Roses produce roses. Apples produce apples.) Why are there lights in the sky? Why are there different kinds of animals? From where did humans come? In that context, the verse about humans being fruitful is an etiology as well. It comes to explain why there are a lot of humans (and animals) and why they are all over the earth and not in just one place. The fruiting and multiplying and filling of the earth have already taken place! This verse is not a commandment to do it. It is an explanation of how it came to be.

How do we know this? Because the text does not express the words of God there as a commandment. It says—repeatedly—that this human fruitfulness is a *blessing*, not a commandment.[1] Here is the full verse:

And God *blessed* them, and God said to them,
"Be fruitful and multiply and fill the earth."
(Gen 1:28)

Eight chapters later, after the flood has wiped out all but one family of humans, the family of Noah, from the earth, God blesses the humans again with the opportunity to refill the earth. The words are almost identical to the verse above:

And God *blessed* Noah and his sons and said to them, "Be fruitful and multiply and fill the earth.'"
(Gen 9:1)

Later God blesses Jacob, who is also known as Israel, with the opportunity to have many progeny. And once again the wording is explicitly in terms of blessing, not commandment, thus:

And He *blessed* him. And God said to him, "Your name is Jacob. Your name will not be called Jacob anymore, but rather Israel will be your name." And He called his name Israel. And God said to him, "I am El Shadday. Be fruitful and multiply."
(Gen 35:9–11)

Then this is fulfilled for Jacob. The text reports about his family:

And they were fruitful and multiplied very much.
(Gen 47:27)[2]

So Jacob tells his son Joseph a few verses later:

El Shadday appeared to me in Luz in the land of Canaan, and He *blessed* me and said to me, 'Here, I'm making you fruitful and multiplying you.'
(Gen 48:3–4)

Later, in Leviticus, there is a blessing-and-curse list that takes up all of Leviticus 26. It enumerates blessings for the people of Israel if they will keep their covenant with their God, and it names curses for them if they will violate it. The list of blessings includes:

> and I shall make you fruitful and make you multiply.
> (Lev 26:9)

In Deuteronomy, Moses makes his farewell speech to his people, and he begins by saying:

> YHWH, your God, has made you multiply, and here today you're like
> the stars of the skies for multitude.
> (Deut 1:10)

And then, in the next verse, he adds:

> May YHWH, your fathers' God, add on to you a thousand times more
> like you! And may He *bless* you as He spoke to you.
> (Deut 1:11)[3]

Later in the speech, too, Moses says:

> And He'll love you and *bless* you and multiply you and *bless* the fruit of
> your womb . . .
> (Deut 7:13)

In all of these cases, the Bible presents the opportunity to spread around the earth as a blessing that the deity offers to humans, not as a decree that they are required to obey. A blessing in the Bible can mean almost anything good. It is not something supernatural. A biblical person regards himself or herself as blessed if things have been going well: good crops, livestock, having children, good health, no fear of enemies, and so on. For specific examples, see the lists of blessings and curses that appear in two places in the Hebrew Bible: Leviticus 26 and Deuteronomy 28.

The point of all this is that the consistent picture of this human multiplying in the Hebrew Bible is that it is always pictured as a blessing, not as a commandment. And there is never a suggestion that the blessing is infinite, that humans can just keep on multiplying until they are shoulder to shoulder all over the earth. That would be no blessing by any biblical standard or by *any* standard. Food is a blessing, but there is a point at which one can eat too much. A blessing that is abused, overdone, or treated irresponsibly can turn into a curse.

Now some may still see a commandment in the words "Be fruitful and multiply and fill the earth" because it is stated in the imperative tense. Or they may base this view on the fact that this is the traditional reading, a reading that people have taught and followed for so many centuries. The biblical scholar Nahum Sarna questioned whether the use of the imperative makes this a commandment, pointing out three other places where the Hebrew imperative is used in contexts that are about blessings and not commands.[4] Still, in fairness to that view we offer a second perspective. We base this perspective on something that one of us (Friedman) wrote ten years ago in *Commentary on the Torah*. That book contains a translation of the first five books of the Bible with commentary on them. One of the shortest comments in the book is on this verse. Following the traditional reading that these words are a commandment, the comment is:

This commandment is now fulfilled.[5]

The filling of the earth has been reached and surpassed. To increase the population of the earth now could be to add to that command, to overdo it. We have often asked our classes and audiences, "What is the most violated commandment in the Bible?" We think that the correct answer to this question, the commandment most frequently broken, without a doubt, is found in Deuteronomy:

You shall not add onto the thing that I command you, and you shall not subtract from it.
(Deut 4:2)

It occurs a second time even more emphatically:

Everything that I command you: you shall be watchful to do it. You shall not add onto it, and you shall not subtract from it.
(Deut 13:1)

To add to a commandment is, in biblical terms, a violation. This is not a criticism of Catholic or Orthodox Jewish interpretation. Our task as scholars is rather to offer this point for biblical interpreters of all denominations to consider and, if they find it to be a correct reading of the text, to declare the first commandment fulfilled. This also is not a criticism of families who have had a lot of children. Here, too, as with all of our discussions in this book, our task as scholars is to help people who value the Bible to understand what this verse means. The important point is that it does not necessarily obligate them to have many children. From either perspective, though, whether it is a blessing or a commandment, the fruiting, multiplying, and filling of the earth has now taken place.

Subdue the earth

In the late 1960s, when we heard that the new big issue was something called "ecology," many of us were shocked, puzzled, or just amused. How could this compare in importance to the issues of those days of war, race, and gender? We were wrong. Each decade since then has seen an expansion of awareness and concerns among humans about our planet. Some of the debates are about whether some of these threats are real. Some of the debates recognize the threats but are about whether human actions are the cause. In what ways is the Bible relevant to any of this?

People sometimes say that one can always make a case for either side of any issue from the Bible. They feel that one can find verses to cite that support either side. "The devil can quote scriptures." We advise not to be too quick to conclude this. Just citing verses on one side of an issue, in the first place, does not make a case. One has to look at the full picture and take as many passages as possible into account. One has to look into the history of each passage, get a refined knowledge of its wording, look into its context in the cultures of the ancient Near East, see if it is prose, poetry, or law, and consider all the other factors we considered in the past chapters. So the texts are not so either-sided as these people imagine, open to all opinions and interpretations. There are *facts* in biblical studies. Still we recognize that there are real issues in which reasonable, learned people can disagree and each conclude that the weight of the biblical evidence comes down mostly toward one side of an issue or the other. After reading the discussions here on homo-sexuality, abortion, gender, and capital punishment, you may feel that on some of these cases the weight of the Hebrew Bible's words falls mainly on one side and that on others it remains open to argument, evidence, and interpretation to reach a conclusion. In the case of the biblical attitude toward the earth and toward humans' place in it, we would say that this is one of those matters in which the weight falls on one side visibly. We do not mean that the Bible gives an answer on a specific current environmental question such as global warming. Whether global warming is a fact and, if so, how to address it—these are not for the Bible to decide. They depend on evidence brought by those who know the science. But on the basic principle of humans' care for the earth, that is something on which the weight of the Bible's evidence and wisdom really does come down on a particular side, namely, that humans do in fact have a responsibility for this and that our moral decisions do affect this. We are willing to say so, but in doing so we are not trying to make a case for the left or the right. We are informing the left and the right what the Bible says. Specifically:

The Bible makes a direct connection between human behavior and the environment. It establishes this connection in several stories at its beginning in Genesis, and it continues to make this point in numerous stories, poems, and laws that follow. A basic biblical principle is: when humans are corrupt, the earth suffers. This is not a subtle concept that one must derive through long, hard interpretation. It is explicit in the text. In the Bible's first story, the account of the Garden of Eden, when the deity reveals to the humans the consequences of their taking the fruit that had been prohibited, those consequences include:

> The *ground is cursed* on your account.
> (Gen 3:17)

One chapter later, when Cain kills his brother Abel, the consequences again include specifically:

> And now you're *cursed from the ground* that opened its mouth to take
> your brother's blood from your hand.
> (Gen 4:11)

Two chapters later comes the story of the flood. Whether one follows a traditional or a critical view of the text, the point is explicit: the entire earth suffers because of human behavior. In traditional reading, the flood story is one long narrative. In critical biblical scholarship, this long narrative has been found to be a combination of two complete, originally separate stories that have been brilliantly combined into one by an editor. The two stories come from two separate sources that run through many books of the Bible.[6] These two sources are known in biblical scholarship by the symbols J and P. The J source begins its version of the flood story this way:

> And YHWH saw that human bad was multiplied in the earth, and every inclination of their heart's thoughts was only bad all the day. And YHWH regretted that He had made humankind in the earth. And He was grieved to His heart. And YHWH said, "I'll wipe out the human (*'ādām*) whom I've created from the face of the ground (*'ădāmāh*), from human to animal to creeping thing to bird of the skies, because I regret that I made them."
> (Gen 6:5–7)

The animals and birds and the earth itself are to be hurt because of humans. The P source likewise explains right at its beginning:

> And the earth was corrupted before God, and the earth was filled with violence. And God saw the earth; and here, it was corrupted because all flesh had corrupted its way on the earth. And God said to Noah, "The end of all flesh has come before me because the earth is filled with violence because of them. And here: I'm destroying them with the earth."
> (Gen 6:11–13)

Humans are portrayed as having become bad, corrupt, and violent. As a result, the earth will suffer. All species will suffer. The interconnectedness of earth and all of its creatures is unequivocal in both versions of the story of earth's inundation. Two of the Bible's greatest authors both saw it this way. And, if you prefer the traditional reading, the final biblical text, which combines both of these passages, makes the point even stronger. Corrupt conduct in the human species causes animals, plants, and the earth itself to suffer.

And take note of the pun in the text: the human (Hebrew *'ādām*) is created out of the earth (Hebrew *'ădāmāh*). This is not the kind of pun that is just meant to be cute or to display an author's literary artistry. It is a pun of meaning. The reciprocal relationship between human and earth is emphasized by this play on words.

Ten chapters after the flood story comes the story of Sodom and Gomorrah, which we looked at in the chapter on homosexuality. As we saw there, the story has nothing to do with homosexuality, but it has everything to do with violence and corruption by an entire community. It is introduced by portraying God as saying:

> The cry of Sodom and Gomorrah: how great it is.
> (Gen 18:20)

The ensuing negotiation between God and Abraham reveals that there are not even ten virtuous people in all of Sodom's population. And this is borne out when "all the people, from the farthest reaches" attack Lot and his guests.[7] The consequence is the annihilation of the people of Sodom and of Gomorrah. But the consequences extend to the ground and to all plant life as well:

> And He overturned these cities and all of the plain and all of the residents of the cities and all the growth of the ground.
> (Gen 19:25)

This is never forgotten. Four biblical books later, hundreds of years later in the story, in the list of blessings and curses at the end of Deuteronomy, Moses includes this terrible threat if the people of Israel betray their covenant with God: the land will be:

> brimstone and salt, all the land a burning, it won't be seeded and won't grow, and not any vegetation will come up in it, like the overturning of Sodom and Gomorrah . . .
> (Deut 28:22)

The destruction of the region of Sodom and Gomorrah becomes a model for what can happen when a society goes wrong. Centuries after

Moses, the prophets Isaiah, Jeremiah, Ezekiel, Amos, and Zephaniah all cite it this way.[8] Indeed, the basic idea of these prose accounts—that a causal link exists between human behavior and the sustainability of their environment—is present in the laws and in biblical poetry as well.

Poetry

In poetry, we find the same basic theology expressed by the biblical prophets. Human behavior is causally connected with the state of creation. When humans sin, the whole earth suffers. The prophet Hosea says:

> Hear the word of YHWH, children of Israel;
> for YHWH has a case with the land's inhabitants.
> There is no faithfulness, and there is no kindness,
> and there is no knowledge of God in the land.
> Swearing and lying and murder,
> and stealing and adultery have broken out;
> and bloodshed follows bloodshed.
> Therefore the land will mourn,
> and everyone who lives in it will languish;
> together with the wild animal
> and the bird of the skies,
> and also the fish of the sea will be gathered away.
> (Hos 4:1–3)

Note that the people's sinning is not just a matter of religious impiety, worshiping other gods, or "knowledge of God," but that the people's bad behavior is tied here directly to their social justice and the way they treat each other as well. Loving one's neighbor as oneself means following the ethical prescriptions of the Ten Commandments, five of which are alluded to here. In the poetry of Hosea, the destructive behavior of humans toward each other has direct ramifications on the natural world: the land, the animals, the birds, and the fish are all in trouble.

In the same vein, Jeremiah pictures Judah's disobedience as producing the collapse of the creation. He directly reverses the picture of creation in Genesis 1:

I looked at the earth,
>   and, here, it was shapeless and formless;
>   and at the skies,
>   and their light was gone.
I looked at the mountains,
>   and, here, they were quaking;
>   all the hills were swaying.
I looked, and, here, there was no human;
>   and every bird of the skies had flown away.
I looked, and, here, the fruitful land was a desert;
>   and all its towns lay in ruins
>   before YHWH, before the flaring of his anger.
For this is what YHWH said:
>   "The whole land will be ruined,
>   though I will not end it completely.
Therefore the earth will mourn,
>   and the skies above grow dark,
>   because I have spoken, have conceived, and have
>   not relented,
>   and I will not turn back."
(Jer 4:23–28)

Elsewhere Jeremiah sees a drought afflicting Judah as a direct result of the people's sins. Here the earth is pictured as both testifying against the people and suffering for their sins:

Judah mourns,
>   and her gates languish;
>   they darken for the land,
>   and Jerusalem's cry has gone up.
And their nobles had sent their youths for water;
>   they came to the cisterns;
>   they found no water.
>   They returned, their jars empty;
>   dismayed and despairing,
>   they covered their heads.

For the ground is cracked
> because there was no rain in the land;
> the farmers are dismayed;
> they covered their heads.

For even the doe in the field
> deserts her newborn fawn
> because there was no grass.

And wild donkeys stood on the barren heights;
> they panted like jackals;
> their eyesight failed
> for lack of pasture.

Although our crimes testify against us,
> YHWH, do something for the sake of your name.
> For our backslidings are great.
> We have sinned against you.

(Jer 14:2–7)

Whether these poetic lines refer to actual conditions or are metaphors, their implication is the same: the environment can suffer when humans go wrong.

Law

The most explicit texts about humans and the earth, though, are the laws. They provide specific cases of what humans are supposed to do. In the first place, humans must protect the earth itself. The law that requires one to let one's land lie fallow every seventh year is a patent example:

> And six years you shall sow your land and gather its produce; and the seventh: you shall let it lie fallow and leave it. And your people's poor will eat, and the animal of the field will eat what they leave. You shall do this to your vineyard, to your olives.
> (Exod 23:10–11)

We should not miss that this law requires something that is good for the land, and that its wording then conveys that this is also meant to be good for the animals and for the plants. And right in the middle it says that this is also for the poor. Like the prose and poetic passages, it connects caring for the environment to caring for human beings. Morality and nature are not separate categories in biblical terms. One cannot be a talented farmer and a jerk at the same time.

It is also hard to miss the obvious analogy to the sabbath. Humans are supposed to have an opportunity to rest every seventh day, and they are directed to give the earth an opportunity to rest every seventh year. This law also appears later, in the priestly laws of Leviticus, and there the connection to the sabbath is explicit:

> When you will come to the land that I am giving to you, then the land shall have a sabbath for YHWH. Six years you shall seed your field, and six years you shall prune your vineyard, and you shall gather its produce. And in the seventh year the land shall have a sabbath, a ceasing, a sabbath for YHWH: you shall not seed your field, and you shall not prune your vineyard, you shall not reap your harvest's free growth, and you shall not cut off your untrimmed grapes. The land shall have a year of ceasing. And the land's sabbath shall be yours for food: for you and for your servant and for your maid and for your employee and for your visitor who are residing with you and for your domestic animal and for the wild animal that are in your land shall be all of its produce to eat.
> (Lev 25:2–7)

And all of this is set in a cosmic context because, in the Bible's very first chapters, God rests on the seventh day of creation. The sabbath command in the Ten Commandments also includes that one must let one's animals rest on the seventh day as well.[9] Humans are thus required to give this benefit to animals, to plants, and to the soil of the earth. The command/blessing to subdue the earth comes with requirements and responsibilities. They must care for the earth and treat it and the life that is on it well.

Some of the laws further make the connection between human behavior and the earth, similar to the connection we saw in the prose and poetry. One of the laws of war especially makes this link. When the people of Israel lay a siege, they are not allowed to cut down a fruit tree to use for building their defenses. Trees are for eating, not for war. Thus:

> When you'll besiege a city many days, fighting against it to capture it, you shall not destroy a tree of it, moving an axe at it, because you'll eat from it, so you shall not cut it down. Because is a tree of the field a human, to go from in front of you in a siege?! Only a tree that you'll know that it isn't a tree for eating: that one you may destroy and cut down so you may build a siege-work against the city that is making war with you until its fall.
>
> (Deut 20:19–20)

As one must treat plants well, so one must treat animals with care, too. For example, one may take eggs or chicks but not along with the mother:

> When a bird's nest will happen to be in front of you on the road in any tree or on the ground—chicks or eggs—and the mother is sitting over the chicks or over the eggs, you shall not take the mother along with the children. You shall *let the mother go*, and you may take the children for you, so that it will be good for you, and you will extend days.
>
> (Deut 22:6–7)

One could argue that this law is meant as a matter of kindness to the mother, or one could argue that it is a practical matter of keeping the mother alive to produce more eggs and chicks. Either way, the law is sensitive to the well-being and future productivity of the environment in which humans live. And in fact the first interpretation is more likely because there is a parallel case:

> An ox or a sheep: you shall not slaughter it and its child on one day.
>
> (Lev 22:28)

And there is also the famous rule:

> You shall not cook a kid in its mother's milk.

It appears three times.[10]

More clearly related to compassion for animals is the commandment against mixing animals of unequal strength for work:

> You shall not plow with an ox and an ass together.
> (Deut 22:10)

Ancient to medieval to contemporary biblical scholars have understood this to be about protection of the weaker animal, which could suffer from being yoked with a much stronger animal for work.

Probably the laws that are most concerned with animal life are the laws about sacrifice. This comes as a surprise to most people in recent generations. They would expect just the opposite: that sacrificing creatures for our own religious purposes is the most blatant act of cruelty to animals. The problem is that so much time has passed since the major Western religions performed sacrifice that most people no longer know what it was, how it worked, or what its purpose was. The Bible requires that all sacrifice must take place only at one central place and nowhere else on earth.[11] For centuries, this meant the Temple in Jerusalem. In 70 CE the Romans destroyed that place. It has never been rebuilt. And so it has been nearly two millennia now that Jews and Christians have not practiced sacrifice. It is perfectly understandable, therefore, that most of us would not know very much about it. People imagine that it meant killing animals and burning up their bodies as a sort of gift to God. That is true of certain categories of offerings, but the vast majority of sacrifices, however, involved no such thing. On the contrary, sacrifice is the Hebrew Bible's regulation of how humans are to treat the animals that we eat. In biblical law, if you want to eat lamb chops, you cannot just take your sheep out in the field and butcher it. You must take it to the central altar, a priest must supervise you, and *you must kill the animal yourself*.[12] The priest is responsible for handling the animal's blood, which may not be eaten:

> because the flesh's life is in the blood.
> (Lev 17:11)

That is: everything about the process appears to be conveying to the people that, if they want to eat meat, they must recognize that they are taking a life. It cannot be casual. It must be done in a way that recognizes that life is sacred. Ironically, people in our age often think that the practice of sacrifice showed lack of care about the animal, when it is we who buy meat wrapped in plastic in markets so that it does not even look like the animal from which it came anymore. And most of us would be horrified if we watched the animals that we eat when they are slaughtered. The biblical practice showed more care and respect for the animal world.

People sometimes say that some of the biblical prophets are against sacrifice. That is not correct. They cite passages that are critical of sacrifice, such as when the prophet Samuel says to King Saul:

> Does YHWH take pleasure in burnt offerings and sacrifices as much as listening to YHWH's voice?! Here, listening is better than sacrifice, paying attention than the fat of rams!
> (1 Sam 15:22)

Some might take the prophet Samuel's words here to mean that he is against sacrificing, but that is manifestly not right. Samuel goes to sacrifice in the very next chapter![13] The issue in this text is rather that King Saul has just committed a violation of spoils in war, and he has tried to cover it up by saying that he kept certain animals for sacrifices. Samuel rejects his excuse and reminds him that their God prefers *listening* to *sacrificing*. It is not a rejection of sacrifice. It is a matter of getting one's priorities straight. Similarly, the prophet Jeremiah says:

> I didn't speak with your fathers and did not command them in the day that I brought them out of the land of Egypt about matters of offering and sacrifice. But rather I commanded them this thing, saying: Listen to my voice, and I shall be your God and you will be my people; and you shall walk in all the way that I shall command you, so that it will be good for you.
> (Jer 7:22f.)

Here, too, the issue is not that Jeremiah is against sacrifices. Jeremiah, who is himself a priest as well as a prophet, is rather engaged in this text in a polemic against other priests, who claim that their laws concerning sacrifice go back to the time of the exodus and Sinai. He quotes God here as denying their claim, but he never rejects sacrifice as the proper way to take animals' lives. He just says that the sacrificial matters were not commanded as part of the legislation at the time of the exodus from Egypt.[14]

Other prophets, as well, make strong statements about how God does not get any pleasure out of animal sacrifices so long as people are not being good to one another. Ministers and rabbis today likewise preach sermons in which they tell their congregations that people cannot lie and cheat all week and then make a donation to the church or synagogue to make it okay. They might even preach a fiery sermon, saying, "If that's how you behave, I don't want your donations!" But that does not mean that they are against donations. It is rather an old and central doctrine in Christianity and Judaism: the ritual without the ethical is meaningless. So the prophet Hosea says:

> I desired kindness and not sacrifice,
> and knowledge of God more than burnt offerings.
> (Hos 6:6)

And Amos says:

> If you make burnt offerings to me and your grain offerings, I won't be
>   pleased,
> And I won't look at a peace offering of your fatlings.
> [But] let judgment run down like water
> And virtue like a mighty stream.
> (Amos 5:22, 24)

Isaiah, too, quotes the deity as being fed up with sacrifices, incense, holidays, and even sabbaths, and even prayer! Instead, he says, learn to do good, help the orphan and the widow.[15] The prophet Micah makes this dramatic point as well in a famous passage.[16] This does not mean that these prophets were against prayer or the sabbath (which is, after all, one of the Ten Commandments!) or sacrifices of grain or animals. Indeed, to say that Samuel, Isaiah, Hosea, Amos, Micah, and Jeremiah were against sacrifice would mean that they were vegetarian or that they ate only game. But there is no basis for this in the texts. Sacrifice in itself, biblically, was about the proper recognition of what it means to take an animal's life. Prophets spoke dramatically, powerfully, and in poetry, so it is easy for one to misunderstand their point. The biblical scholar Gary Anderson makes this point well: "One should not mistake the prophetic critique of the cult for systematic theology. Prophetic discourse occurs in a highly charged atmosphere. It is a mixture of hyperbole, exalted rhetoric, and even polemic."[17] As in cases we saw in earlier chapters, the lesson is to use great caution when reading biblical texts that are in poetry.

While referring to being vegetarian, we should address the larger matter of vegetarianism here because it is the most frequently occurring aspect of humans' relationship to animal life on earth, and it is another issue of our time. Does one find support for it in the Bible or not? A common understanding is that, in the biblical creation account, humans are given only plants for food. Then, ten generations later, after the flood, God makes a covenant with Noah, giving all humans permission to eat animals as well. The creation account says:

> And God said, "Here, I have placed all the vegetation that produces seed that is on the face of all the earth for you and every tree, which has in it the fruit of a tree producing seed. It will be food for you."
> (Gen 1:29)

The post-flood covenant text says:

> Every creeping animal that is alive will be yours for food; I've given every one to you like a plant of vegetation, except you shall not eat meat in its life, its blood.
> (Gen 9:3–4)

So humans are pictured as being vegetarians for their first ten generations and then carnivorous after that. Whether one believes that this is history or understands it to be a story, the lesson is the same: a change takes place in the way humans relate to animals. The text does not say why this change occurs. One likely understanding is that humans have saved the lives of all of the animal species and thus have earned this power. Others see God making a concession to human appetites for meat in this story. The Bible only rarely depicts God's reasons for divine decisions, so we cannot know for sure.

Now this picture of a transition from plant-eating to plant-and-animal-eating is not quite as certain as we have implied so far. That humans before Noah do not eat animals is not entirely clear. Nine generations before Noah, Abel sacrifices animals (while Cain offers plants). And, contrary to most Bible art, Noah brings seven pairs of the sacrificeable animals onto the ark and only one pair of the others.[18] That is, there are fourteen cows and fourteen sheep on the ark, but there are two lions and two elephants. And in fact Noah offers a sacrifice as the first thing he does after the flood—and this is before God gives the permission to eat animals.[19] This is presumably the reason why he brought the extra sacrificeable animals onboard in the first place: if you have only two sheep, and you sacrifice one of them—no more sheep! We might imagine that Abel raises sheep only for wool and that Noah sacrifices only burnt offerings to God, not for his own food. But this is uncertain, so we cannot say for sure that the Bible pictures this two-stage development in humans' relationship to animals. Now, in critical biblical scholarship, the stories of Abel and of Noah's extra sacrificeable animals and of Noah's sacrifice after the flood are all part of one source (the text known as J), and the story of God changing the command from plants-only to plants-and-animals is from a separate source (the text known as P).[20] So, from this point of view, it is possible that these two source texts represented two different ideas of the development of meat-eating—and this would be the reason for the uncertainty in the present text.

Notably, the covenant that allows humans to eat meat includes a limitation: "you shall not eat meat in its life, its blood." One may understand this to be a prohibition against eating blood.[21] More commonly, though, it has been understood to mean that one must not eat a limb from a living animal.[22] Either way, though, it establishes that in the biblical perspective there are limitations. Humans' power over animals is not regarded as absolute, and it does not include cruelty.

The bottom line: one can make a case for or against vegetarianism on biblical grounds. On the one hand, one can say: the Bible (or at least one of its sources) regards vegetarianism to be humans' original, natural condition. On the other hand, one can say: yes, that is the original condition, but then the creator gives humans explicit permission to change and eat meat. We might consider the famous words of Isaiah:

A wolf will live with a sheep,
And a leopard will lie down with a kid,

> And a calf and a lion and a fatling together. . . .
> (Isa 11:6)

And even more relevant:

> A wolf and a lamb will feed as one,
> And a lion will eat straw like cattle.
> (Isa 65:25)

These prophecies suggest that humans might look forward to a future time when animals (including us) will no longer eat each other. (Though we might recall Woody Allen's cautionary words: "The lion will lie down with the lamb, but the lamb won't get much sleep.") In that case, from Eden to Isaiah, the Bible's overall picture would be that being vegetarian is the world's condition at the beginning of life on earth and is the condition to which it will return at a later stage. In the meantime—that is, in our time—we are in a middle condition in which some humans (and animals) eat animals while others choose not to. This is similar to the point we reached in our discussion of capital punishment. The Bible presents a picture of our world as it is in a middle period, a period of thousands of years between an ideal beginning and an ideal destiny. It presents humans on a course of growing up, and it offers some counsel on how to get there.

Cultural context

In the preceding chapters we pointed out many parallels with texts from the ancient Near East that helped picture biblical Israel in its historical context. Sometimes this showed connections, and sometimes it revealed interesting contrasts. In the case of the earth, we would say that the parallels are fewer, especially when it comes to connecting humans' virtue or corruption with the environment's fate.

The best-known ancient Mesopotamian creation myth pictures the gods creating humans in order to do work for the gods, not to subdue the earth or have dominion over it.[23]

There are ancient Mesopotamian versions of the flood story that have visible parallels to the Bible's account: a god tells a human (named Utnapishtim or Atrahasis) to build a boat and take pairs of animals. A flood comes, everything not on the boat dies, the boat settles on a mountain, the hero sends out three birds to see if the earth has dried, and when it is safe the humans disembark and offer a sacrifice. But there is an important difference: the Mesopotamian flood story does not connect that destruction of the environment to human corruption. Rather, the divine flood occurs because humans make noise, and this disturbs the gods.[24]

In the ancient Mesopotamian epic of Gilgamesh, the hero acquires a plant that enables a human who eats from it to become youthful again. It is not eternal life but at least very long life. But as Gilgamesh bathes in a cool pool, a snake steals this life-renewing plant from humans. (This is the etiology of why snakes slough their skin and seemingly come out youthful and live on.) So the story has the biblical element of a snake depriving humans of a "tree of life," but, unlike the Bible, it does not connect the snake and the loss of the tree of life to human wrongdoing.[25]

The law code of Hammurabi does not contain laws about yoking unequal animals together or driving mother birds away or cooking a kid in its mother's milk or any other laws like the biblical laws concerning animals' well-being. It contains many laws about harm done to animals, trees, and fields, but in every case it is about the financial loss to the owners, not about the animal or plant itself.[26]

There are ancient Mesopotamian laws such as the *mesharum* concerning periodic canceling of people's debts and their release from servitude, but they do not include the Bible's element of releasing the land by letting it lie fallow.[27]

The ancient Near Eastern religions are not based on covenants in which gods reward humans with blessings for their plants, animals, and land in return for the humans' following ethical and ritual laws.[28]

And Egyptians used fruit trees for building siege-works.[29]

We have heard people say that such things mean that the Bible and Israelite religion were thus morally superior to the pagan world. So we want to clarify right here that we do not mean that. We are making an observation about a distinction between the pagan and the biblical texts regarding humans' relationship with animals. We are only making that observation. We are not making chauvinist judgments about which culture was higher.

The overarching biblical idea, then, is this linking of human destiny with the plants and animals. The Bible begins with two accounts of creation,[30] and in both accounts the creations of humans, animals, and plants are told as part of a whole, within a few verses of each other. In the first creation story the plants and animals come first. In the second creation story the humans come first. But, for the Bible, there is no telling about the arrival of one without the other. In the Hebrew Bible it is not a picture of humans against nature. Humans are a part of nature.

This is an important fact in the context of the ancient Near East. In ancient Near Eastern pagan religion the gods are the forces in nature. The Mesopotamian god Enlil, known in Canaan as Baal, is the wind. Anu is the sky. Enki is the earth. Shamash is the sun. Yamm is the sea. Dagon is grain. Asherah is fertility. In Israelite religion, however, the deity is not any one of the forces of nature. Nothing in nature is more revealing about God than anything else. You cannot learn more about YHWH by contemplating the sea or the sky than by contemplating the sun or the wind or fire. The pagan gods as the forces in nature means that these forces are separate from humans, on a different plane of existence. But in Israelite religion the forces of nature and humanity are all on the same plane, all connected, while God is outside of all of that. The traditional thinking about this is: since in pagan religions the gods are nature personified, and in biblical theology God transcends nature, this is the origin of Western religions' lack of care for nature. But we think that the texts that we have seen indicate the exact opposite. Israelite religion, by taking away the divinity of natural forces, put those natural forces into the world of men and women. Humans were no longer seen as lower than nature. They were now part of it, related, connected, and, above all, *responsible* for it. The Hebrew Bible pictured God as giving humans power over nature. But, as we had occasion to quote earlier, with great power came great responsibility.

We commonly make the distinction: pagan religion was about nature, while Israelite religion was about history.[31] That is essentially true. But it does not mean that Israelite religion was oblivious to nature. Rather, from those first stories of Genesis, nature and human history are pictured as intertwined—inseparably intertwined. So the irony is that pagan religion was the most nature-centered religion of all time: Nature was sacred. Nature was the gods. But Israel's turn away from that religion of the divinity of nature led to a whole new commitment to nature and to responsibility for it—to all of it: animals, plants, and the earth itself.

This is not a radical view. It is not left wing or right wing. And it should come as no surprise. After all:

The first setting in the Bible is a garden.

The Bible's first story is about two trees.

Its second story is about a brother who tends animals and a brother who tends plants.

Its third story is about the devastation of the animals and plants and earth by a flood.

This is the context in which the rest of the Bible's stories, laws, and poetry are embedded. It did not have to start this way. There are a hundred other ways that the Bible might sensibly, meaningfully have begun. But it begins with the earth, with nature, with the environment, and humans' place in it. And in critical scholarship, in which scholars understand the Bible's opening chapters to come from two sources, this means that two different biblical authors saw the story this way. And, in both traditional and critical scholarship, it resonated in authors who came after them: in prophets, in historians, in their psalms, in wisdom texts, in laws.

One might think that it is only natural that the Bible should have such sensitivity toward nature because it came from a pastoral society. Its authors were countryfolk: shepherds and farmers. That makes sense, but only in the movies. Ancient Israel was primarily urban. The majority of its population and nearly all of its authors were city people. They may have been closer to the soil than most city people in industrial society today, but they lived in houses, not tents; they wore hats or helmets, not kaffiyehs; they worked in business or the military or the priesthood or were landowners or writers or poets or fishermen or scribes or metalworkers or musicians or builders. They farmed and raised animals as well, but that does not mean that they spent their days lying in the grass contemplating their relationship to the trees. The biblical passages that show care for the earth and its plants and animals do not come from a lost age of innocence. They come from a sophisticated, urban culture that still saw value in caring about the environment.

Implications for current issues

As with many sociopolitical issues, people use the Bible on all sides of debates about the environment. Some argue that the Bible empowers humans to control nature and use it indiscriminately for our purposes. Others argue that the Bible admonishes humans to care for nature as God's partners in sustaining creation. In 1967, a medieval historian, Lynn White Jr., published a brief essay in which he blamed biblically-based religions for justifying Western exploitation and abuse of the environment. He claimed that "by destroying pagan animism, Christianity made it possible to exploit nature in a mood of indifference to the feelings of natural objects."[32] Further, he felt qualified to interpret the Bible, writing that the biblical separation of humans from nature and the general anthropocentrism of the Bible lead biblical religions to the conclusion that "it is God's will that man exploit nature for his proper ends."

White's essay prompted an enormous variety of responses, some defending the Bible, others agreeing with his thesis, and others pointing to indigenous and Eastern religions as alternative spiritualities that were more environmentally friendly. The latter position argues that religions that sacralize nature inherently treat the earth better than those that relegate the divine to a separate realm of existence. The conclusion of many was that the key problem with the Bible's stance on the environment lay in God's words to the humans:

> Be fruitful and multiply and fill the earth and subdue it and dominate
> the fish of the sea and the birds of the skies and every animal that creeps
> on the earth.
> (Gen 1:28)

To scholars like White, this statement constituted a blank check to humans with respect to the earth: according to "the Bible," then, the earth is ours to rule, to use and abuse as we see fit. Indeed, there are politicians and policymakers who justify anti-environmental policies based on just such an understanding of this passage.[33] Most famous perhaps in this regard is a remark attributed to James Watt, Secretary of the Interior of the United States in the Reagan administration, who felt qualified to interpret the Bible, saying: "God gave us these things to use. After the last tree is felled, Christ will come back."[34] Political columnist and author Ann Coulter, who felt qualified to interpret the Bible, wrote: "The ethic of conservation is the explicit abnegation of man's dominion over the Earth. The lower species are here for our use. God said so: Go forth, be fruitful, multiply, and rape the planet—it's yours. That's our job: drilling, mining and stripping. Sweaters are the anti-Biblical view. Big gas-guzzling cars with phones and CD players and wet bars—that's the Biblical view."[35] The Interfaith Council for Environmental Stewardship, a Christian organization founded by radio evangelist James Dobson, dispensationalist[36] Rev. D. James Kennedy, Rev. Jerry Falwell, and Robert Sirico, a Catholic priest, also drew on this passage to shape its environmental policy. For them, Gen 1:28 proves human superiority over nature and allows for unchecked population growth and unrestrained resource use.[37] An Evangelical high school history textbook likewise argues that overpopulation and conservation are non-issues because "the Christian knows that the potential in God is unlimited and that there is no shortage of resources in God's Earth. The resources are waiting to be tapped."[38]

In the light of all the biblical texts we have seen here, we have to say that these views are utterly contrary to the evidence.[39] It would not even be out of line to say that they are a gross misinterpretation. We have written with reserve in preceding chapters about some common misunderstandings about biblical passages, but it is frankly incredible that anyone could take the biblical text about human dominion to mean a license to do whatever we want with the earth—as if a divine commandment does not mean to use dominion *well*, to use it for *good*. The boss leaves an employee in charge. The employee bullies everyone else and runs things irresponsibly and wastefully. He or she tells them, "The boss left me in charge, and I can do whatever I want." Would we admire this person's wisdom? And just wait until the boss gets back. Will he or she say, "Great job. That's just what I wanted you to do"?

The evidence from the prose, poetry, and law indicates rather that the biblical command must mean good use of dominion. From the story of Eden at the beginning of the Bible to Moses' closing words to his people at the end of Deuteronomy, the Bible is about humans making choices. The Five Books of Moses, the Torah, culminates with this idea that humans have to make a *choice* about how to use the power that they have acquired, a choice for good or bad, a choice for life or death. Moses concludes:

> I've put in front of you today life and good, and death and bad.
> I've put life and death in front of you, blessing and curse.
> And you shall choose life, so you'll live.
> (Deut 30:15, 19)[40]

We have seen this error many times: people read Genesis, or even just the beginning of Genesis, and form conclusions about what THE BIBLE says—missing where the story goes in the next thousand pages completely. What other book would we read this way? Would we do it with *Gone with the Wind*—and thus conclude that it is a book about a Southern family and interpret it without knowing that it involves a little thing called the Civil War? Or try it with *The Wizard of Oz*, and you'll never get past Kansas. (You may then find the title a little confusing.)

It may be that whether such human characteristics of "subduing" and "ruling" are creative or destructive is a matter of human free will. But there are consequences. The consequences demonstrate that, in the biblical texts, there is an inextricable link between human behavior and obedience to God's commandments, on the one hand, and our ability to live in harmony with the earth, on the other. In Leviticus 26 God lists blessings for the Israelites that include their own fertility and the fertility of the earth:

> If you will go by my laws, and if you will observe my commandments,
> and you will do them: then I shall give your rains in their time, and
> the earth will give its crop, and the tree of the field will give its fruit,
> and threshing will extend to vintage for you, and vintage will extend
> to seeding, and you will eat your bread to the full, and you will live in
> security in your land, and I shall give peace in the land, and you will
> lie down with no one making you afraid, and I shall make wild ani-
> mals cease from the land, and a sword will not pass through your
> land. . . .
> (Lev 26:3-6)

Conversely, the curses in Leviticus 26 threaten:

But if you will not listen to me and not do all these commandments, and if you will reject my laws, and if your souls will scorn my judgments so as not to do all my commandments, so that you break my covenant, I too, I shall do this to you. . . . I shall make your skies like iron and your land like bronze, and your power will be used up in vain, and your land will not give its crop, and the tree of the land will not give its fruit . . .
(Lev 26:14–20)

In other words, human moral, ritual, and ethical actions impact the land on which we live. This is not the kind of link between human action and environmental reaction that most people may think about; in our age's sense, the impact of humanity on creation is much more direct and immediate. In the biblical view, moral pollution leads to a lack of sustainability in a way that is not immediately relevant to current political talk about the environment. However, understanding this context does impact our understanding of the charge in Gen 1:28 to "dominate it and subdue" earth's creatures. Some, like Lynn White Jr., might argue that being made in the image of God and given dominion could suggest that, biblically, humans may reign as despots over the natural world. But in the Bible this seems to be more of a responsibility to maintain and sustain creation than to use and abuse it indiscriminately.

More consistent with the biblical conception was the conclusion of Pope Benedict XVI:

We cannot simply do what we want with this Earth of ours, with what has been entrusted to us.[41]

Elsewhere he urged:

Respect for creation is of immense consequence, not least because creation is the beginning and the foundation of all God's works, and its preservation has now become essential for the pacific coexistence of mankind.

Can we remain impassive in the face of actual and potential conflicts involving access to natural resources? All these are issues with a profound impact on the exercise of human rights, such as the right to life, food, health and development.

For this reason, it is imperative that mankind renew and strengthen that covenant between human beings and the environment, which should mirror the creative love of God, from whom we come and toward whom we are journeying.[42]

The very fact that there are principles established in the biblical laws about animals and plants reflects the fact that the human dominion over the earth is not a free-for-all. There are limits. And the dominion must be for *good*. Whether one turns to the Bible as authority or as a guide or just to see what is there, the point of the texts in this matter seems clear enough and consistent: humans have acquired enough power in the earth to do huge good or huge harm. Having eaten from the tree of knowledge of good and bad, they know the difference. Humans have a choice, and humans have the knowledge necessary to make that choice. As it says in Deuteronomy: choose life.

Afterword

You do not have to agree with everything here. Look to others as well, but be sure that they have real learning—and not just that they happen to know more about the Bible than you do. We have warned about doing Bible when one is not trained in it. It is a bad thing to do in general. But, if this book shows anything, it should be just how bad it is to do this on these questions that really matter to people, where the stakes are clear and high. These are matters with huge implications. Women's status, homosexuality—they involve humans' happiness and hurts, justice and injustice. Capital punishment and abortion—these are about life and death. The earth—this is about everyone and everything. These are not matters to be trifled with or practiced on. The texts about these things are not to be explained by people who cannot read them unless someone else does translations for them. Do not let unskilled, untrained people cut your hair, fix your car, treat your illnesses, invest your savings, defend you in court, or tell you what the Bible means.

We do not mean that biblical scholars are the only ones who can contribute to understanding the Bible. We know of wonderful contributions from non-biblical scholars, whose insights have been felt far afield from biblical studies. We have especial appreciation for some of Freud's insights[1] and for observations by literary critics Erich Auerbach[2] and our colleague Robert Alter, who brought perspectives from their own fields to share with us.[3] And we have had the pleasure of exchanging thoughts (and arguments) with our friend Mary Douglas, who has contributed to the anthropological perspective of many biblical scholars.[4] And one of the great joys of being university teachers is meeting colleagues from all different fields, sharing meals with them, talking with them, and learning facts, approaches, and methods from them. Our great friend, colleague, and teacher David Noel Freedman took this to the ultimate stage, saying that, since the Bible is something that matters to everyone, everyone has something important to say about it. He said that even the most outlandish, implausible, and even *ignorant* opinions about the Bible had merit because they prompted scholars to have to *defend their scholarship*. Non-experts with their opinions were the ones who enforced in scholars the need for method, for transparency of that method, for the gathering of sound evidence and the marshaling of scholarly arguments.

But one might say: scholars get things wrong, too. That is a fair point. Scholars have most certainly gotten things wrong. But, still, medical doctors have gotten things wrong as well, but we would not advise that therefore you should not go to them when you are sick. Rather, in any field, from Bible to medicine to law to history, we must find a balance between using our own judgment and common sense, on one hand, and knowing when to turn to professionals, on the other. So, we urge you, turn to the best sources you can, in person or through their books. Turn to men and women with advanced training and knowledge and, if you are fortunate, with wisdom as well.

We have often spoken of left versus right or of liberal versus conservative. Really, though, we recognize that these are an illusion. In reality, not so many things come down to two sides. Rather, there is a spectrum of beliefs, and there are varieties of points of view. Among those who oppose abortion, there are different views of what, if any, are acceptable exceptions. Among those who favor permitting abortion, there are different views of under what conditions they should occur. And there are many who are personally opposed to abortion but still hold the view that the woman involved must have a right to make the choice whether to have an abortion or not. Likewise with capital punishment, we see not only the either-or views of being for it or against it. Among people who favor it, there are still differing views of what crimes can be punished by execution, what means of execution are acceptable, at what age one can be executed, and whether one who is not completely mentally competent can be executed.

The more complicated these things get, the more they become a matter of wisdom.

Most wisdom comes from life experience, but we can also get wisdom from reading and studying the Bible, wrestling with its stories and laws and poetry, liking many of the things we find there, being troubled by others, studying the contradictions and differences among its many texts, arguing with other people about its meanings and its qualities, questioning our own values and opinions, contemplating what it was like to live in its world.

For many readers, the Bible itself is not the last stop on the journey. There is also the authority of their particular religious communities. In Catholicism, there is not just what the text says but also what the Church teaches about the meaning of that text. In post-biblical, rabbinic Judaism, which is now most retained in Orthodox and Haredi Judaism, there is not just what the text says but, rather, what the rabbis have taught that it means, with the rabbis claiming to have received an additional revelation, an oral Torah, from God. Even recognizing the more direct focus on the Bible itself, the doctrine of *Sola Scriptura*, in Protestant Christianity, there are still doctrinal matters of interpretation and authority in the various Protestant denominations as well. For some, the history of interpretation is interesting as a subject in its own right. For others it is far more than merely interesting. It is a matter of authority. The text means what the Church says it means. The text means what the rabbis have traditionally said it means. That is not our perspective—our first love is the text itself—but it is not a goal of this book to argue about that point.[5] For those who believe in these things within the context of their particular religious movements, denominations, or churches, that is a decision of faith on their part. Our task as biblical scholars here is only to treat the text itself, with recourse to archaeology and what we know of the ancient Near East's cultures when they provide helpful knowledge. What people do with this information, how they understand it, and how they relate to it is between them and their particular communities. What we hope is that those individuals and those religious authorities will agree with us that the goal is, in the first place, to be true to the text. After all, it is the Bible, for heaven's sake.

NOTES

Chapter 1

1. R. E. Friedman has made the case that the two stories are in fact by the same author in *The Hidden Book in the Bible* (San Francisco: HarperCollins, 1998), esp. pp. 17–19.

2. Gen 6:4; 12:20; 18:2; 20:8; 24:13, 32, 54, 59; 26:7; 29:22; 32:29; 34:20, 21, 22; 37:28; 38:21, 22; 39:11, 14; 46:32, 34.

3. Gen 17:23; 32:8.

4. Gen 13:8; 14:24; 17:27; 34:7; 43:15, 16, 17, 18, 24, 33; 44:3, 4; 47:2, 6.

5. See chapter 3, on women's status in the Bible.

6. Gen 19:25.

7. Gen 10:19; 13:10, 12, 13; 14:2, 8, 10, 11, 12, 17, 21, 22; 18:16, 20, 22, 26; 19:1, 4, 24, 28; Deut 29:22; 32:32; Isa 1:9, 10; 3:9; 13:19; Jer 23:14; 49:18; 50:40; Ezek 16:46, 48, 49, 53, 55, 56; Amos 4:11; Zeph 2:9; Lam 4:6.

8. The story of Noah's son Ham (Gen 9:20–27) may or may not be relevant to the question of homosexuality in the Bible. One cannot be sure of what Ham does to his father in this strange episode. Some think that he castrates his father; some think that he rapes him. Both are horrible, and the text complicates things further by having Noah curse Ham's son Canaan rather than Ham himself for whatever Ham has done. So we cannot know if this story involves homosexuality, and even if it does, it would be about homosexual rape, and of one's own father, rather than about homosexual acts in general. It is hardly a good source to use in forming a view of homosexuality and the Bible.

9. 2 Sam 1:26.

10. Similarly, see 1 Sam 18:1, 3, which says: "And Jonathan's soul was bound up with David's soul, and Jonathan loved him as himself. . . . And Jonathan and David made a pact because of his loving him as himself." This is a very hard passage to capture in English. The Hebrew word *nepeš* is translated here both as "soul" and as "self." It can also mean "life" or "person." No one English

term corresponds to its range of meaning. So it does not necessarily mean romantic, physical love between them, any more than the famous command to "love your neighbor as yourself" means that we should have romantic or physical love with everyone.

Also, the text ties their love to their making a pact. That indicates that this is a case of the technical use of the word *love* in the Bible in covenants. It is a legal term for the loyalty of one covenant party to the other. See Saul Olyan, "'And with a Male You Shall Not Lie the Lying Down of a Woman': On the Meaning and Significance of Leviticus 18:22 and 20:13," *Journal of the History of Sexuality* 5, no. 2 (October 1994), n. 3, for references, especially the work of W. L. Moran; and see R. E. Friedman, "Torah and Covenant," in *The Oxford Study Bible*, ed. J. Suggs (New York: Oxford University Press, 1991), pp. 154–63. Olyan acknowledges the covenantal language (love, brother) in 1 Samuel 18, but he rejects the idea that "more wondrous to me than the love of women" has anything to do with covenantal love. We agree. He says that this is because such a comparison is without parallel in the ancient Near Eastern texts. We say that it is just noncovenantal on the face of it. Who would say such a thing in the legal setting of a covenant? It is poetry.

11. 1 Sam 30:18; 2 Sam 3:2–5, 15:16. Perhaps more of a potential issue is 1 Sam 20:30, in which King Saul criticizes his son Jonathan's support of David, saying, "Son of a rebellious girl, haven't I known that you choose the son of Jesse [viz., David] to your shame and to the shame of your mother's nakedness!" But since Saul's tongue-lashing of Jonathan begins with cursing Jonathan's mother (calling Jonathan an s.o.b.) and then speaks of Jonathan's shame and the shame of *his mother's nakedness*, one usually takes it not as a reference to sex between David and Jonathan (that would presumably involve exposing David's nakedness, not Jonathan's mother's) but, rather, "the uncovering of Jonathan's mother's nakedness" by Saul at Jonathan's conception. Saul is saying that Jonathan is shaming his own birth and future bloodline. Thus the next line is "for as long as the son of Jesse lives upon the earth, neither you nor your kingdom shall be established."

On the other hand, though virtually everyone takes the phrase *na'ăwat hammardût* here as a cursing of Jonathan's mother, it really makes no sense when Saul is saying in the second part that Jonathan is doing wrong to shame that mother. And how does that phrase have anything to do with Jonathan's mother anyway? Literally it means "(someone or something) bent (or twisted) of rebellion." What does that mean? And putting the word *ben* in front of it does not have to mean that he is literally the son of it. It just means that he is a member of the class *na'ăwat hammardût*. And even the word *mardût* for rebellion occurs only here and nowhere else in the Hebrew Bible. They make it a reference to his mother by changing the *waw* to a *resh*, emending the text to read *na'ărat* instead of *na'ăwat*. But that is just speculation because they do not know what to make of the text. All we know is that Saul is accusing

Jonathan of being something bad in terms of being rebellious. Saul's larger point is that Jonathan is shaming his own birth, expressed in gross terms about Jonathan's mother's nakedness in order to dramatize that point. But the fact remains that he words it in terms of Jonathan's *choosing* David; that he twice uses the word *shame*, which is uncalled for if all that Saul means is that Jonathan is making a terrible political error; and that he uses the term *nakedness*, which is not a neutral term when it comes to the Bible's treatment of forbidden sexual relationships. (It is used that way about forty times in P and also twice in the J story of whatever Ham does to Noah.) The bottom line: The passage probably does not allude to homosexuality; but one cannot be 100 percent certain of that.

12. E.g., 2 Sam 3:7–11, 16:21–22; and see also Ken Stone, "Sexual Power and Political Prestige," *Bible Review*, August 1994: pp. 28–31, 52–53.
13. See Jacob Milgrom, *Leviticus 17–22*, The Anchor Bible (New Haven: Yale University Press, 2000), vol. 2, pp.1567–68; Howard Eilberg-Schwartz, *The Savage in Judaism* (Bloomington: University of Indiana Press, 1990), p. 183; David Biale, *Eros and the Jews* (Berkeley: University of California Press, 1997), p. 29.
14. Lev 15:16, 17, 18, 32; 22:4; Num 5:13.
15. Lev 18:20.
16. Milgrom supposes that Israel's priests would have favored postmenopausal sex because they could point proudly to the case of Abraham and Sarah (Gen 17:17; 18:9–13) who give birth to Isaac in their old age (Milgrom, *Leviticus 17–22*. The Anchor Bible, Yale University Press, 2000: p. 1568). That story, however, could just as easily show the opposite. After all, it is a story of a miracle, a birth announced in advance by God Himself. It sheds no authoritative light on the legal question of when every other couple on earth would cease to expect to achieve pregnancy through sex.
17. The story of Noah and his son Ham, the story about Sodom, and this story of Onan were all written by the same author: the composer of the text known as J and other texts. This author's works involve the least law of any of the documents that the Torah contains. And this author's works rarely include an implication that all people are supposed to learn how to behave from these stories. See Friedman, *Hidden Book in the Bible*.
18. Milgrom, *Leviticus 17–22*, p. 1568, criticizing the view of E. S. Gerstenberger, *Das Tritte Buch Mose: Leviticus* (Göttingen: Vandenhoeck und Ruprecht, 1993); English translation by D. W. Stott, *Leviticus* (Louisville: Westminster-John Knox), p. 297.
19. Douglas argues that the pattern of forbidden foods in Leviticus 11 and Deuteronomy 14 indicates that categories of clean and unclean foods were determined by whether a creature is a pure example of its type or transgresses boundaries (fish that do not swim with fins, birds that dive into the water, animals that have "hands," insects that fly instead of creep). Mary Douglas,

Purity and Danger: An Analysis of Concepts of Pollution and Taboo (New York: Frederick A. Praeger, 1966; reprint, London: Harmondsworth, 1970), 54–72. Building on this premise, Thomas M. Thurston ("Leviticus 18:22 and the Prohibition of Homosexual Acts," in *Homophobia and the Judaeo-Christian Tradition*, ed. M. L. Stemmeler and J. M. Clark (Dallas: Monument Press, 1990), pp. 7–23) suggests that the prohibition of male homosexuality in Leviticus should be understood in the same way; the receptive male in anal intercourse transgresses the boundaries of male and female. Frederick Greenspahn refers to this argument, citing Mary Douglas, in "Homosexuality and the Bible," *CCAR Journal*, Fall 2002, p. 42. Saul Olyan cites Douglas in "'And with a Male You Shall Not Lie the Lying Down of a Woman,'" p. 200n.

20. Richard Elliott Friedman, *Commentary on the Torah* (San Francisco: HarperCollins, 2001), pp. 346–48.

21. This law code is known in biblical scholarship as the Holiness Code: Leviticus 17 to 25. Various scholars see it as larger or smaller than these chapters. Two scholars recently have regarded it as far larger, extending through much of the Torah. They trace it to a "Holiness School," a community of priests who interacted with the Priestly source of the Torah over a long period of time. We have questioned this entire claim to the existence of a Holiness School; R. E. Friedman, *The Bible with Sources Revealed* (San Francisco: HarperCollins, 2003), 218n, 296–97n.

22. See note 30 below.

23. On the identification and dates of the Bible's source texts, see R. E. Friedman and Shawna Dolansky, "Pentateuch," in *Encyclopedia Judaica* (Farmington Hills, Mich.: Thomson Gale, 2007), vol. 15, pp. 730–53; R. E. Friedman, *Who Wrote the Bible?* 2nd ed. (San Francisco: HarperCollins, 1996); Friedman, *The Bible with Sources Revealed*; R. E. Friedman, "Torah," in *The Anchor Bible Dictionary* (New York: Doubleday, 1992), vol. 6, pp. 605–22; and bibliographies therein of works on this subject.

24. See the comments on Lev 18:21 and 20:2 in Friedman, *Commentary on the Torah*; and L. E. Stager, "Carthage: A View from the Tophet," in *Phonizier im Westen*, ed. H. G. Niemeyer (Mainz: Madrider Beitriige 8, 1982), pp. 155–66.

25. Num 31:17–18, 35; Judg 21:11–12.

26. Olyan, "'And with a Male You Shall Not Lie the Lying Down of a Woman,'" n. 15.

27. Friedman, *Commentary on the Torah*, pp. 377, 387; Friedman, *The Bible with Sources Revealed*, pp. 220, 222.

28. Olyan, "'And with a Male You Shall Not Lie the Lying Down of a Woman,'" p. 203.

29. Richard Elliot Friedman, "The Deuteronomistic School," in *Fortunate the Eyes That See, David Noel Freedman Festschrift*, ed. Astrid B. Beck, Andrew H. Bartelt, Paul R. Raabe, and Chris A. Franke (Grand Rapids: Eerdmans, 1995), pp. 70–80.

30. Olyan accepts Israel Knohl's (and Jacob Milgrom's) division of the Priestly portions of the Torah into sources and editing from two schools: the Holiness School (H) and the Priestly School (P). But this is not a proposal that has yet been proven (and in our view it is wrong). Its fulcrum (Numbers 15) is incorrect, and it has not yet addressed the major evidence against it (notably the continuity of the P texts). Olyan talks about "the H Source" and "H tradents" and "the final H redactors" and an "H School." He says that the prophet Ezekiel "is widely viewed as sharing H's purity system (in other words, Ezekiel belonged to the Holiness School)." Olyan says, "The laws of Lev 18 and 20 must also be analyzed with reference to the larger Holiness Source" ("'And with a Male You Shall Not Lie the Lying Down of a Woman,'" p. 197). But he does not know that the Holiness source exists. And then he criticizes many others' studies because they do not take this H editorial development into account: "the possibility that these laws had a prehistory before the activity of the final H tradents and redactors . . . either is never raised or is given insufficient attention" ("'And with a Male You Shall Not Lie the Lying Down of a Woman,'" p. 198). But we do not know that there were H tradents and redactors. (On the other hand, Olyan's critique of each of these studies on actual errors of fact and assumptions is excellent.)

    Olyan defends the distinction between H and P in one case: sex with a menstruating woman ("'And with a Male You Shall Not Lie the Lying Down of a Woman,'" p. 204). He says that both Lev 20:18, which he ascribes to H, and Lev 15:24, which he ascribes to P, prohibit this but that they each have a different treatment for this same offense: uncleanness in H, *karet* (cutting off) in P. But Olyan is not correct. These two laws are about two different things. Lev 15:24 is about what happens if some menstrual blood gets on a man during sex: he, like the woman, is unclean for seven days. Lev 20:18 is about a man who deliberately takes action to expose a woman's menstruating genitals and have sex with her: he and she are both cut off.

31. Milgrom, *Leviticus 17–22*, p.1569.

32. Our former student Joshua Van Ee, in an unpublished paper, "Homosexuality in the Hebrew Bible," cites Milgrom, *Leviticus 17–22*, pp. 1786ff, claiming that this law applies only in the land, and Van Ee rejects that view, as we do.

33. Lev 18:3–4, 24–28; 20:22–24.

34. Frederick Greenspahn raises this point also: "One might go even further and observe that it is physically impossible for men to have sex with other men in (exactly) the same way that they would with women" ("Homosexuality and the Bible," p. 43).

35. These reservations about the term are expressed in Friedman, *Commentary on the Torah*, p. 637.

36. See N. H. Snaith, *Leviticus and Numbers* (London: Nelson, 1967), p. 126; and John Boswell, *Christianity, Social Tolerance, and Homosexuality* (Chicago: University of Chicago Press, 1980), p. 100. Olyan rightly questions this

assumption; see Olyan, "'And with a Male You Shall Not Lie the Lying Down of a Woman,'" p. 181n.6, p. 197.

37. 1 Kgs 14:24. We should note that the Greek text here reads a different word (*qešer*) rather than *qadeš*, so we cannot be sure of the correct reading.

38. 1 Kgs 15:9–12, 22:47, 23:7. Many English translations since the King James Version have translated this term as "sodomite," which is unjustified and misleading since we do not know what the *qĕdēšîm* were or what acts they performed and with whom. Several recent translations have corrected this and no longer use the term *sodomites* in these passages.

39. A. Bray, *Homosexuality in Renaissance England* (New York: Columbia University Press, 1995); D. F. Greenberg, *The Construction of Homosexuality* (Chicago: University of Chicago Press, 1988), pp. 24–29, 344; R. B. Parkinson, "'Homosexual' Desire and Middle Kingdom Literature," *Journal of Egyptian Archaeology* 81 (1995): pp. 57–76.

40. See, for example, Lawrence Stager, "The Archaeology of the Family in Ancient Israel," *BASOR* 260 (1985): pp. 1–3; L. G. Purdue, J. Blenkinsopp, J. J. Collins, and Carol Meyers, *Families in Ancient Israel* (Louisville, Ky.: Westminster John Knox Press, 1997), esp.pp. 1–103. See also our discussion in chapter 3.

41. Stager, "Archaeology of the Family in Ancient Israel"; Carol Meyers, "The Family in Early Israel," in Purdue et al., *Families in Ancient Israel*, pp. 26–32; Beth Nakhai, "Female Infanticide in Iron II Israel and Judah," in *Sacred History, Sacred Literature: Essays on Ancient Israel, the Bible and Religion in Honor of R. E. Friedman on His Sixtieth Birthday*, ed. S. Dolansky (Winona Lake, Ind.: Eisenbrauns, 2008), pp. 257–72.

42. See Meyers, "Family in Early Israel," esp. pp. 26–32: "the labor of juveniles was essential to the household economy. . . . The essential role of child labor in agrarian households meant, of course, that childbearing was an additional component of a woman's life. Reproduction in such a context was not simply a biological process; and it certainly was not a process subject to the choice of an individual woman as she reached childbearing age. Rather, it was integral to the fundamental issue of family survival. . . . Economic conditions mandated large families."

43. L. Stager, "Archaeology of the Family"; C. Meyers "Family in Early Israel," and J. Blenkinsopp, "The Family in First Temple Israel," pp. 48–103, in Purdue et al., *Families in Ancient Israel*.

44. Carol Meyers, *Discovering Eve: Ancient Israelite Women in Context* (Oxford: Oxford University Press, 1988), pp. 112–13.

45. "If a man violates his own mother, it is a capital crime. If a man violates his daughter, it is a capital crime. If a man violates his son, it is a capital crime," in G. R. Driver and J. C. Miles, *Assyrian Laws*, vol. I (London: Oxford University Press, 1952), 71 #189.

46. Middle Babylonian period: 1595–1000 BCE.

47. From Martti Nissinen, *Homoeroticism in the Biblical World: A Historical Perspective* (Minneapolis: Augsburg Fortress, 1998), p. 27. As Nissinen explains it, *assinnu* are men whom Ishtar has made into women (biologically male, socially female) and who have special healing powers.

48. Middle Assyrian Law (MAL) A 19.[

49. MAL A 18.

50. MAL A 20.

51. *The Contendings of Horus and Seth* (Papyrus Chester Beatty I) dates to the twelfth century BCE.

52. Egyptian Middle Kingdom: 2040–1640 BCE; Egyptian New Kingdom: 1550–1070 BCE.

53. Parkinson, "'Homosexual' Desire and Middle Kingdom Literature," p. 67.

54. Greenberg, *Construction of Homosexuality*, p. 149.

55. Ibid., esp. p. 142. See also K. J. Dover, *Greek Homosexuality*, 2nd ed. (Cambridge: Cambridge University Press, 1989); D. M. Halperin, *One Hundred Years of Homosexuality* (New York: Routledge, 1990), esp. pp. 4–16; A. Richlin, *The Garden of Priapus* (New York: Oxford University Press, 1992); A. Richlin, "Not before Homosexuality," *Journal of the History of Sexuality* 3 (1993): pp. 523–73; D. M. Halperin , John J. Winkler, Froma I. Zeitlin, eds., *Before Sexuality: The Construction of Erotic Experience in the Ancient Greek World* (Princeton: Princeton University Press, 1990); R. Padgug, "Sexual Matters: Rethinking Sexuality in History" (1979), reprinted in *Hidden from History: Reclaiming the Lesbian and Gay Past*, ed. M. B. Duberman, Martha Vicinus, and George Chauncey (London: Penguin Books Limited, 1989), pp. 54–64.

56. Plato, *Symposium* 8.21.

57. Plato, *Laws* 837C.

58. Plutarch, *Moralia* 768E.

59. Plato, *Symposium* 181D.

60. For example, Lev 24:22.

61. Olyan argues that the original form of the laws in Leviticus 18 and 20 did make this distinction and that only the penetrating partner was intended. But this is dependent on his view that the law is only about anal intercourse. As we discussed above, we do not believe that that view is justified by the language of the text (the plural *miškĕbê 'iššāh*). If it is not just about anal intercourse, then this distinguishing of the penetrating partner from the passive one is not correct. Also, the text in Lev 20:13 does specifically refer to both partners, without this distinction between them, and condemn them to identical punishment. Olyan argues that this part of the verse was added by an editor, so that "we may speak of at least two identifiable stages in the development of Lev 18:22 and 20:13" ("'And with a Male You Shall Not Lie the Lying Down of a Woman,'" 187–88). In the first stage, it only prohibited and punished the insertive partner, not the receptive partner. In the second stage,

an editor changed it to be a complete ban on male–male sex. But this is based on Olyan's undefended acceptance of Israel Knohl's theory of composition and editing by a "Holiness School," which we have questioned. See note 30 above. He bases his claim of an editorial change in Lev 20:13 on the fact that there is a change from singular to plural in that verse, but such singular-to-plural transitions are so common in the wording of biblical laws that it would be inconceivable to trace all of them to editors. They occur in the two verses that precede this one (Lev 20:11–12) and in the last verse of Leviticus 18, which Olyan himself attributes entirely to a single editor. The singular-to-plural switches simply do not mean what Olyan thought. They are a normal formulation, not a mark of editors changing a text. In each of these passages, it is just as easy to see the author of the text wording it this way as to see a second person coming in and wording a change this way.

62. Lev 18:25, 28; 20:22.

63. Lev 18:29.

64. Gen 46:34.

65. Gen 43:32.

66. Gen 14:18, 29:22.

67. Exod 8:22. The cases involving Joseph and his brothers come from the biblical source J. This case involving Moses and Pharaoh comes from the biblical source E. So this understanding of the word *tōʿēbāh* as a relative term is not just the view of one biblical author. It appears in both of the Bible's foundational prose sources.

68. See Olyan's note on the term in its ancient Near Eastern context, which has a sense of "the violation of a socially constructed boundary" ("'And with a Male You Shall Not Lie the Lying Down of a Woman,'" p. 180 n. 3).

69. We credit Joshua van Ee for this and other interesting insights.

70. Deut 7:25, 12:31, 17:1, 18:12, 22:5, 23:19, 25:16, 27:15; Prov 3:32; 11:1, 20; 12:22; 15:8–9, 26; 16:5; 17:15; 20:10, 23.

71. Robert Gagnon, in *The Bible and Homosexual Practice* (Nashville: Abingdon, 2001), says, "It is contextually clear that what is generally meant by *tôʿēbâ* is something that 'Yahweh hates' (Deut 12:31; Prov 6:16)," p. 120. But this is not at all "contextually clear." And it is not what the verse he cites in Deuteronomy says. It refers only to a *tōʿēbāt yhwh*, which homosexuality (and other cases) is *not*. And the poem in Proverbs that he cites likewise relates to *tōʿēbôt* to *God*. Contextually they mean the opposite of what Gagnon asserts. Gagnon, a New Testament scholar, makes strong assertions on several other matters in the Hebrew Bible where matters are more complex than he indicates.

72. Deut 17:4.

73. Deut 32:8; Ps 82.

74. For example, Gen 6:6–7; Exod 32:14; Num 14:11–20.

75. Gen 3:22.

76. Spider-Man.

Chapter 2

1. Bruce Metzger and Michael D. Coogan, eds., *The Oxford Companion to the Bible* (New York: Oxford University Press, 1993), p. 4.

2. Num 35:16, 17, 18, 21, 31; Deut 22:26; Judg 20:4; 1 Kgs 21:19; 2 Kgs 6:22; Isa 1:21; Jer 7:9; Hos 4:2; 6:9; Ps 62:4 (62:3 in English); 94:6. The Hebrew term *rṣḥ* can also be used in certain cases of manslaughter, in which the manslayer takes a life by accident and has to flee to one of the cities of refuge for judgment, which we shall discuss in the chapter on capital punishment; Num 35:6, 11, 25–28; Deut 4:42; 19:3–6; Josh 20:3–6; 21:13, 21, 27, 32, 36. In one anomalous passage it refers to the execution of a murderer ("the murderer shall be murdered"), apparently to convey the principle of justice matching the crime; Num 35:27, 30. It is not the usual term for execution. In poetry, it can refer to the slaughter of a human by an animal; Prov 22:13.

3. Laws 209–13.

4. Tablet I, laws 17–18; see James B. Pritchard, ed., *Ancient Near Eastern Texts Relating to the Old Testament*, 3rd edition (Princeton: Princeton University Press, 1969), hereafter: ANET, p. 190, for changes in the compensatory amounts over time.

5. MAL A 50–52; see ANET, p. 185, and Victor H. Matthews and Don C. Benjamin, *Old Testament Parallels: Laws and Stories from the Ancient Near East* (Mahwah, N.J.: Paulist Press, 2007), p. 129.

6. William Propp, *Exodus 19–40*, The Anchor Bible (New York: Doubleday, 2006), pp. 221–30.

7. 1 Sam 17:51; and see 14:13.

8. 2 Sam 1:9, 10, 16; and see Judg 9:54. David has the Amalekite executed, but not for murder. He is executed for having "killed YHWH's anointed [Hebrew *mašíaḥ*]."

9. Ps 34:22.

10. Ps 109:16.

11. Eccl 6:3.

12. Eccl 7:1.

13. Gen 6:17 and 7:15 in the Priestly source (P); Gen 2:7 and 7:22 in J.

14. Isa 42:5; Job 27:3.

15. John M. Riddle, *Eve's Herbs: A History of Contraception and Abortion in the West* (Cambridge: Harvard University Press, 1997), p. 35.

16. Riddle, pp. 35–36. Riddle notes that the Egyptians also manufactured medicines for use as contraceptives as early as 1900 BCE, based on recipes in the Kahun Papyrus.

17. *BAM* 246; see translation and discussion in R. D. Biggs, "Conception, Contraception, and Abortion in Ancient Mesopotamia," in *Wisdom, Gods and Literature: Studies in Assyriology in Honour of W. G. Lambert*, ed. A. R. George and I. L. Finkel (Winona Lake, Ind.: Eisenbrauns, 2000), pp. 1–14.

18. See, for example, Kahun Papyrii Nos. 21 (3/6), 22 (3/7), in Hildegard von Dienes, Hermann Grapow, and Wolfhart Westendorf, *Ubersetzung der medizinischen Texte*, 2 vols. (Berlin: Grundriss der Medizin de Alten Agypter, iv, 1958), vol. 1, p. 277, vol. 2, p. 211. For further discussion, see John M. Riddle, "Oral Contraceptives and Early-Term Abortifacients during Classical Antiquity and the Middle Ages," *Past and Present*, no. 132 (August 1991), pp. 3–32; and G. Devereux, "A Typological Study of Abortion in 350 Primitive, Ancient, and Pre-industrial Societies," in Harold Rosen, *Abortion in America: Medical, Psychiatric, Legal, Anthropological, and Religious Considerations* (Boston: Beacon Press, 1967).

19. MAL A 53; see ANET, p. 185; and Matthews and Benjamin, *Old Testament Parallels*, p. 129.

20. Abortion was legal in ancient Greece and Rome, with various texts describing herbal and other methods used to induce abortions. In his *Theaetetus*, Plato mentions a midwife's ability to induce abortion in the early stages of pregnancy (149d). Although the Hippocratic Oath forbade abortion by vaginal suppository, other methods were advocated: Hippocrates himself advised a prostitute to induce a miscarriage by jumping up and down, touching her buttocks with her heels at each leap (see further Mary R. Lefkowitz and Maureen R. Fant, "Intercourse, Conception and Pregnancy," in *Women's Life in Greece and Rome: A Source Book in Translation* [Baltimore: Johns Hopkins University Press, 1992], p . 341). Aristotle advised: "When couples have children in excess, let abortion be procured before sense and life have begun; what may or may not be lawfully done in these cases depends on the question of life and sensation" (*Politics* 7.16).

21. Code of Hammurabi, Laws 131 and 132.

22. G. R. Driver, "Two Problems in the Old Testament Examined in the Light of Assyriology," *Syria* 33 (1956): p. 75.

23. Josephus, *Antiquities* III:vi:6.

24. Tikva Frymer-Kensky, "The Strange Case of the Suspected *Sotah* (Numbers V 11–31)," in *Women in the Hebrew Bible*, ed. Alice Bach (New York: Routledge, 1999), pp. 463–74.

25. Gen 46:26; Exod 1:5.

26. Gen 24:2, 9.

27. So W. McKane, "Poison, Trial by Ordeal and the Cup of Wrath," *Vetus Testamentum* 30 (1980): p. 474; Bach, *Women in the Hebrew Bible*, p. 461; Jacob Milgrom, "The Case of the Suspected Adulteress," in *The Creation of Sacred Literature*, ed. Richard Elliott Friedman (Berkeley: University of California Press, 1981), p. 75; H. C. Brichto, "The Case of the *Sota* and a Reconsideration of Biblical 'Law,'" *Hebrew Union College Annual* 46 (1975): pp. 55–70.

28. Milgrom, "Case of the Suspected Adulteress," p. 74.

29. Matt 1:18–25.

30. Gen 25:23, 24; 30:2; 38:27; Deut 7:13; 28:4, 11, 18, 30, 53.
31. The phrase *taḥat yad*, "under the hand," is the way to say that, as in Gen 41:35.
32. Admittedly, the text says in Num 5:22 "to swell the womb and make the thigh sag," but it is not certain whether God causes this (see verse 21) or the water causes it. Also the verse may mean "at the womb's swelling and the thigh's sagging" in the unvocalized text; the vowel points that we read in the text now were inserted in the medieval period by scribes who already understood the text to refer to something other than pregnancy.
33. Num 35:30; Deut 17:6.
34. Richard Elliott Friedman, *Commentary on the Torah* (San Francisco: HarperCollins, 2001), pp. 440–41; Shawna Dolansky, *Now You See It, Now You Don't* (Winona Lake, Ind.: Eisenbrauns, 2008), p. 80.
35. G. B. Gray, *A Critical and Exegetical Commentary on Numbers* (Edinburgh: T&T Clark, 1903), p. 49.
36. Driver, "Two Problems in the Old Testament Examined in the Light of Assyriology," pp. 73–77. Driver went on to say that, since the procedure would not in fact produce these results, it was psychological.
37. Frymer-Kensky, "Strange Case of the Suspected *Sotah*," pp. 467–68.

Chapter 3

1. On the role of the Nazirite, who can be male or female, see the comment on Num 6:2 in Richard Elliott Friedman, *Commentary on the Torah* (San Francisco: HarperCollins, 2001), pp. 442–43.
2. 2 Kgs 11:1–16; 2 Chr 22:10–23:15.
3. Carol Newsom and Sharon Ringe, eds., *The Women's Bible Commentary* (Louisville: Westminster/John Knox, 1982), p. xiii.
4. *The Women's Bible Commentary*, p. xv.
5. Frank Moore Cross and David Noel Freedman, *Studies in Ancient Yahwistic Poetry*, 2nd ed. (Grand Rapids, Mich.: Eerdmans, 1997), p. x.
6. See Katharine Doob Sakenfeld, *Just Wives? Stories of Power and Survival in the Old Testament and Today* (Louisville, Ky.: Westminster/John Knox, 2003).
7. D. N. Freedman, "Early Israelite Poetry and Historical Reconstructions," in *Pottery, Poetry, and Prophecy* (Winona Lake, Ind.: Eisenbrauns, 1980), pp. 167–78; Robert G. Boling, *The Early Biblical Community in Transjordan* (Decatur, Ga: Scholars Press, 1988), pp. 57–63.
8. Baruch Halpern, *The Emergence of Israel in Canaan* (Chico, Calif.: Scholars Press, 1983), p. 47. Susan Ackerman, too, has emphasized the enormous importance of Deborah's leadership role in the Judges account. See her "Digging Up Deborah: Recent Hebrew Bible Scholarship on Gender and the Contribution of Archaeology," *Near Eastern Archaeology* 66, no. 4 (December 2003): pp. 176–77; and *Warrior, Dancer, Seductress, Queen: Women in Judges and Biblical Israel* (New York: Doubleday, 1998).

9. A cover story in *Newsweek* on "Women of the Bible" (December 8, 2003, pp. 48–59) mentions only Eve, Sarah, Rebekah, Rachel, Miriam, and Hagar. And Sarah, Rebekah, and Rachel are noted only in terms of their being wives of patriarchs. Hagar, too, is discussed with regard to her being Abraham's concubine. And Miriam is mentioned only as being the sister of Moses.

10. Some other political terms likewise use familial words to express political relationships. Halpern mentions *bĕrît 'aḥîm* (a "covenant of brothers") in Amos 1:9.

11. Halpern, *Emergence of Israel in Canaan*, p. 149. Jean Bottéro also recognized the phrase to mean "Mother of Israel" (*Mere d'Israël*) in *Naissance de Dieu: La Bible et l'historien* (Paris: Editions Gallimard, 1986); English translation by Kees Bollw, *The Birth of God: The Bible and the Historian* (University Park: Pennsylvania State University Press, 2003), p. 111. Bottéro also acknowledges the antiquity of the Song of Deborah, calling it "The Oldest Biblical Poem," pp. 107–18.

12. 2 Sam 1:21.

13. Danna Nolan Fewell, in *The Women's Bible Commentary*, Carol Newsom and Sharon Ringe, eds., *Women's Bible Commentary* (Louisville, Ky.: Westminster/John Knox, 1982), p. 69. Cf. Barnabas Lindars, "Deborah's Song: Women in the Old Testament," *Bulletin of the John Rylands Library of Manchester* 65, no. 2 (Spring 1983): pp. 158–75.

14. For other recent studies on the Song of Deborah, see Charles L. Echols, *"Tell Me, O Muse": The Song of Deborah (Judges 5) in the Light of Heroic Poetry*, Library of Hebrew Bible/Old Testament Studies 487 (New York: T&T Clark, 2008); and the excellent bibliography in T. Mayfield, "The Accounts of Deborah (Judges 4–5) in Recent Research," *Currents in Biblical Research* 7, no. 3 (2009): pp. 306–35.

15. Ex 15:1.

16. This is discussed in Friedman, *Who Wrote the Bible?* pp. 190–91.

17. C. Fontaine discusses this in *With Eyes of Flesh: The Bible, Gender and Human Rights* (Sheffield Phoenix, 2008) and points out that "Though we may explicate all the various meanings of his grammatical ambiguities and put forth gentler readings, interpreters should not and cannot ignore the very real, negative effects on the lives of actual women that the 'plain sense' of this text, read over the centuries, created" (207). As our discussion here will emphasize, however, the plain sense of the text may be quite different from what people understood it to be. The negative effects may derive from readers' misunderstandings rather than from something that was native to the text itself.

18. See Eccl 12:8.

19. Robert Gordis declared it "an erroneous division of the words *'mr hqhlt*," in *Koheleth—The Man and His World* (New York: Schocken, 1951) p. 284. He notes that this is in fact how it is written in Eccl 12:8. True, but that is just as likely to disprove this claim of a scribe's mistake as to prove it. Why would the

scribe get it wrong in one place and right in another? More supportive of Gordis's view is that the Greek text reads it the same (with a masculine verb) in both passages.

20. This is treated in detail, and the photo appears, in Richard Elliott Friedman, *The Disappearance of God* (Boston: Little, Brown, 1995), pp. 150–52; and in H. F. Peters, *My Sister, My Spouse: A Biography of Lou Andreas-Salome* (New York: Norton, 1962), pp. 103, 141.

21. See Eccl 9:9.

22. The first account is in Gen 1:1 to 2:3. The second is in 2:4b–24. The first is attributed in critical scholarship to the source known as P. The second is attributed to the source known as J.

23. Gen 2:18, 20.

24. This was first pointed out by R. David Freedman. He noted a number of cases in which *'ezer* occurs in biblical poetry in parallel with the word *'ōz*, which means strength (see, e.g., Ps 46:2). Richard Friedman also noted that the King of Judah whose name is Uzziah ("YHWH is my *'ōz*") in the book of Chronicles is usually called Azariah ("YHWH is my *'ezer*") in the book of Kings, which likewise suggests that the two words are interchangeable.

25. Pss 121:2; 124:8; 146:5, 33:20; 115:9–11; Ex 18:4; Deut 33:72, 629. Philip King and Lawrence Stager also cite Ps 70:6 in this regard in *Life in Biblical Israel* (Louisville, Ky.: Westminster/John Knox, 2001), p. 49.

26. Phyllis Trible likewise writes, "we misread if we assume that these judgments are mandates. They describe; they do not prescribe." ("Depatriarchalizing in Biblical Interpretation," *Journal of the American Academy of Religion* 41, no. 1 [March 1973]: p. 41).

   If the story is polemical or prescriptive at all, it is about goddesses, not women: all of the elements of ancient Near Eastern mother goddesses appear in the story—the serpent and the magical trees, the fertile earth from which humanity emerges, and the etymology of Eve as "the mother of all living"—and yet the story is explicitly, insistently, about a male God who creates alone. See further Shawna Dolansky, "A Goddess in the Garden? The Fall of Eve," in *Milk and Honey: Essays on Ancient Israel and the Bible in Appreciation of the Judaic Studies Program at the University of California, San Diego*, ed. S. Malena and D. Miano (Winona Lake, Ind.: Eisenbrauns, 2006), pp. 3–21.

27. The *śāṭān* in Job, for example, is not the wicked creature of Milton and rabbinic literature.

28. At the other end of the spectrum, Susan Niditch writes in Newsom and Ringe's *Women's Bible Commentary*, p. 14, "The woman gives him the fruit and he eats as if he were a baby (3:6)." That reading, unjustifiably denigrating the man, is no more defensible from the text than the readings that unjustifiably denigrate the woman.

29. Gen 25:1–4.

30. Known as Sarai until the blessing that brings her a son also changes her name to Sarah, Gen 17:15–16.

31. Gen 11:29–30:. "Abram's wife's name was Sarai. . . . And Sarai was infertile. She did not have a child."

32. See the provocative analysis and appended bibliography by J. Cheryl Exum, "Who's Afraid of the Endangered Ancestress?" in *Women in the Hebrew Bible*, ed. Alice Bach (New York: Routledge, 1999), pp. 141–56.

33. Gen 16:2.

34. Gen 30:1–13.

35. Gen 17:16.

36. Gen 16:6.

37. Gen 17:17.

38. Gen 17:21.

39. This is discussed in Friedman, *Commentary on the Torah*, on Gen 25:23; and in *The Disappearance of God*, pp. 111–12.

40. Gen 27:13.

41. Gen 27:37.

42. Gen 27:46.

43. In the context of the narrative, this may even be understood as yet another deception by Rebekah: so that Isaac will not know the real reason why Jacob is going to her family (viz., to flee before Esau's fury), she tells him that it is because she wants him to marry family. Esau's wives had been a source of aggravation to her anyway (Gen 26:35), so she uses this. This speculation is complicated because the matter of Esau's foreign wives is in the source known in critical scholarship as P. The merger of that source with the other story, which is from the source known as J, by an editor thus created something new and tantalizing in the final narrative.

44. This later becomes a law in Deut 25:5–10.

45. Gen 38:9.

46. 2 Samuel 13.

47. Genesis 34.

48. Ex 1:11–12; Gen 16:6.

49. Judg 19:24; 20:5.

50. See below, pp. 100–101.

51. An important recent women's Bible commentary published by the Union for Reform Judaism unfortunately translates the last two terms as "he lay her down" and "raped her." The discussion of the story and of that wording in the translation there is by one of the authors of this book. See Shawna Dolansky and Risa Levitt Kohn, "Dinah and Shechem: Sex and Social Status," in *The Torah: A Women's Commentary* (New York: URJ Press, 2007), pp. 190–95. Despite the translation provided therein, Dolansky and Levitt Kohn insist in their commentary that "the word *'innah* should not be translated as rape." ("he lay her down" is grammatically wrong in any case. The form in English

is "laid her down"—past tense of a transitive verb. If ever there was a case in which one should not make the common error in the grammar of *lie* and *lay*, it is in translating this biblical text.)

52. For example, M. Weinfeld, *Deuteronomy and the Deuteronomistic School* (Oxford: Oxford University Press, 1972), p. 286; L. M. Bechtel, "What if Dinah Is Not Raped? (Genesis 34)," *JSOT* 62 (1994): pp. 19–36; and Victor P. Hamilton, *The Book of Genesis: Chapters 18–50, vol. 2*, New International Commentary on the Old Testament (Grand Rapids: Eerdmans, 1995), pp. 351–73.

53. Susanne Scholz, "Was It Really Rape in Genesis 34? Biblical Scholarship as a Reflection of Cultural Assumptions," in *Escaping Eden*, ed. H. C. Washington, S. L. Graham, and P. Thimmes (New York: New York University Press, 1999), pp. 182–98.

54. A building has been excavated that may have been the palace of David. That is the opinion of the archaeologist who directed the excavation, Eilat Mazar. She discussed this in "Did I Find King David's Palace?" *Biblical Archaeology Review* 32, no. 1 (January/February 2006): pp. 16–27. See also "King David's Palace Is Found, Archaeologist Says," *New York Times*, August 5, 2005; and the challenges raised by Israel Finkelstein, Ze'ev Herzog, Lily Singer-Avitz, and David Ussishkin in "Has King David's Palace in Jerusalem Been Found?" *Journal of the Institute of Archaeology of Tel Aviv University* 34, no. 2 (2007): pp. 142–64.

55. 2 Sam 11:27.

56. 2 Sam 12:10–12.

57. 2 Sam 12:22.

58. 2 Sam 18:24.

59. See Alice Ogden Bellis, *Helpmates, Harlots, and Heroes: Women's Stories in the Hebrew Bible* (Louisville, Ky.: Westminster/John Knox, 1994), pp. 149ff., for discussion and references.

60. 1 Kings 1.

61. Another biblical example is instructive. The Torah refers to "women who worked at the entrance of the Tent of Meeting." Later, in the book of 1 Samuel, the high priest Eli's sons have illicit sex with these women who work at the Tabernacle at Shiloh (1 Sam 2:22–26). As pointed out in Friedman, *Commentary on the Torah*, "The temptation of males in power to take advantage of their high position in the eyes of women who work under them has persisted for centuries. It is criticized in the *Tanak*. In the case of the Shiloh priests, it is one of the acts that leads to the downfall of that priestly house" (comment on Ex 38:8).

62. Ex 20:14 in the Hebrew text (20:13 in the English text); Deut 5:18 in the Hebrew text (5:17 in the English text).

63. Deut 22:22. On execution as a penalty for adultery, see the chapter on capital punishment below.

64. Betrothal in the Bible is an intermediary step on the way to marriage. It is more than getting engaged and less than actual marriage.

65. Code of Hammurabi, Article 129; see ANET, p. 171.

66. Code of Hammurabi, Article 130; see ANET, p. 171.

67. Hittite Law, Article 197; see ANET, p. 196.

68. Middle Assyrian Law (MAL), Tablet A, Article 15, indicates that such punishments can include death, setting her free, or cutting off his wife's nose. If the husband chooses the latter option, the male adulterer is castrated and his face is mutilated.

69. MAL, Tablet A, Articles 12–14; see ANET, p. 181.

70. MAL A 59; ANET, p. 185.

71. Notice that the word *degraded* occurs here, the same word that people have taken to mean rape in the case of Dinah. Here a man is said to have degraded the woman even though it is a law that explicitly prevented a rape. So, again, it is absolutely incorrect to claim that the terms in the Dinah story establish the episode as a rape.

72. MAL A 41; ANET, p. 183.

73. Deut 15:12.

74. There are complex textual problems. William Propp shows these and treats them in detail in *Exodus 19–40*, The Anchor Bible (New York: Doubleday, 2006), pp. 118–20, 196–203.

75. Gen 3:16.

76. See Friedman, *Commentary on the Torah*, p. 241: "Here we are told of a case in which a man is explicitly not free to dominate a woman. Even in that worldview that recognized male control of women, there was an understanding that this control is not unlimited. This point of respect for women and recognition of a legal right that they possessed was a first small step in the breakdown of that worldview. And this passage teaches that a commandment can change or become limited even within the Torah itself."

77. Shalom Paul, *Studies in the Book of the Covenant in the Light of Cuneiform and Biblical Law* (Leiden: Brill, 1970).

78. Deut 22:28–29.

79. MAL A 55; ANET, p. 185.

80. MAL A 56; ANET, p. 185.

81. Gen 24:57–58.

82. Ex 20:12; Deut 5:16.

83. Lev 19:3.

84. We should acknowledge that the Greek text, the Septuagint, has the reverse order in Lev 19:3, with the father coming first, as in the Ten Commandments. The Qumran text (the Dead Sea scrolls) has the same as the Masoretic Text, which we have cited here, with the mother coming first. The Septuagint also has the father preceding the mother in Lev 21:2, while the Masoretic Text and the Qumran text have the mother first.

85. Ex 21:15.
86. Lev 20:9.
87. Deut 27:16.
88. Lev 12:2. See Friedman, *Commentary on the Torah*, on this verse and on Lev 10:10.
89. Deut 22:19.
90. Deut 22:17.
91. It comes in post-biblical rabbinic Jewish law.
92. Deut 24:1–4; Jer 3:1–5. Compare MAL A 37 (ANET, p. 183), which states that a man can divorce his wife with impunity, and he can do so with or without giving her any money, property, or alimony.
93. The ceremonies related to birth, puberty, marriage, and death in Judaism are largely established in post-biblical, rabbinic sources. They are not found in the Bible.
94. Lev 21:13–14.
95. Ex 7:11–12, 22; 8:3.
96. Ex 8:14–15; 9:11.
97. Deut 18:10; cf. 2 Chr 33:6; Mal 3:5; (and Babylonian magicians in Dan 2:2). On the meaning of magic in the Bible, see Shawna Dolansky, *Now You See It, Now You Don't* (Winona Lake, Ind.: Eisenbrauns, 2008).
98. There are two other possibilities, as proposed in D. N. Freedman and Shawna Dolansky, "Omitting the Omissions: The Case for Haplography in the Transmission of the Biblical Texts," in *"Imagining" Biblical Worlds: Studies in Spatial, Social, and Historical Constructs in Honor of James W. Flanagan*, ed. David M. Gunn and Paula M. McNutt (New York: Sheffield, 2002), pp. 99–116, with preference given to the second: first, this is the only place in the entire Hebrew Bible where we find the (presumably) feminine form of this word—it is possible that *mkšph* here is masculine, in agreement with LXX, and the final *h* is the rare accusative singular ending. Second, Syriac and two versions of the Targum also have *mkšp* in agreement with LXX *pharmakous*: perhaps the original text read *mkšp 'w mkšph l' thyh*—quadruple homoeoarcton causes the masculine singular form of the verb to be lost by haplography as the scribe's eye skipped from *mkšp* to *mkšph*, preserving only the feminine form.
99. 1 Samuel 28.
100. Friedman and Dolansky Overton, "Death and Afterlife: The Biblical Silence," in *Judaism in Late Antiquity, Volume Four: Death, Afterlife, Resurrection, and the World to Come*, ed. Alan J. Avery-Peck and Jacob Neusner (Leiden: Brill, 2001), pp. 35–59.
101. Lev 20:27.
102. In the law of the goring ox, women are explicitly distinguished from slaves. If an ox gores a woman, the law is the same as when an ox gores a man: execution of the owner of the ox (if it is not the first time the ox has gored).

If an ox gores a slave, male or female, the penalty is less severe: a payment to the slave's owner (Ex 21: 28–32).

103. C. J. H. Wright also challenges this view on the basis of the biblical laws and stories about women ("Family," in *The Anchor Bible Dictionary* [New York: Doubleday, 1992], vol. 2, p. 766), as do Phyllis Bird, who contends that although wives were included among a man's possessions, they were not reckoned as property ("Women [OT]," in *The Anchor Bible Dictionary*, vol. 6, p. 956), and King and Stager, (*Life in Biblical Israel*, p. 49). See also Carol Meyers, *Discovering Eve: Ancient Israelite Women in Context* (Oxford: Oxford University Press, 1988), pp. 182–83; and Phyllis Trible, *Texts of Terror: Literary-Feminist Reading of Biblical Narratives* (Philadelphia: Fortress, 1984).

104. Compare, for example, Middle Assyrian Law (1114–1076 BCE), Article 59, which states that "Except in those instances prescribed by law, a husband may punish his wife, without liability, whipping her, pulling out her hair, or mutilating her ears" (Victor H. Matthews and Don C. Benjamin, *Old Testament Parallels: Laws and Stories from the Ancient Near East* [New Jersey: Paulist Press, 1997]). As noted above, Middle Assyrian Law also allows a man to determine his wife's punishment in certain cases of adultery. The Bible does not arrogate such power and authority to husbands.

105. Drorah O'Donnell Setel, in Newsom and Ringe, *Women's Bible Commentary*, p. 33.

106. Ex 1:9, 20; 3:12; 4:16, 21; 7:14; 8:4, 25, 28; 9:6; 10:7; 11:2–3; 12:27, 33–34, 36; 13:17–18, 22; 14:5, 31; 17:1, 6; 18:10.

107. Deut 17:17.

108. Numbers 30.

109. Or "the Queen of heaven"; Jer 7:18, 44:17ff.

110. William G. Dever, *Did God Have a Wife?* (Grand Rapids: Eerdmans, 2005); David Noel Freedman, "Yahweh of Samaria and His Asherah," *Biblical Archaeologist*, (December 1987): pp. 243ff.

111. 2 Kings 23.

112. So Dever, *Did God Have a Wife?* p. 94.

113. So Meyers, *Discovering Eve: Ancient Israelite Women in Context* (Oxford: Oxford University, 1998), pp. 162–63, and *Households and Holiness: The Religious Culture of Israelite Women* (Minneapolis: Augsberg Fortress, 2005), pp. 28–29; and Ziony Zevit, *The Religions of Ancient Israel: A Synthesis of Parallactic Approaches* (London: Continuum, 2001), pp. 271–72.

114. Shawna Dolansky, "Re-Figuring 'Fertility' Figurines from Biblical Judah," forthcoming.

115. For a discussion of this perspective, see A. Brenner, *A Feminist Companion to the Song of Songs* (London: Sheffield Academic Press, 1993), pp. 58–97.

116. J and the other source texts can now each be read individually in R. E. Friedman, *The Bible with Sources Revealed* (San Francisco: HarperCollins, 2003). This book contains the first five books of the Bible, the Torah, with

its sources identified by distinct colors and fonts. It includes a presentation of the evidence and arguments concerning the analysis of the sources.

117. *Who Wrote the Bible?* p. 86.

118. Jo Ann Hackett, "Women's Studies and the Hebrew Bible," in *The Future of Biblical Studies: The Hebrew Scriptures*, eds. R. E. Friedman and H. G. M. Williamson (Atlanta: Scholars Press, 1987), pp. 141–67.

119. Including the comparative literature scholar Harold Bloom, but see R. E. Friedman, "Is Everybody an Expert on the Bible?" *Bible Review* 7, no. 2 (1991): pp. 16–18, 50–51; and "Scholar, Heal Thyself," *Iowa Review* 21 (1991): pp. 33–47.

120. Friedman, *The Hidden Book in the Bible* (San Francisco: HarperCollins, 1998). This book contains a restoration and an English translation of the entire work along with the evidence and arguments for its being the first great work of prose.

121. Hannelis Schulte, *Die Enstehung der Gerschichtsschreibung im Alten Israel*, published in Beihefte zur Zeitschrift für die alttestamentliche Wissenschaft, 128 (Berlin: De Gruyter, 1972).

122. Schulte's and Friedman's work and the early date of the text are discussed by John Barton, "Dating the 'Succession Narrative,'" in *In Search of Pre-Exilic Israel*, ed. John Day (London: T&T Clark, 2004), pp. 100–104.

123. King and Stager, *Life in Biblical Israel*, p. 49.

124. Ackerman, "Digging Up Deborah," 173; emphasis added. See also on p. 174: "None of the texts of our primary written source, the Hebrew Bible, for example, *can be said* to have been authored by a woman, and neither do any of the extra-biblical texts that we have from ancient Israel show any indication of female authorship. We thus lack the direct witness such texts might provide regarding the nature of ancient Israelite women's lives and experiences."

125. Meyers, *Discovering Eve*, p. 6.

126. For an excellent summary of this history, see R. Radford Ruether, *Goddesses and the Divine Feminine: A Western Religious History* (Berkeley: University of California Press, 2005), especially chapters 1 and 9.

127. General scholarship on this issue is represented well in M. Conkey and R. Tringham, "Archaeology and the Goddess: Exploring the Contours of Feminist Archaeology," in *Feminisms in the Academy*, eds. D. Stanton and A. Stewart (Ann Arbor: University of Michigan Press, 1995), pp. 199–247.

128. Elizabeth Cady Stanton, *The Woman's Bible* (Seattle: Coalition Task Force on Women and Religion, 1974 [1895, 1898]), p. 25.

129. *The Woman's Bible*, p. 21. Actually, the garden of Eden story (attributed to the source J) was written before the creation story in Genesis 1 (attributed to the source P).

130. See, for example, Carol P. Christ and Judith Plaskow, eds., *Womanspirit Rising* (San Francisco: Harper and Row, 1979); Naomi Goldenberg,

Changing of the God (Boston: Beacon Press, 1979); and Ruether, *Goddesses and the Divine Feminine*. For a useful discussion of the origins of a split between "Reformers" and "Revolutionaries," see M. Weaver, "Who Is the Goddess and Where Does She Get Us?" *Journal of Feminist Studies* 5 (Spring 1989), pp. 49–64.

131. See the useful delineation of these positions in Alice A. Keefe, "Stepping In/ Stepping Out: A Conversation between Ideological and Social Scientific Feminist Approaches to the Bible," *Journal of Religion and Society*, (1999) pp. 1–14.

132. For example, Esther Fuchs, *Sexual Politics in Biblical Narrative*, JSOT Supplement Series (Sheffield Academic Press, 2000); L. R. Russell, ed., *Feminist Interpretation of the Bible* (Philadelphia: Westminster, 1985). In *Discovering Eve*, Carol Meyers further critiques such feminist scholarship on the basis of a faulty set of assumptions and biases regarding what constitutes "patriarchy": "While broadly correct in associating patriarchy with ancient Israel, their assessment of patriarchy as a limiting, harsh, enslaving, or oppressive system, or as a fact that is painful to consider, reveals a serious methodological flaw. They are misusing the term patriarchy as a synonym for male dominance or for a system in which male traits are valued over female ones. Worst of all, their judgmental response to biblical patriarchy unfairly uses contemporary feminist standards (which hope for an elimination of sexist tradition by seeking to promulgate equality between the sexes) to measure the cultural patterns of an ancient society struggling to establish its viability under circumstances radically different from contemporary western conditions," pp. 25–26. See also the recent compilation of essays entitled *With Eyes of Flesh* by C. Fontaine, in which she uses "gender and a focus on universal Human Rights, especially the rights of women and girls, to explore the roles that biblical religion *interpreted in the present* may play in both empowering and obstructing such concepts" (p. xi). We added the emphasis in the quotation above; as we have been arguing all along, the relationship between what the text says in its context and the way in which it is read today is crucial in seeking its meaning.

133. See, for example, the variety of works by Marija Gimbutas, in addition to Riane Eisler, *The Chalice and the Blade, Our History Our Future* (Peter Smith, 1994); and Merlin Stone, *When God Was a Woman* (New York: Harcourt Brace Jovanovich 1978).

134. See Conkey and Tringham, "Archaeology and the Goddess."

135. For example, in his best-selling *Listen, America!* Jerry Falwell wrote that the Bible advocates unequivocal patriarchy: "In the Christian home the father is responsible to exercise spiritual control and to be the head over his wife and children. . . . In the Christian home, the woman is to be submissive." (New York: Bantam Books, 1989), p. 159.

Chapter 4

1. Exod 21:13; Numbers 35; Deut 19:1–13; Josh 20:7f.

2. Julius Wellhausen, *Prolegomena to the History of Ancient Israel*, trans. J. S. Black and A. Menzies (Edinburgh: Adam and Charles Black, 1885), p. 33 [German edition, 1883]. See Moshe Greenberg, *Studies in the Bible and Jewish Thought* (Philadelphia: JPS, 1995), p. 44.

3. Robert Polzin, *Late Biblical Hebrew: Toward an Historical Typology of Biblical Hebrew Prose* (Atlanta: Scholars Press, 1976); Gary Rendsburg, "Late Biblical Hebrew and the Date of P," *Journal of the Ancient Near Eastern Society* 12 (1980): pp. 65–80; Ziony Zevit, "Converging Lines of Evidence Bearing on the Date of P," *Zeitschrift für die Alttestamentliche Wissenschaft* 94 (1982): pp. 502–9; Jacob Milgrom, *Leviticus 1–16*, The Anchor Bible (New York: Doubleday, 1991), pp. 3–13; "Numbers, Book of," in *The Anchor Bible Dictionary* (New York: Doubleday, 1992), vol. 4, pp. 1148–49; Avi Hurvitz, "The Evidence of Language in Dating the Priestly Code," *Revue Biblique* 81 (1974): pp. 24–56; Avi Hurvitz, *A Linguistic Study of the Relationship between the Priestly Source and the Book of Ezekiel*, Cahiers de la Revue Biblique (Paris: Gabalda, 1982); בין לשון ללשון (Jerusalem: Bialik Institute, 1972); "Continuity and Innovation in Biblical Hebrew—The Case of 'Semantic Change' in Post-Exilic Writings," *Abr-Naharaim*, supp. 4 (1995): pp. 1–10; "The Usage of שׁשׁ and בוץ in the Bible and Its Implication for the Date of P," *Harvard Theological Review* 60 (1967): pp. 117–21; Ronald Hendel, "'Begetting' and 'Being Born' in the Pentateuch: Notes on Historical Linguistics and Source Criticism," *Vetus Testamentum* 50 (2000): pp. 38–46.

4. Leviticus 16.

5. Lev 16:32.

6. Greenberg, *Studies in the Bible and Jewish Thought*, p. 48. He cites the gold plate on the high priest's forehead as expiatory in Exod 28:36ff.

7. Exod 21:28–32. On this and the related law in Hammurabi (Laws 250–52), see Brettler, *How to Read the Bible* (Philadelphia: Jewish Publication Society, 2005), pp. 69–71; William Propp, *Exodus 19–40*, The Anchor Bible (New York: Doubleday, 2006), pp. 122–23, 233–36. In Hammurabi, there is not capital punishment; the owner pays a penalty.

8. The ox is killed in any case. One might argue that this constitutes an expiation, but this is uncertain since normally one cannot equate an animal's life to a human's in law. Lev 24:17–18 says explicitly: "A man who will strike any human's life shall be *put to death*, and one who strikes an animal's life shall pay for it."

9. J. J. Villenga, in J. M. Martinez, W. D. Richardson, and C. A. Brown, *The Leviathan's Choice: Capital Punishment in the Twenty-First Century* (Lanham, Md.: Rowman & Littlefield, 2002), p. 110, calls the law about execution for murder in Exod 21:12, 14, "the commentary on the commandment" and

criticizes those who take the Decalogue commandment "out of its context and interpret it without regard to its qualifying words." But the law in the Covenant Code in Exodus 21 is most certainly not commentary on the Decalogue commandment. The Covenant Code and the Decalogue are different sources and had no such relationship.

10. Greenberg, *Studies in the Bible and Jewish Thought*, p. 47.

11. Hammurabi, laws 6–11, 21, 25; Middle Assyrian Laws, law 3; Laws of Eshnunna, law 13. Hittite law is an exception. See Greenberg, *Studies in the Bible and Jewish Thought*, p. 47.

12. J. M. Martinez, W. D. Richardson, and C. A. Brown, in *Leviathan's Choice*, assert that the Old Testament use of the death penalty includes "stealing some types of property" among acts that "are not capital offenses today, but they were terrible offenses for the children of Israel" (p. 11). As we have seen, however, a distinguishing feature of the Bible is that there is no capital punishment for property offenses. Since Martinez et al. never say what property they have in mind, at best we can surmise that they may have misunderstood the *ḥerem* laws to be about stealing property. We shall discuss this later in this chapter.

13. R. E. Friedman, "The Tabernacle in the Temple," *Biblical Archaeologist* 43 (1980): pp. 241–48; R. E. Friedman, *The Exile and Biblical Narrative*, Harvard Semitic Monographs (Atlanta: Scholars Press, 1981), pp. 48–61, 137–40; *Who Wrote the Bible?* pp. 174–87; "Tabernacle," in *The Anchor Bible Dictionary*, vol. 6, pp. 292–300.

14. The case of Jephthah of course comes to mind, but its many complexities make it well beyond the scope of a treatment here, where all we are pointing out is that human sacrifice and murder are two separate offenses in biblical law codes.

15. Shawna Dolansky, *Now You See It, Now You Don't* (Winona Lake, Ind.: Eisenbrauns, 2008); Richard Elliott Friedman and Shawna Dolansky Overton, "Death and Afterlife: The Biblical Silence," in *Judaism in Late Antiquity*, vol. 4: *Death, Afterlife, Resurrection, and the World to Come*, ed. Alan J. Avery-Peck and Jacob Neusner (Leiden: Brill, 2001), pp. 35–59.

16. And one cannot avoid the implications of this verse by suggesting that it comes from a different source than the creation story in Genesis 1. In critical biblical scholarship, both of these texts (Genesis 1 and 9) come from the same source (P).

17. If they were ever practiced, it was only in the biblical period, because the Jews never again had courts with the power to carry out executions through biblical law.

18. As pointed out in *Commentary on the Torah*, older translations make this: "The voice of your brother's blood is crying," but that is wrong. The word for "voice" or "sound" is singular. The word for blood is plural and must therefore be the subject of the plural verb "crying." The word "sound" must be understood as an interjection.

19. 2 Samuel 14. We have made the case that this story and the Cain and Abel story were written by the same author. See Friedman, *The Hidden Book in the Bible* (San Francisco: HarperCollins, 1998).

20. Gen 4:8.

21. Lev 24:10–16, 23.

22. Num 15:32–36.

23. Many centuries later, rabbinic sources categorized for Judaism the kinds of acts that constituted violations of the law against sabbath labor, but these are not found in the biblical text.

24. Joshua 7 (and 6:18).

25. Greenberg, *Studies in the Bible and Jewish Thought*, p. 36.

26. 2 Kgs 12:21–22; 14:6; 2 Chr 24:25–26; 25:4.

27. Deut 24:16.

28. Joshua 9.

29. Gen 37:24; 39:20ff.; Jer 38:6ff.

30. Jer 37:15.

31. 1 Kgs 22:27; 2 Chr 18:25–27.

32. Jer 37:21; see 32:2–12; 33:1; 37:21; 38:6, 13, 28; 39:14,15.

33. Jer 20:2; 29:26.

34. F. Brown, S. R. Driver, C. A. Briggs, and W. Gesenius, *A Hebrew and English Lexicon of the Old Testament* (Oxford: Oxford University Press, 1979).

35. Ezra 7:26.

36. Neh 3:25 and 12:39 speak of a gate and a court of *maṭṭārāh* in this period, but we do not know what they are, and we are never told for what they were used.

37. Raymond Westbrook, "Punishments and Crimes," in *The Anchor Bible Dictionary*, vol. 5, p. 555.

38. Edward M. Peters, "Prison before the Prison: The Ancient and Medieval Worlds," in *The Oxford History of the Prison*, ed. N. Morris and D. J. Rothman (Oxford: Oxford University Press, 1995), pp. 3–47.

39. Judg 16:21.

40. The Hebrew (Masoretic) text has *bêt happĕquddôt*. See K. van der Toorn, "Judges XVI 21 in the Light of the Akkadian Sources," *Vetus Testamentum* 36 (1986) pp. 248–53. K. van der Toorn and Moshe Weinfeld ("The Covenant of Grant in the Old Testament and in the Ancient Near East," *Journal of the American Oriental Society* 90 [1970]: pp. 190, 193), refer to *bit kili* ("house of detention"), cognate to the Hebrew *bêt hakkele'*. The Judean King Manasseh is also bound in fetters; 2 Chr 33:11.

41. 2 Kgs 17:4; 25:27; Jer 52:31; 2 Chr 36:6.

42. Deut 25:1–3. The law code of Hammurabi allows sixty strokes (law 202). The Middle Assyrian laws allow from twenty to one hundred twenty.

43. There is a similar (though not identical) law in the Middle Assyrian laws (law A 8).

44. The other passage is Lev 24:19–20.
45. *Law* 195.
46. *Law* 95.
47. *Law* 95.
48. *Law* A 9.
49. *Law* A 15.
50. There is a law concerning a thief who cannot pay back for his theft: "He shall be sold for his theft" (Exod 22:2). As William Propp noted in his commentary on Exodus, this is "so that he may repay his victim from the proceeds." It does not establish that sale into slavery is an option that the courts could use as a punishment. See Propp, *Exodus 19–40*, p. 241.
51. 1 Kgs 2:26.
52. 1 Kgs 2:36f.
53. Greenberg (*Studies in the Bible and Jewish Thought*, p. 34), gives numerous examples of such vicarious punishments in other ancient Near Eastern law codes.
54. Lev 5:1, 17; 7:18; 17:16; 19:18; 20:17, 19; Num 5:31; 30:16. W. Zimmerli, *ZAW* 66 (1954), pp. 8–11; Tikva Frymer-Kensky, "The Strange Case of the Suspected *Sotah* (Numbers V 11–31)," in *Women in the Hebrew Bible*, ed. Alice Bach (New York: Routledge, 1999), p. 469: "in the Priestly writings [it] means in effect that there is to be no human penalty; punishment is to be expected from God."
55. Gen 17:14; Exod 30:33, 38; Lev 7:20, 21, 25, 27; 17:4, 9, 14; 18:29; 19:8; 20:17, 18; 22:3; 23:29; Num 9:13; 15:30, 31; 19:13, 20.
56. Lev 22:3.
57. Lev 5:21–26.
58. Deut 17:6.
59. Glen H. Stassen, "Deliverance from the Vicious Cycles of Murder," in Martinez et al., *Leviathan's Choice*, p. 127.
60. Deut 16:20.
61. For a thorough discussion of the ethics involved in the issue of capital punishment, see Stephen Nathanson, *An Eye for An Eye? The Immorality of Punishing by Death*, 2nd ed. (Lanham, Md.: Rowman & Littlefield Publishers, 2001).

Chapter 5

1. The German biblical scholar Gerhard von Rad observed long ago that this is the meaning of Gen 1:28, thus: "Man also receives from God's hand the blessing that enables him to propagate and increase." See *Genesis: A Commentary*, trans. J. H. Marks (Philadelphia: Westminster, 1961), p. 58; original German edition, *Das erste Buch Mose, Genesis* (Göttingen: Vandenhoeck und Ruprecht, 1956). Likewise the distinguished legal scholar David Daube in *The Duty to*

Procreate (Edinburgh: Edinburgh University Press, 1977), pp. 1–42; and the biblical scholar Calum Carmichael: "We have, then, in Genesis 1:28 a blessing, not a duty." In *Sex and Religion in the Bible* (New Haven: Yale University Press, 2010), pp. 2, 182n.

2. See also Exod 1:7. Also Exod 23:25–30 begins with a promise of divine blessing (v. 25) and later says "you will be fruitful" (v. 30).

3. Cf. Deut 6:3.

4. Nahum Sarna, *Genesis: The Traditional Hebrew Text with New JPS Translation/ Commentary* (Philadelphia: JPS, 1989), pp. 13, 353, note 23.

5. Comment on Gen 1:28, in Richard Elliott Friedman, *Commentary on the Torah* (San Francisco: HarperCollins, 2001), p. 13.

6. For those who are interested in this matter of the Bible's authors and how it came to be written, see R. E. Friedman, *Who Wrote the Bible?* 2nd ed. (San Francisco: HarperCollins, 1997). The flood story with the two sources identified appears there on pp. 54–59. It also appears on the NOVA Web site with the sources distinguished by distinct colors, readable separately or combined, at http://www.pbs.org/wgbh/nova/bible/flood.html. A translation of the entire Pentateuch with the sources identified by distinct colors and fonts appears in R. E. Friedman, *The Bible with Sources Revealed* (San Francisco: HarperCollins, 2003).

7. Gen 19:4.

8. Isa 1:9,10; 3:9; 13:19; Jer 23:14; 49:18; 50:40; Ezek 16:46, 48, 49, 53, 55, 56; Amos 4:11; Zeph 2:9.

9. Deut 5:14.

10. Exod 23:19; 34:26; Deut 14:21. Some have argued that this ban is a ritual matter rather than a concern for the animals. William Propp thoroughly rejects this view. See his commentary, *Exodus 19–40*, The Anchor Bible (New York: Doubleday, 2006), pp. 284–86; Jeffrey Tigay likewise, *The JPS Torah Commentary: Deuteronomy* (Philadelphia: JPS, 1996), p. 140; and Friedman, *Commentary on the Torah*, pp. 250, 612.

11. Leviticus 17; Deuteronomy 12.

12. Lev 1:5, 11; 4:15. Gary Anderson, "Sacrifice and Sacrificial Offerings (OT)," in *The Anchor Bible Dictionary* (New York: Doubleday, 1992), vol. 5, p. 875.

13. 1 Sam 16:2–5.

14. Cf. John Bright on this passage in his Anchor Bible commentary on *Jeremiah* (Garden City, N.Y.: Doubleday, 1965), p. 57: "It is unlikely that it is to be taken either as a categorical rejection of the sacrificial system as such, or as a statement that there was no sacrifice in the wilderness." The specific issue involved in Jeremiah's polemic is discussed in R. E. Friedman, *The Exile and Biblical Narrative*, Harvard Semitic Monographs (Atlanta: Scholars Press, 1981), pp. 74–75.

15. Isa 1:11–17.

16. Mic 6:7–8.

17. Anderson, "Sacrifice and Sacrificial Offerings," p. 882.

18. Gen 7:2.

19. Gen 8:20.

20. Friedman, *The Bible with Sources Revealed*, pp. 33–46.

21. So von Rad, *Genesis*, pp. 127–28.

22. This is the traditional rabbinic view, found in the commentaries of Rashi and Sforno on Gen 9:4. The rabbis are divided on the question of whether this also prohibits the consumption of blood as a separate command. See the commentary of Ramban (Nachmanides) on Gen 9:4; and Sarna, *Genesis*, pp. 60–61, 377.

23. *Enuma Elish*; ANET, pp. 61–72; Thorkild Jacobsen, *The Treasures of Darkness: A History of Mesopotamian Religion* (New Haven: Yale University Press, 1976), pp. 117–18; William P. Brown, *The Seven Pillars of Creation: The Bible, Science, and the Ecology of Wonder* (New York: Oxford University Press, 2010), pp. 26–27; Alexander Heidel, *The Babylonian Genesis*, 2nd ed. (Chicago: University of Chicago Press, 1951).

24. Tablet 11 of the *Epic of Gilgamesh*; ANET, pp. 93–95; Jacobsen, *Treasures of Darkness*, p. 119; Brown, *Seven Pillars of Creation*, p. 27.

25. ANET, p. 96. Alexander Heidel, *The Gilgamesh Epic and Old Testament Parallels*, 2nd ed. (Chicago: University of Chicago Press, 1949); David Ferry, *Gilgamesh: A New Rendering in English Verse*, with Introduction by William L. Moran (New York: Noonday Press, Farrar, Straus and Giroux, 1992).

26. ANET, pp. 166–77.

27. Richard S. Hess, "Alalakh Studies and the Bible: Obstacle or Contribution?" in *Scripture and Other Artifacts: Essays on the Bible and Archaeology in Honor of Philip J. King*, ed. M. Coogan, C. Exum, and L. Stager (Louisville, Ky.: Westminster/John Knox, 1994), pp. 202–3; J. J. M. Roberts, *The Bible and the Ancient Near East: Collected Essays* (Winona Lake, Ind.: Eisenbrauns, 2002), p. 46.

28. Roberts, *The Bible and the Ancient Near East*, p. 46: "the concept of the commandments as the stipulations of a covenant between the gods and the people is simply unknown in Mesopotamia."

29. Miriam Lichthein, *Ancient Egyptian Literature* (Berkeley: University of California Press, 1976), vol. 2, p. 33. Jeffrey Tigay discusses the use of trees for siege-works among Egyptians, Assyrians, and Greeks in *Deuteronomy*, pp. 190–91, 380, notes 40 and 41.

30. Gen 1:1–2:3; and Gen 2:4b–25.

31. See G. Ernest Wright, *The Old Testament against Its Environment* (London: SCM, 1950); Henri Frankfort et al., *The Intellectual Adventure of Ancient Man* (Chicago: University of Chicago Press, 1946); and discussion in Theodore Hiebert, *The Yahwist's Landscape: Nature and Religion in Early Israel* (Oxford: Oxford University Press, 1996), pp. 6ff. Hiebert provides an insightful discussion and critique of traditional scholarship that dichotomizes ancient religions

in this way, that see nature as a "problem" in biblical theology; see especially his first chapter. Hiebert then gives an analysis of the J source in the Pentateuch and arrives at a similar conclusion to ours: the biblical authors perceived humanity and nature as interrelated in a way that has been overlooked by biblical scholars and ecologists alike.

32. Lynn White, Jr., "The Historical Roots of Our Ecologic Crisis," *Science* 155 (March 10, 1967): p. 1205.

33. For a history of the relationship between Christianity and ecology, see Ernest L. Fortin, "The Bible Made Me Do It: Christianity, Science, and the Environment," *Review of Politics* 57, no. 2 (Spring 1995): pp. 197–223; and Gene M. Tucker, "Rain on a Land Where No One Lives: The Hebrew Bible on the Environment," *Journal of Biblical Literature* 116, no. 1 (1997): pp. 3–17.

34. Watt charges that this quotation was taken out of context: see Glenn Scherer, "The Godly Must Be Crazy: Christian-Right Views Are Swaying Politicians and Threatening the Environment," *Grist*, October 27, 2004, available at http://www.grist.org/news/maindish/2004/10/27/scherer-christian/index. html; and James Watt, "The Religious Left's Lies," *Washington Post*, May 21, 2005: A19, available at http://www.washingtonpost.com/wp-dyn/content/ article/2005/05/20/AR2005052001333.html.

35. Ann Coulter, "Oil Good; Democrats Bad," October 12, 2000, in her syndicated column on townhall.com.

36. Dispensationalism is a Protestant evangelical and eschatological movement originating in the nineteenth century. It holds that God relates to Israel through a series of covenants that differ in each successive era (or "dispensation"). Dispensationalists interpret modern social and ecological crises as signs that we are the "terminal generation," and that soon all believers will be taken up to heaven in apocalyptic rapture.

37. See Glenn Scherer's comprehensive article on politics, fundamentalism, and environmental policy, "The Godly Must Be Crazy," at http://www.grist.org/ article/scherer-christian/.

38. Ibid.

39. Other biblical scholars have written similarly on this issue: Leonard Greenspoon, "From Dominion to Stewardship? The Ecology of Biblical Translation," in "Religion and the Environment," ed. Ronald A. Simkins, *Journal of Religion and Society*, suppl. series 3 (2008): pp. 159–83; and Ronald A. Simkins, "The End of Nature: Humans and the Natural World in the History of Creation," in "Religion and the Environment," ed. Ronald A. Simkins, *Journal of Religion and Society*, suppl. series 3 (2008): pp. 47–65; both available at http://moses.creighton.edu/jrs/toc/SS03.html.

40. The Hebrew Bible scholar Bernhard W. Anderson makes this point, also citing this verse, in "'Subdue the Earth': What Does It Mean?" *Bible Review* (October 1992:) pp. 4, 10.

41. Pope Benedict XVI, Catholic News Agency, July 26, 2007.
42. Pope Benedict XVI, CNN World, January 1, 2010.

Afterword

1. Sigmund Freud, *Moses and Monotheism* (London: Hogarth Press and the Institute of Psycho-analysis, 1974); original German edition published in Amsterdam, 1939; published in English in *The Standard Edition of the Complete Psychological Works of Sigmund Freud*, ed. James Strachey (London: Hogarth Press).

2. Erich Auerbach, *Mimesis*, trans. W. R. Trask (Princeton: Princeton University Press, 1953); original German edition published in Berne, 1946.

3. Robert Alter, starting with his essay "Sacred History and Prose Fiction," in *The Creation of Sacred Literature*, ed. Richard Elliott Friedman (Berkeley: University of California Press, 1981), pp. 7–24; and including Robert Alter, *The Art of Biblical Narrative* (New York: Basic Books, 1983); Robert Alter, *The Art of Biblical Poetry* (New York: Basic Books, 1987); Robert Alter and Frank Kermode, eds., *The Literary Guide to the Bible* (Cambridge: Belknap/Harvard University Press, 1990); and others.

4. Mary Douglas, *Purity and Danger* (London: Routledge, 1966).

5. For those who are interested, one of us has argued this point in an exchange with James Kugel, a scholar of the history of interpretation of the Bible. R. E. Friedman, "Ancient Biblical Interpreters vs. Archaeology and Modern Scholars," *Biblical Archaeology Review* 34, no. 1 (January/February 2008): pp. 62–67; and Kugel's response in the following issue.

SUBJECT INDEX

SCRIPTURE INDEX

Printed in the USA/Agawam, MA
August 14, 2014

595155.020